AF560586

Priests, Kings, and Women in the Early Upaniṣads

Priests, Kings, and Women in the Early Upaniṣads

The Character of the Self in Ancient India

BRIAN BLACK

MOTILAL BANARSIDASS PUBLISHERS
PRIVATE LIMITED • DELHI (INDIA)

First Indian Edition: Delhi, 2014

ISBN: 978-81-208-3702-7

MOTILAL BANARSIDASS
41 U.A. Bungalow Road, Jawahar Nagar, Delhi 110 007
8 Mahalaxmi Chamber, 22 Bhulabhai Desai Road, Mumbai 400 026
203 Royapettah High Road, Mylapore, Chennai 600 004
236, 9th Main III Block, Jayanagar, Bengaluru 560 011
Sanas Plaza, 1302 Baji Rao Road, Pune 411 002
8 Camac Street, Kolkata 700 017
Ashok Rajpath, Patna 800 004
Chowk, Varanasi 221 001

For Sale in South Asia only

Library of Congress Cataloging-in-Publication Data
Black, Brian, 1970-
The character of the self in ancient India : priests, kings, and women in the early Upanisads / Brian Black.
p. cm. — (SUNY series in Hindu studies)
Includes bibliographical references and index.
1. Upanishads—Criticism, interpretation, etc. 2. Hindu literature, Sanskrit—History and criticism. 3. Character in literature. 4. Self in literature. I. Title. II. Series
BL1124.57.B63 2007
294.5'9218—dc22

Printed in India

by RP Jain at NAB Printing Unit
A-44, Naraina Industrial Area, Phase I, New Delhi–110028
and published by JP Jain for Motilal Banarsidass Publishers (P) Ltd
41 U.A. Bungalow Road, Jawahar Nagar, Delhi-110007

In memory of my father, Jerry Black,
my most inspirational dialogical companion

Contents

Acknowledgments

One of the fundamental arguments of this book is that philosophy, as well as academic work in general, is not the result of solitary reflection, but rather is generated and produced through an active engagement with other people. Nowhere have I learned this more profoundly than in the process of researching and writing this book. This work has emerged out of the conversations, discussions, debates, and arguments I have had with my supervisors, teachers, colleagues, students, friends, and family members during the past several years.

I would first like to thank my father, who passed away before this book was completed. I dedicate this work to him.

I would also like to thank my doctoral supervisors, Ted Proferes and Daud Ali, both of whom offered incisive comments and invaluable suggestions to earlier drafts of this work. I also thank my examiners, Julius Lipner and Cosimo Zene, both of whom offered extremely important feedback that has assisted me in transforming my doctoral thesis into this book.

In addition to my supervisors, my colleague Simon Brodbeck has been particularly helpful by providing me with detailed written responses to an earlier draft.

A number of people in the Department of the Study of Religions at the School of Oriental and African Studies (SOAS) have been significant sources of help, inspiration, and support. In particular I would like to mention Peter Flügel, Paul Gifford, Sîan Hawthorne, Douglas Osto, Alexander Piatigorsky, Vena Ramphal, Tadeusz Skorupski, Paul-François Tremlett, Simon Weightman, and Ronit Yoeli-Tlalim. I would like to offer special thanks to the late Julia Leslie for her enthusiastic encouragement. I am also grateful to my students at SOAS and Birkbeck, whose questions and insights contributed greatly to this work.

I am deeply indebted to Pushpa Kale for reading the Upaniṣads with me in Sanskrit while I was studying for an academic year in

Pune. A number of other people were welcoming and supportive during that year: Saroja Bhate, M. A. Mehendale, Steven Lindquist, Jane Hobson, and Laurie Patton.

I would never have been interested in the Upaniṣads in the first place if I had not spent a formative year of my life in India in 1991–92 with the University of California Education Abroad Program. I am grateful to Gerald Larson who organized this program and who was the supervisor for my first paper on Indian philosophy. And I would like to give a special thanks to my dearest friends, with whom I had the pleasure of sharing this wonderful experience: Suanne Buggy, Lawrence Manzo, Jed Olson, Jasmine Sharma, and Joseph Sorrentino. Thanks to them for being there when it all started, and their love and support ever since.

I am indebted to Ilona Schäfer and Nicole Wolf, and to Susan Clark for reading an earlier draft. I would like to offer a special thanks to my dear friend Nakissa Etemad for proofreading a recent draft and for offering feedback as a "first reader."

I thank Wendy Doniger, Nancy Ellegate, Judith Block, Marilyn Semerad, and the staff at SUNY for all their help and support during the publication process; and I thank Sona Datta for suggesting the cover art and the British Museum for kindly lending permission to use it.

Finally, and most of all, I thank my family: my wife, Yulia; my son, Harrison; and my mother, Mary. Writing this book would not have been possible without their unceasing love, support, and encouragement.

Abbreviations

AĀ	Aitareya Āraṇyaka
AU	Aitareya Upaniṣad
BU	Bṛhadāraṇyaka Upaniṣad
CU	Chāndogya Upaniṣad
DN	Dīgha Nikāya
JB	Jaiminīya Brāhmaṇa
JUB	Jaiminīya Upaniṣad Brāhmaṇa
KaU	Kaṭha Upaniṣad
KṣU	Kauṣītaki Upaniṣad
MDS	Mānava Dharmaśastra
ṚV	Ṛgveda
ŚĀ	Śāṅkhāyana Āraṇyaka
ŚB	Śatapatha Brāhmaṇa
ŚU	Śvetāśvatara Upaniṣad
TĀ	Taittirīya Āraṇyaka
TU	Taittirīya Upaniṣad

Introduction

OPENING STATEMENT

The seventh section of the *Chāndogya Upaniṣad* begins with a dialogue between Nārada and Sanatkumāra. Nārada approaches his teacher and asks for instruction in the typical manner for Upanishadic students. Sanatkumāra, however, demands to know his educational background before taking on Nārada as his pupil. Nārada responds:

> Sir, I know the *Ṛgveda*, the *Yajurveda*, the *Sāmaveda*, the *Ātharvaṇa* as the fourth, the history and legend (*itihāsa purāṇa*) as the fifth Veda, the grammar, ancestral rites, mathematics, fortune telling, treasure-finding, the dialogues, the narrow path, the knowledge of the gods, the knowledge of brahmins, the knowledge of the spirits, the knowledge of *kṣatriyas*, astrology, and the knowledge about serpent beings. So I am, sir, a knower of the *mantras*, but not a knower of the self (*ātman*). (7.1.2–3)[1]

Nārada's response is illustrative of the interests of a number of individuals throughout the Upaniṣads. He is unhappy with the traditional education that he has already received and recognizes that to be truly knowledgeable he must learn about the self (*ātman*). As we will see in this book, the Upaniṣads present several different, and sometimes conflicting, teachings about the nature of the self, but throughout the texts the self remains a central concern.

The Upanishadic orientation towards the self marks a significant transformation in relation to previous Vedic literature, which primarily focuses on the description and meaning of ritual actions. Indeed, this shift has been recognized by the Indian tradition, as exemplified in the traditional Vedānta division of the Vedas into *karmakāṇḍa* and *jñānakāṇḍa*.

According to this classification, the Saṃhitās and Brāhmaṇas are considered *karmakāṇḍa* as they are the sections of the Veda that deal with ritual, while the Upaniṣads, as well as the Āraṇyakas, are called *jñānakāṇḍa* as they deal with more philosophical subjects.

Modern readers have also noticed the change in orientation from the ritual texts to the Upaniṣads. Romila Thapar, for example, describes the emergence of the Upanishadic material as a paradigm shift in the constitution of knowledge in ancient India, observing that "the nature of the change was a shift from the acceptance of the Vedas as revealed and as controlled by ritual to the possibility that knowledge could derive from intuition, observation and analysis" (1993, 307). Modern translators of the Upaniṣads, including Max Müller ([1879–84] 2000), Paul Deussen ([1897] 2004), Robert Ernest Hume ([1921] 1975), Sarvepalli Radhakrishnan ([1953] 1992), Patrick Olivelle (1996), and Valerie Roebuck (2003), have all recognized this philosophical orientation of the Upaniṣads, especially in discussions relating to the self.[2]

Similarly, this book addresses knowledge about the self in the Upaniṣads. However, what makes this study different is that it will approach the texts paying close attention to the literary presentation of the ideas. Included in the diverse material contained in the Upaniṣads are a number of stories and dialogues.[3] These sections use narrative to introduce teachings about the self (*ātman*), and related ideas such as the bodily winds (*prāṇās*), and the knowledge of the five fires (*pañcāgnividyā*). I will demonstrate that these narrative sections are not merely literary ornaments, but are integral to an understanding of the philosophical claims of the texts. In fact, the paradigm shift noted by other scholars does not pertain merely to a change in the content of the Vedic texts, but also, as I will argue, is marked by innovations in the style and structure of the texts. As such, much of what makes the Upaniṣads unique in relation to previous material is the literary presentation of the texts themselves.

As in the dialogues of Plato, in the Upaniṣads philosophical claims are often introduced in the form of a conversation, thereby presenting philosophical ideas within the context of specific individuals and social situations. The dialogues tell us who is speaking, to whom, where, under what conditions, and what is at stake in the discussions. When we pay attention to these details, we see that the narratives not only contextualize the teachings, but also characterize the knowledge, and outline how and by whom these teachings should be practiced in the social world. While the teachings emphasize the *ātman*, the dialogues reinforce this focus on the individual by presenting us with specific selves, the literary characters. In this way, the distinct characters and how they achieve selfhood are an integral part of the Upanishadic discourses about the self. As such, the Upanishadic notion of self is not merely a philosophical insight, but a way of being in the world.

WHAT ARE THE UPANIṢADS?

The Upaniṣads are some of the most well-known and well-appreciated philosophical texts in the world. In the modern era a number of intellectuals from Europe and India not only have recognized their profundity, but also have developed a personal affinity for these texts. For example, Arthur Schopenhauer viewed the Upaniṣads as "the most profitable and sublime reading that is possible in the world; [they have] been the consolation of my life and will be that of my death" ([1851] 1974: 397). In the preface to his translation of the Upaniṣads, which constitutes the first installment to the Sacred Books of the East series, Max Müller proclaimed: "My real love for Sanskrit literature was first kindled by the Upanishads" (1879–84, lxv). Vivekananda, one of the first Indian reformers to relate his reading of the Upaniṣads with the nationalist movement, declared before an audience in Madras: "The truths of the Upanishads are before you. Take them up, live up to them, and the salvation of India will be at hand" ([1922] 1973, 225). Similarly, Radhakrishnan connected the Upaniṣads to a national Indian identity: "For us Indians, a study of the Upaniṣads is essential, if we are to preserve our national being and character. To discover the main lines of our traditional life, we must turn to our classics, the Vedas and the Upaniṣads, the *Bhagavad-gītā* and the *Dhamma-pada*" ([1953] 1992, 9). As we can see from these quotations, the Upaniṣads have made a personal impact on Indian and Western scholars alike, inspiring distinct interpretations among different audiences. Before describing my own approach and the structure of this book in more detail, let us first familiarize ourselves with what the Upaniṣads are and which specific texts will constitute the source material for this study.

The Upaniṣads are ancient texts from India that are traditionally regarded as the fourth and final section of a larger group of texts called the Vedas. The oldest parts of the Vedas are the Saṃhitas, followed by the Brāhmaṇas, the Āraṇyakas, and then the Upaniṣads. In addition to the four types of Vedic text, there are four different collections or branches (*śākhā*) of Vedic material: the *Ṛgveda*, the *Yajurveda* (consisting of two sub-branches: the Black *Yajurveda* and White *Yajurveda*), the *Sāmaveda*, and the *Atharvaveda*. In this book we will concentrate on the Upaniṣads that constitute part of the first three of these four branches of the Vedas. The dates of the Upaniṣads—as well as the other sections of the Vedas—continue to be contested, yet most scholars estimate that they were composed between 700 and 300 BCE (see Olivelle 1996, xxxvi–xxxvii; Roebuck 2003, xxiv–xxvi).[4] It is important to point out, however, that there are hundreds of texts that are known as Upaniṣads, because texts that called themselves by this name continued to be composed long after the Vedic corpus was closed. After the Vedic period, a number of devotional texts have referred to themselves as Upaniṣads, with the *Bhagavad Gītā* (18:78: *śrīmadbhagavadgītā upaniṣadaḥ*) as the most famous example. Additionally, there is a Muslim devotional text composed during the Mughal period called the *Allopaniṣad*.

A number of scholars claim that the Vedic Upaniṣads mark the birth of philosophy in ancient India.[5] There are, of course, potential problems with this claim because the earlier Vedic texts also contain material that could be considered philosophical, and contention surrounds the word 'philosophy' itself as not appropriate for the Indian context.[6] Despite these hesitations, it seems fair to say that the Upaniṣads occupy a similar place within the Indian tradition as the writings of the pre-Socratic philosophers do in the history of Western philosophy. Like the pre-Socratics, the Upaniṣads mark the beginning of a reasoned enquiry into a number of perennial philosophical questions concerning the nature of being, the nature of the self, the foundation of life, what happens to the self at the time of death, how one should live one's life. In this way, the Upaniṣads establish a set of questions and provide a terminology for addressing these questions that would remain influential throughout the subsequent Indian textual tradition. This book, like so many others that engage the Upaniṣads, assumes their status as the birth of philosophy in ancient India. However, rather than focus on the philosophy as such, we will pay particular attention to how the Upaniṣads present their ideas.

Our primary focus will be on the *Bṛhadāraṇyaka Upaniṣad*, the *Chāndogya Upaniṣad*, the *Kauṣītaki Upaniṣad*, the *Taittirīya Upaniṣad*, and the *Aitareya Upaniṣad*, all of which are considered to be the early Upaniṣads, composed sometime before the time of the Buddha and Mahāvīra, most probably between the eighth and sixth centuries BCE. These five early Upaniṣads are composed in prose, as opposed to the post-Buddhist Upaniṣads, which are presented in verse form. The later Vedic Upaniṣads, which would include the *Kena Upaniṣad*, the *Kaṭha Upaniṣad*, the *Īśā Upaniṣad*, and *Śvetāśvatara Upaniṣad*, represent a further shift in philosophical orientation.[7] It is important to distinguish the early Upaniṣads from these later texts, because a number of important ideas generally assumed to be representative of the Upaniṣads as a whole—such as *saṃsāra* (cycle of life, death, and rebirth), *mokṣa* (final liberation), and *yoga*—are only developed in the later texts.

As our focus is on the literary presentation of ideas, we will concern ourselves primarily with the sections of the early Upaniṣads that contain narratives and dialogues. We will also be looking closely at some other sections, including speculations about the Vedic sacrifice, creation myths, genealogies of teachers and students, magical formulas, and procreation rites, insofar as this material helps contextualize the stories and dialogues. As will become clear, the early Upaniṣads consist of a diverse set of material, much of which either existed independently or formed parts of other texts before being collected in one of the Upaniṣads.

We will also consider sections from the Brāhmaṇas and Āraṇyakas, particularly the *Śatapatha Brāhmaṇa* and *Jaiminīya Brāhmaṇa*, as they contain some of the initial examples of the kinds of narratives that appear in the Upaniṣads, and the later portions of these texts are connected to the Upaniṣads based on how they have been handed down in the oral tradition. In this respect, the Āraṇyakas are especially intertwined with the Upaniṣads, as a number of the early Upaniṣads have been transmitted as material entirely embedded within the Āraṇyakas. For example, in the textual tradition of the *Ṛgveda*, the *Aitareya Upaniṣad* appears within the *Aitareya Āraṇyaka*.[8] In the school of the Black *Yajurveda*, the *Taittirīya Upaniṣad* consists of a portion of the *Taittirīya Āraṇyaka*.[9] In the White *Yajurveda*, the *Bṛhadāraṇyaka Upaniṣad*, as the name suggests, is considered both an Āraṇyaka and an Upaniṣad.

In addition to a connection at the textual level, another common feature of the late Brāhmaṇas, Āraṇyakas, and early Upaniṣads is a shift in focus to the meaning of ritual actions, rather than the literal descriptions of how to perform the ritual. The Āraṇyakas, for example, have a number of discourses that are considered secret and equivalent to ritual performance.[10] A. B Keith argues that this knowledge does not replace ritual activity, but rather consists of teachings that are connected to it:

> The Āraṇyaka seems originally to have existed to give secret explanations of the ritual, and to have presupposed that the ritual was still in use and was known. No doubt the tendency

> was for the secret explanation to grow independent of the ritual until the stage is reached where the Āraṇyaka passes into the Upaniṣad . . . But originally an Āraṇyaka must have merely meant a book of instruction to be given in the forest. ([1909] 1995, 15–16)

Similarly, in a number of dialogues in the Upaniṣads, knowledge does not replace ritual, as it seems likely that rituals, including large-scale Vedic sacrifices, continued to be performed. Nevertheless, in the Upaniṣads a number of teachings are considered independent from traditional rituals and in many cases they are cast as superior to them. Additionally, the emphasis on secret or hidden knowledge that is established in the Brāhmaṇas and the Āraṇyakas continues throughout the early Upaniṣads, with several discourses claiming that the gods love what is secret (*paro'kṣakāmā hi devāḥ*) (ŚB 6.1.1.1–15; BU 4.2.2; AU 1.3.14).

Indeed, the notion of esoteric knowledge is closely intertwined with the meaning of the term *upaniṣad*. According to tradition the significance of the word is derived from the sum of its parts: *upa* (near) + *ni* (down) + *sad* (to sit), meaning "to sit down near." This rendering of the term conjures up the image of the student sitting by the feet of the teacher. Although this is undoubtedly what the word has come to mean, scholars have challenged this as the original connotation on the grounds that this is not how the word is employed in its initial occurrences, or indeed anywhere in the texts that we now call the Upaniṣads. Rather than defining the word by its etymology, scholars have noticed that in its earliest textual contexts, *upaniṣad* is used to describe a connection between things, often presented in a hierarchical relationship. According to Harry Falk (1986), in the Brāhmaṇas, *upaniṣad* refers to the dominant power in a chain of dependency in which the *upaniṣad* is the final component in a list, or the final teaching that is the foundation for everything else. As Joel Brereton explains, "The purpose of arranging things in such a progression is finally to identify the dominant reality behind an object" (1990, 124–25). As such, an *upaniṣad* is not immediate or transparent, but rather remains concealed and obscure. Patrick Olivelle suggests that due to the hidden nature of an *upaniṣad* as the connecting power in a hierarchy, it "came to mean a secret, especially secret knowledge or doctrine. It is probably as an extension of this meaning that the term came finally to be used with reference to entire texts containing such secret doctrines, that is, our Upaniṣads" (1996, liii). According to Roebuck, this notion of an esoteric teaching returns us to a meaning of *upaniṣad* that focuses on teacher and student: "An Upaniṣad recounts one or more sessions of teaching, often setting each within the story of how it came to be taught" (2003, xv). As we will see, the connotation of secrecy that is conjured up by the word *upaniṣad*, as well as other narrative details, is a central feature of the texts. However, this book will concentrate more on the formal features of secrecy rather than claiming to uncover the secrets themselves.

THE SELF, LIFE, DEATH, AND IMMORTALITY

This book will focus primarily on the teachings that are highlighted by the dialogues in the Upaniṣads, and those that are generally characterized as new in relation to Vedic ritualism. Among these teachings there are a number of interrelated ideas that concentrate on the self, the processes of life and death, and how to achieve immortality.

Ātman, the religio-philosophical idea that is discussed most in the dialogues, has a number of different meanings and usages in Vedic literature. Originally, in the earliest Vedic material, *ātman* was a reflexive pronoun meaning 'self.' The word continued to be used as a pronoun, but by the time of the late Brāhmaṇas and early Upaniṣads, *ātman* also became a philosophical term that could be associated with a wide range of meanings including body and soul, and could sometimes refer to the ontological principle underlying all reality. Although there are a number of distinct and contradictory definitions of *ātman*, throughout the Upaniṣads, teachings about *ātman* indicate a general interest in the human body and the processes of life and death.

Discussions about the human body in ancient Indian literature, however, are by no means new to the Upaniṣads. One of the most prevailing myths in the Vedic ritual texts is that the universe began with the sacrifice and dismemberment of the primordial male body. In the *Puruṣasūkta* hymn of the *Ṛgveda* (10.90), the body of Puruṣa is dissected and the elements of his body are reassembled to create an ordered universe. Thus, the initial body of Puruṣa is considered imperfect or incomplete, and only when his body is reassembled does creation really begin. In the Brāhmaṇas, the mythology of Puruṣa becomes extended to the creator god Prajāpati.[11] Prajāpati creates the world from his own corporality and his creation is considered incomplete, as his creatures are without breath, suffering from hunger or lack of food, without firm foundation, or without name or form.[12] As in the *Puruṣasūkta*, creation is imagined in terms of restoring and reordering rather than making something from nothing (ŚB 10.4.2.3).

One of the functions of the Vedic sacrifice was to complete the creation process begun by Prajāpati. Throughout this mythology the universe not only is made from a primordial male body, but also shares with both Puruṣa and Prajāpati the same fundamental structure, thus pointing to a correspondence between microcosm and macrocosm.

In some passages in the Upaniṣads, *ātman* assumes the character of the cosmic bodies of Puruṣa and Prajāpati. The *Aitareya Upaniṣad* (1.1), for example, begins with a creation myth in which *ātman* creates the universe from the body of Puruṣa.[13] As with Puruṣa and Prajāpati, *ātman*'s creation is incomplete without a sacrifice. The gods reject both a cow and a horse as inadequate sacrificial victims. Finally *ātman* offers a *puruṣa* (a man) and the gods are pleased. The result of this sacrifice is that the original creation folds back on itself. Originally, *ātman* created fire from speech and speech from the mouth of Puruṣa. Now, after the sacrifice, fire returns to speech and enters the mouth. Like Puruṣa and Prajāpati, *ātman* is cast as a creator god who creates the universe by means of sacrificing, dismembering, and reconstructing a body.

Although in this passage *ātman* assumes the mythological status of Puruṣa and Prajāpati, most of the teachings concerning *ātman* represent a different set of concerns from those found in the ritual discourse. Rather than assume a correspondence between the human body and the universe, many teachings in the Upaniṣads show an interest in the fundamental essence of life. As Brereton explains. "While the Brāhmaṇas sought . . . correlations within the domains of the ritual and outside world, the Upaniṣads search primarily for those that exist within and among the human and natural domains" (1990, 119). Several sections describe *ātman* as a life force or something that keeps the body alive. For example, the *Aitareya Āraṇyaka* (2.3.2) describes *ātman* as taking different forms in different living beings. In plants and trees *ātman* is equated with sap, while in animals *ātman* is consciousness. In humans, however, *ātman* is said to be clearer than in other beings. In the *Chāndogya Upaniṣad* (6.1–16) Uddālaka Āruṇi teaches that *ātman* is the finest essence in all living beings.

In chapter 1 we will look at how different Upanishadic teachers have different teachings about *ātman*. Here, however, it is important to point out that despite the differences, there are some general tendencies. Most of these teachings assume that *ātman* is immortal, that *ātman* dwells within the body when it is alive, and in one way or another that *ātman* is responsible for the body being alive. *Ātman* does not die when the body dies, but rather finds a dwelling place in another body.

As Yājñavalkya, one of the most prominent figures in the Upaniṣads, explains, "Just as a caterpillar, having reached the end of a blade of grass, as it takes another step, draws itself together. So the self (*ātman*), having thrown down the body and having dispelled ignorance, in taking another step, draws itself together" (BU 4.4.3).[14] As the *ātman* is immortal, it is also characterized as permanent and unchanging.

Closely related to these discussions about *ātman* are discourses about *prāṇa*. The *Taittirīya Upaniṣad* (2.2.1), for example, describes the *ātman* as consisting of *prāṇa*, while in the *Bṛhadāraṇyaka Upaniṣad* (2.1.20) King Ajātaśatru teaches that the *ātman* and the *prāṇās* have an interdependent relationship. Indeed, these teachings explain that the *ātman*, as a living organism, cannot exist without *prāṇa*. As H. W. Bodewitz suggests, generally *prāṇa* refers to breath and can mean both exhalation and life-breath (1973, 22).

It is difficult to define *prāṇa* because it means different things in different contexts. In its plural form, the *prāṇās* refer to either the bodily winds or to the five vital functions (breath, sight, hearing, speech, and mind).[15] Although these distinctly different categories are both called *prāṇās*, in its singular form, *prāṇa* appears in both groups, retaining its connection to breath. The *Bṛhadāraṇyaka Upaniṣad* (1.5.21) explains that because the *prāṇa* is superior, the other vital functions take on the name collectively. Importantly, the composers of the Upaniṣads did not associate the life breaths of the human body with the lungs, but rather the breaths are usually described in terms of how they move and where they operate within the body. For example, the *Bṛhadāraṇyaka Upaniṣad* (1.3.19) describes the *prāṇās* as the essence (*rasa*) of the bodily parts (*aṅga*), articulating the close connection between the breaths and the material body. In another passage, the *Kauṣītaki Upaniṣad* (3.2) associates life with *prāṇa*, stating that as long as *prāṇa* remains within the body, the body remains alive.

In the *Aitareya Āraṇyaka* (2.1.4) we see one of the earliest appearances of a recurring myth about the competition between *prāṇa* and the other vital functions. There are a number of variations of this myth.[16] Whatever the variations, however, the events in the story are always the same: all the vital functions agree to leave the body to discover which one of them is most central to keeping the body alive. As they leave one by one, the body continues to have life. Only when *prāṇa* departs does the body die. Then, when *prāṇa* returns the body is restored to life.

The various versions of the *prāṇa* myth assume that knowledge of how the body works and what is responsible for life can contribute to keeping the body alive and to averting death. Accordingly, *ātman* and *prāṇa* are often discussed in relation to sleep and death. The *Śatapatha Brāhmaṇa* describes how the *prāṇā*s, during sleep, take possession of the *ātman* and descend into the cavity of the heart (10.5.2.14).[17] In the *Chāndogya Upaniṣad* (4.3.3), Raikva teaches that during sleep, all the vital functions pass into the *prāṇa*. The union of the *prāṇā*s in the interior of the body explains why someone who is asleep is unaware of what goes on. The *Śatapatha Brāhmaṇa* (10.5.2.14) warns that someone who is in this state of deep sleep should not be woken. In this passage, as well as others, the process of sleeping is likened to the process of dying.

Death is generally described as the departure of *prāṇā*s from the body. In the *Bṛhadāraṇyaka Upaniṣad* (4.3.38; 4.4.1), Yājñavalkya teaches King Janaka that death occurs when *prāṇa* leaves the body. The similarity between sleeping and dying is that when the *ātman* or *prāṇa* retreats into the cavity of the heart, the person loses all consciousness of the outside world. The difference is that after sleep, the *ātman*/*prāṇa* leaves the cavity of the heart and returns to the rest of the body, whereas in death the *ātman*/*prāṇa* leaves the body altogether. The *Chāndogya Upaniṣad* (8.6.3) describes these two processes together: in the state of sleep a man slips into his veins and "no evil thing touches him."[18] Similarly, in the following passage (8.6.4), a dying man is described as slipping into unconsciousness and unable to recognize his relatives. This passage ends by stating that knowledge of these processes affects what happens after death, and that the door to the world beyond is an entrance for those who know, but an obstacle for those who do not know (8.6.5). Thus, when a man knows the connection between the *prāṇās*, he is joined with death and becomes immortal. In an example from the *Śatapatha Brāhmaṇa* (10.6.3.11), Śāṇḍilya teaches that a person obtains *ātman* during death, indicating that people's knowledge is connected to what happens to them when they die.

These discussions of *ātman* and *prāṇa* are not merely indicative of a general interest in bodily functions, but are closely connected with the Upanishadic goal of immortality (*amṛta*). As Dermot Killingley points out, the Vedic literature considers life after death in a much different way than later texts that emphasize ideas about *saṃsāra* and *mokṣa*: "The main way in which Vedic thought on the subject differs from later Hindu thought is that it usually regards life after death as something to be achieved, rather than as something to be escaped from" (1997, 2). In the Vedic period immortality is understood in a number of different ways, including being preserved in the social memory, becoming one with the essential being of the universe, and surviving death in the heavenly world.[19] As Killingley describes, different understandings of immortality assume different ways for achieving the deathless state: "Firstly, one can become immortal through one's offspring . . . A second idea is survival through dispersal of the person into the corresponding parts of the universe . . . Thirdly, there is the idea of survival in one's deeds (*iṣṭāpūrta*), particularly ritual deeds, which prepare a place for the deceased in the next world" (1997, 2–3). Another common understanding of *amṛta,* which literally means "not dying," is a long life.[20] For example, in the *Chāndogya Upaniṣad* (3.16.7), Mahidāsa Aitareya claims that he will overcome death because of his knowledge. The text then states that he lived to be 116 and that anyone who knows this teaching will also be able to live to the same advanced age.

Despite sharing with the ritual texts similar ideas about avoiding death and securing immortality, the Upaniṣads offer different methods as to how to achieve these goals. In the ritual context, immortality is gained through ritual action, as the sacrifice feeds the gods and ancestors, providing for their nourishment and continued survival in the heavenly world. In the Upanishadic discussions about *ātman* and *prāṇa,* however, immortality is often gained through manipulation of the life process. To know *ātman* is to understand how the *prāṇā*s work and how *ātman* leaves the body at the time of death.

As we will see, Yājñavalkya teaches that immortality can be secured through knowledge alone. However most Upanishadic teachers assume the earlier Vedic notion that achieving immortality requires having male children. The difference is that in the ritual texts, male children are important because they inherit ritual knowledge and continue to feed and keep alive their deceased ancestors. In the early Upaniṣads, however, the desire for male offspring is linked to more naturalistic views of the self and the human body, as a man can avert death by being reborn in his son. As Olivelle explains, "A man's sperm is viewed as his *rasa* or essence. In other words, a man replicates himself, creates a second self for himself, in his sperm" (1997a, 432).

This point is illustrated in the *Aitareya Upaniṣad* (2.1–6), where Vāmadeva teaches that *ātman* has three births: conception, birth, and death/rebirth. As *ātman* is understood as generating life, these passages explain how *ātman* is passed from one body to give life to another body. This passage, as well as others, considers *ātman* in terms of a specifically male body and describes sexual activity as the male passing the *ātman* to the female. In Vāmadeva's teaching the female body is basically a receptacle for the *ātman* to be reborn in another male body:

> In a man, indeed, one first becomes an embryo (*garbha*). That which is semen (*retas*) is the energy (*tejas*) proceeding from all the limbs (*aṅga*). In the self (*ātman*) one bears a self (*ātman*). When he emits this in a woman he begets it. That is his first birth. It becomes one with the woman, just as her own limbs, so it does not harm her. She nourishes this self (*ātman*) of his that has come to her. (AU 2.1–2)[21]

This teaching of *ātman* has significant gender implications, which we will explore in chapter 4. For now, however, I merely want to point out that the connection between immortality and progeny implies that access to immortality privileges men who are married and have children. Although *ātman* is sometimes defined as a universal life-force that is present in all living beings, knowledge of *ātman*, and consequently the ability to secure immortality through *ātman*, is limited to very few. As we will see, the dialogues define for whom this knowledge is available and outline practices to be performed in order to attain this knowledge.

THE HISTORICAL AND SOCIAL CONTEXT

The changes in the presentation of Vedic literature, as well as the new orientation towards the self and the processes of life and death, are related to political and social changes that were taking place in ancient India. Several scholars have suggested that the Upaniṣads were composed during a time of dynamic change in north India. Both the textual and archeological evidence point to pivotal social and economic developments such as increasing sedentarization, a spread in agriculture, an emergence of a mercantile economy, craft specialization, and increased urbanization. Indeed, several scholars have argued that the Upaniṣads reflect these political and social changes (Thapar 1984, 1993; R. S. Sharma 1983; Olivelle 1992). That the dialogues take place in Videha and Kāśi, both of which became prosperous cities by the time of early Buddhism, has been taken to indicate a process of urbanization. Also, the diversity of geographical locations known to the participants in Upanishadic discussions suggests that travel and trade were already extensive. It is important to keep in mind, however, that there is no conclusive evidence that these particular social changes were taking place. The mere mention of names of cities does not necessarily imply urbanization, and the diversity of geographical locations visited by literary characters does not establish anything concrete about trade or commerce. Admittedly, the early Upaniṣads certainly seem to fit this picture of radical social change, but it is not the aim of this book to anchor the texts conclusively to these general historical changes.

Nevertheless, there are a number of specific changes that are directly reflected in the early Upaniṣads: a shift in geographical orientation, changing attitudes about the sacrifice, and changing definitions about the status of brahmins. It is my opinion that these three issues explored by the texts reflect social changes that were taking place during the time of the composition and compilation of the Upaniṣads, yet it would be impossible to prove such a claim. We can say for certain, however, that these are fundamental issues in the texts and that the philosophical ideas are defined in the context of these changes at a textual level.

One of the most interesting social dynamics that is reflected in the early Upaniṣads is the geographical rivalry between the Vedic heartland of Kuru-Pañcāla and the emerging eastern cities of Videha and Kāśi. As Michael Witzel (1997) and Olivelle (1999) demonstrate, the *Chāndogya Upaniṣad* is set in the western Kuru-Pañcāla area, whereas the *Bṛhadāraṇyaka Upaniṣad* champions the eastern city of Videha, which it presents as superior to the more orthodox western region. The emergence of the east as an important center of Vedic culture is indicated by an often cited passage in the *Śatapatha Brāhmaṇa* (1.4.1.14–7), which recounts the story of King Videgha Māthava, his priest Gotama Rāhūgaṇa, and their move with Agni Vaiśvānara from Pañcāla to Kosala. Agni Vaiśvānara means '*agni* of all people' and represents the sacrificial fire. Both Agni Vaiśvānara and Gotama Rāhūgaṇa are prominent figures in the *Ṛgveda*, and their appearance as part of this legend links the newly emerging cultural center of Kosala with the traditions of the oldest Brahmanical text.[22] Witzel characterizes their symbolic role as linking the Videha dynasty with the 'sacred time' of the *Ṛgveda* (1997, 311). In this way, the arrival of Agni Vaiśvānara is presented as a civilizing process: before his arrival the eastern region is described as uncultivated and marshy, whereas due to the brahmins bringing sacrifice it becomes "sweetened" (311).

This passage also suggests that the emergence of the east as a cultural center was not due to a large-scale migration, but rather represents the movement of specific schools of brahmins who sought to align themselves with newly emerging political leaders.[23] While leaders in the east could offer brahmins new opportunities for patronage and employment, the brahmins could give aspiring kings claims to divine authority through ritual. Witzel shows that textual composers who moved east, especially the Aitareyins, incorporated various eastern tribes into older Vedic legends. These tribes, many of whom had no historical connection with the west, adopted Brahmanical texts and practices as a means of competing with each other.

It was in the east where there emerged the first larger and more centralized states, as indicated by the fact that the final portions of the Brāhmaṇas, which give the most importance to royal rituals such as the *aśvamedha* and *rājasūya,* were composed in the eastern regions. This shift in the focus of the texts suggests that eastern kings not only appropriated Brahmanical texts and practices, but also initiated a number of changes.

That Vedic culture had been imported to the east and that ascending cultural centers such as Videha and Kāśi were in competition with Kuru-Pañcāla is suggested on numerous occasions in the Upanishadic narratives. In the *Bṛhadāraṇyaka Upaniṣad,* King Janaka of Videha stages a competition between his own court priest, Yājñavalkya, and several brahmins from Kuru-Pañcāla. As we will explore further in chapter 2, this competition is not merely about contesting philosophical points of view, but represents a political and regional rivalry between Janaka, as an eastern king gaining power and authority, and established leaders from the west. Janaka uses the assembly of Kuru-Pañcāla brahmins as a way of linking his power with the prestige of the ancient Brahmanical tradition. Accordingly, the shift eastwards can be seen as a process of appropriation in which elites from the east were attempting to model themselves after the legendary rulers from the west, as well as manipulating Vedic texts and practices for their own purposes, inevitably contributing their own ideas and practices in the process.

One of the most important changes to the textual material is an attempt to establish a complete canon. As Witzel explains, "It is thus in these eastern territories of Northern India that a thorough reorganization of the *brāhmaṇa* style texts were carried out (ŚB), including a rethinking of many of the earlier [Yajurveda] 'theological positions' " (1997, 328). One of the indications of this is that the same material is organized differently by various groups. Also, the textual innovations in the east are represented in the hybrid nature of many of the texts. According to Witzel, the various ruptures and breaks that are present in the Vedic texts represent a social situation in which texts were changing hands and employed for different purposes (1997: 319–29). The Vedic schools needed to organize their canon periodically in order to survive in the competitive business of performing sacrifices and gaining patronage. That Janaka invites a number of noted textual composers to his court perhaps represents this process.

This reorganization of Vedic material in the east is also reflected in the composition of the early Upaniṣads. As we will see, a number of characters in the narratives introduce their teachings as new, yet on many occasions the teachings that are ascribed to them consist of material that had already appeared in previous Vedic texts. Bodewitz, for example, points out that much of the material spoken by kings, or members of the *kṣatriya* class (rulers and warriors) in general, that is presented as new to the Brahmanical tradition appears in older sections of the *Jaiminīya Brāhmaṇa* and *Śatapatha Brāhmaṇa*.[24] This is a crucial point because it shows that often what is new about the Upaniṣads is not the teachings themselves, but rather how they are presented. As such, what is particularly innovative about teachings of *ātman*, *prāṇa*, and the five fires is that they appear as the instructions of specific individuals. When we consider this change in the literature within the context of the movement from west to east, narratives and dialogues appear to be attempts by brahmin composers to make older Vedic material seem relevant to a new audience.[25]

Another social change reflected in the Upaniṣads is a movement away from the practice of sacrifice. Scholars remain in disagreement about the fate of the sacrifice in ancient India. Romila Thapar has argued that the Vedic sacrifice became too much of an economic strain and as a consequence went into decline. She describes the process of burning excess wealth as a "prestige economy" that restricted Vedic societies to remain in a prolonged state of "arrested development" (1984, 66). She maintains that because the sacrifice was the central institution and practice in defining social relations, its demise opened up radically new ways for defining social relations, especially political relations: "The discontinuance of the Vedic sacrificial ritual would break the nexus between the *brāhmaṇa* and the *kṣatriya* and would provide a new role for the *kṣatriya*, more in consonance with the broader changes of the time" (1994, 318). Thapar concludes that both the Upaniṣads and the rise of Buddhism reflect this decline of the sacrifice, as well as the emergence of new practices and institutions. Thapar is right to notice that the Upaniṣads and, to a much greater extent the early Buddhist literature, challenge the centrality of sacrifice. However, it is far from clear that the sacrifice went through the radical decline that she portrays. If the importance of the sacrifice had already ceased, then why did the early Buddhist texts criticize it so strongly?[26] Laurie Patton has recently suggested that during the time that the brahmin composers of the Upaniṣads challenged the sacrifice, the brahmin composers of the Gṛhyasūtras continued to perform Vedic rituals and invest them with new meanings and purposes: "We should acknowledge all the while that the sacrifices were still happening, and the old ways still existed while the . . . Upaniṣadic ways emerged" (2005, 185). It is also important to point out that later texts such as the *Mahābhārata* and Dharmaśāstras indicate that the sacrifice continued to be practiced long after the time of the composition of the early Upaniṣads and the early Buddhist texts.

Although it is unlikely that the Vedic sacrifice ceased to be performed, it is significant that the early Upaniṣads show a radical reinterpretation of sacrifice; it is not rejected completely, yet it is not as centrally important as it is in the earlier Vedic texts. One of the most innovative aspects of the narratives and dialogues is that they often assume a sacrificial context, yet they focus on a different set of practices, all of which are defined, often explicitly, in contradistinction to sacrifice. The four practices that are most fully developed by the narratives and dialogues are teaching, debating, advising the king, and controlling procreation, all of which we will explore throughout this book.

Connected to the move away from the practice of sacrifice is the redefinition of the status of brahmin. In the earlier Vedic texts, brahmins are defined by their participation in ritual, and the status of brahmin is established through family lines. In contrast, the Upaniṣads show us a number of nontraditional brahmins who earn their status through learning specific teachings and engaging in a different set of practices. Many of the narrative sections in particular are critical of those who are brahmins only by birth and those brahmins who continue to perform sacrifices. In other words, the Upaniṣads both criticize the old ways of achieving the status of brahmin and establish new ways of becoming a brahmin. One of the central arguments of this book is that through narrative the Upaniṣads actively portray new representations of what it means to be a brahmin and that the attainment of selfhood is closely connected to this new ideal.

CHARACTERIZING THE SELF

Now that we have briefly outlined the texts, ideas, and contexts, let us return to the central arguments of this book. Previous scholars have already acknowledged the shift in focus from ritualism to the self. But, for whom are these teachings about the self available? How does one pursue this knowledge? In what kinds of circumstances can one learn about the self? This book will demonstrate that the stories and dialogues that often introduce discussions about the self are integral to addressing these questions.

As Yohanan Grinshpon has pointed out, traditional commentators such as Śaṅkara have not placed much value on the narrative sections of the Upaniṣads, making a clear distinction between the story (*ākhyāna*) and the knowledge (*vidyā*): "For Śaṅkara . . . all the stories are alike in the sense that they provide an occasion for the transmission of the Upanishadic 'teaching' " (1998, 379–80). As we will see, however, the Upanishadic narratives do much more than merely provide an occasion for teaching. Crucially, they bring attention to how knowledge is transmitted, in what contexts, to whom, and by whom. This is not to say that the situations represented are based on real historical events, but that the literary realism of Upanishadic narrative serves to present philosophy as taking place within the realm of ordinary, everyday experiences.

Moreover, in addition to providing a context, the dialogues constitute an integral part of the teachings of the Upaniṣads. Whereas the doctrinal sections address the ontological status of the *ātman,* the narratives teach how to achieve this status. In other words, the narrative frames suggest that there is a social dimension to the teachings about the self. Although *ātman* is described in universal terms, the stories and dialogues define which individuals can attain knowledge of *ātman,* as well as situate knowledge about *ātman* in specific social situations. The Upanishadic narratives present knowledge of *ātman* as largely restricted to brahmins, and the social situations where *ātman* is discussed are fundamental events in establishing an identity within the brahmin community.

In addition to brahmins, the Upanishadic narratives address their dialogical partners and opponents. In order for brahmins to achieve their goals in this world and the next, they have to enter into dialogical relationships with others. The two groups of people whose participation is necessary for brahmins to earn wealth and status in this world, as well as immortality in the next, are kings and women. Kings are vital because they are the brahmins' employers. Kings reinforce the authority of brahmins and even give them political importance. Women are necessary for brahmins primarily as wives and childbearers. They are most often represented and defined so as to ensure that their role in reproduction will produce male offspring, which is considered necessary for the immortality of brahmin men. Importantly, for both kings and women, their participation requires at least some knowledge of the teachings, suggesting that, in addition to brahmins, kings and women also have access to the kind of knowledge contained in the Upaniṣads. However the extent of their participation in the dialogues is not the same. Kings are often portrayed teaching brahmins, and even when they are cast as students they are sometimes represented as more knowledgeable than brahmins. In their roles as both teachers and students, kings have a potential access to most of the rewards that the teachings offer, including wealth, power, and immortality. Women, although their presence is necessary, have only restricted and indirect access to the Upanishadic goals of knowing the self and achieving immortality. As we will see, in their dialogues with both kings and women, brahmins model their relationships in ways that reinforce their superiority as brahmins.

This book will explore the interactive dimension of Upanishadic teachings by analyzing the dialogues according to four different groups. All the dialogues in the Upaniṣads feature at least one brahmin, but this book distinguishes the different types of dialogues from each other by the brahmins' different dialogical partners. The four different types of dialogues are discussions between: 1) brahmins and students; 2) brahmins and other brahmins; 3) brahmins and kings; and 4) brahmins and women. It is not my intention to claim that the composers and compilers of the Upaniṣads organized the dialogues according to these groups, but rather in this book I use these categories for heuristic purposes to illustrate that as the dialogical partners change, so do the dynamics between individuals, as well as the practices that accompany the discussion and what is at stake for brahmins. This book will show that the brahmins say and do different things according to whom they are speaking.

Additionally, we will use these four categories of dialogue as a way to explore four different social situations. The first category represents education and how one joins the brahmin community. The second type of dialogue features debate and addresses how brahmins establish their reputation and their relative hierarchy among each other. The discussions between brahmins and kings are about patronage and how brahmins earn wealth, accommodation and even political power. The fourth category addresses how brahmins set up a household and secure immortality through progeny. Importantly, all of these different social situations represent fundamental aspects of a brahmin's life.

We will explore these social dimensions of the dialogues by looking at three narrative components: character, social context, and the description of the teaching. With respect to the characters, we will be asking the following questions: How are individual characters represented? What do they do? How do they interact with each other? How are they represented differently in different texts? Concerning the social situations, we will examine: Where and in what situations do these dialogues take place? What is the structure of the scene? What kinds of situations are represented? What modes of address and conduct accompany different situations? What kinds of rewards are promised? With regard to the description of the teaching, we will be examining the following: What is the link between the frame story and the teaching? How is the knowledge characterized?

LITERARY CHARACTERS

This book is not the first study to focus on the characters or dialogues of the Upaniṣads. For example, James Helfer (1968) portrays the dialogue between Naciketas and Yama as an initiation ritual; Ivo Fišer (1984) analyzes the development of Yājñavalkya's character from the early sections of the *Śatapatha Brāhmaṇa* to the *Bṛhadāraṇyaka Upaniṣad*; Grinshpon (1998) argues that there is a hidden *vidyā* (teaching) in the third section of the *Bṛhadāraṇyaka Upaniṣad*; Bodewitz (1973) discusses the dialogues between priests and kings; and Ellison Banks Findly (1985) points out the innovative qualities of Gārgī's argument in her debate with Yājñavalkya.[27] These studies, as well as others that have focused on a particular character or a particular dialogue, have made important contributions to our understanding of the Upaniṣads. What makes this book different from previous investigations is that it will demonstrate that there are common characteristics among the dialogues, and that when we examine these common characteristics together they comprise a consistent set of teachings that are integral to understanding ideas such as *ātman*, *prāṇa*, and immortality.

One of the best studies to date in illustrating how the portrayal of character contributes to the philosophical position of the texts is Patrick Olivelle's examination (1999) of Śvetaketu, a character who appears in a story featured in three different Upaniṣads (BU 6.2.1–16; CU 5.3.1–5.10.10; KṣU 1.1–2). Olivelle's work is a key moment in the history of scholarship about the Upaniṣads, because he moves away from the classical philological approach that looks for an authentic doctrine or an original text. Instead, Olivelle asks, what can be learned about the different Upaniṣads that present the same story in different ways? He argues that the variation in presentation is deliberate and that each version has its own narrative logic. The additions, substitutions, and modifications can be seen as part of the narrative strategies of the respective authors or editors. In this way, the different portrayals of Śvetaketu, as well as of his father, Uddālaka Āruṇi, and of Pravāhaṇa Jaivali, tell us something about the overall stance of the different Upaniṣads. Olivelle concludes that the *Bṛhadāraṇyaka Upaniṣad*, which favors the east, is critical of Kuru-Pañcāla brahmins and presents Śvetaketu as rude and spoiled, while the *Chāndogya Upaniṣad* is more conservative and presents Śvetaketu and Uddālaka Āruṇi more positively. Thus, Olivelle illustrates that the portrayal of specific characters in the Upaniṣads is part of the narrative strategy and political positioning of the texts.

This book will draw from a number of Olivelle's conclusions, including the differences between the *Bṛhadāraṇyaka Upaniṣad* and the *Chāndogya Upaniṣad*. However, whereas Olivelle concentrates on the competing philosophical orientations among the different Upaniṣads, this book will demonstrate that the dialogues throughout the late Brāhmaṇas and early Upaniṣads share a number of common features in terms of structure, motifs, and the relationship to the teachings. One of the most notable aspects of the three versions of Śvetaketu's story, for example, is that they show that three different textual traditions considered the dialogue as an effective means for presenting philosophical ideas. In the *Bṛhadāraṇyaka Upaniṣad* and the *Chāndogya Upaniṣad*, the Śvetaketu story introduces the teachings of the five fires and the two paths, while in the *Kauṣītaki Upaniṣad* it introduces the doctrine of the path to heaven. Throughout this book, I will show that the Upaniṣads use dialogues to convey teachings in similar ways, following comparable patterns and narrative structures, all of which address changes in the lives of brahmins. Although the priests of the *Chāndogya Upaniṣad* seem to emphasize formal instructions between teachers and students more than the priests of the *Bṛhadāraṇyaka Upaniṣad* who focus on debate, both texts use dialogues to connect these practices to the teachings.

Additionally, rather than focus on only one individual, in this book I will examine all the major characters in the Upanishadic dialogues. Importantly, the texts do not tell us what individual characters physically look like, nor does the narrative voice describe their psychology. Rather, literary personae are characterized almost entirely by what they say and what they do, as almost every action is an action of speech. Nevertheless, despite the lack of literary descriptions, the Upaniṣads portray a number of unique personalities.

One of the striking features of the characters is that they are all portrayed as true-to-life individuals. This is not to say that the narratives are historically accurate, but rather that the characters are presented as human and that their actions take place in the human world. In this way, there is a realistic thrust to the narrative. The characters are mere mortals who do things that are quite ordinary, such as discuss and debate, exchange greetings and offer hospitality, and seek material wealth and large families. There are some extraordinary events that take place: fires and animals that talk, women who are possessed by celestial beings, gods and demons learning from the creator god, a person whose head shatters apart. Nonetheless, most of the characters are humans, and their actions take place in the human world in real locations in ancient India. In contrast to many of the tales in the Brāhmaṇas that take place on a mythic time scale and record the actions of gods (*devas*) and celestial beings (*gandharvas*), the Upanishadic narratives are firmly rooted in everyday life.

Furthermore, a number of characters are based on individuals that were already authoritative figures in Vedic literature. Characters such as Śāṇḍilya, Uddālaka Āruṇi, and Yājñavalkya were already known as famous priests before they appeared in the stories and dialogues of the Upaniṣads. The fact that the narratives further develop the personalities and authority of already esteemed figures suggests that a principal function of Upanishadic narrative was to record and create legends about these specific individuals. As we will see, these individuals first appear merely as names that add authority to particular teachings, but by the time of the Upaniṣads, these famous textual composers are developed into literary personalities in extended narrative scenes.

In addition to elevating the status of already legendary figures, the characters function to highlight particular teachings, while discrediting others. While characters such as Yājñavalkya and Satyakāma are depicted positively and serve to endorse particular teachings, characters such as Virocana largely function as an example of what not to say or what not to do. In this way, the characters who are portrayed negatively serve to define Upanishadic philosophy through what it is not. The two groups of people who are criticized by means of the portrayal of individual characters are (1) the orthodox Vedic ritualist, and (2) the non-*ārya*.[28] As we will see, brahmin ritualists are depicted as ignorant of the most valuable teachings, and they are described performing sacrifices that they do not understand. Worse still, Virocana is portrayed as outside the Vedic culture altogether. He does not observe the proper rituals, but rather adheres to non-Vedic practices. Through negative descriptions of brahmin ritualists on the one hand, and non-*ārya*s on the other, the early Upaniṣads present themselves as texts that contain new teachings that oppose the sacrifice, yet as texts firmly rooted within the Brahmanical tradition.

Alternatively, characters such as Yājñavalkya and Satyakāma embody a certain way of life that is presented in contradistinction to that of the ritual priests. As the Upaniṣads are critical of the stereotypical Vedic ritualists, they offer up different models of how to be a brahmin, with Yājñavalkya and Satyakāma serving as two of the best examples. In this way, the literary characters embody or "flesh out" particular teachings of the texts, anchoring abstract claims in the reality of particular individuals in real-life situations.

Generally speaking, all the brahmins who are depicted positively serve as examples for how to be a brahmin. What distinguishes Yājñavalkya and Satyakāma is that the texts give us more information about their lives. In the way that the texts are edited, originally distinct episodes are strung together to offer the outlines of a life story. In both cases their lives are more of a sketch than a comprehensive biography. Nevertheless, distinct episodes are collected together in a chronological order and we are presented with enough information to reconstruct a coherent life story. Whereas Satyakāma lives the life of a teacher and married householder, Yājñavalkya represents a challenge to this ideal as the priest who debates in the court and leaves his household without any male heirs. Both Satyakāma and Yājñavalkya embody their teachings, offering two distinct models of how to be a brahmin.

THE SOCIAL CONDITIONS OF KNOWLEDGE

In addition to anchoring the teachings to specific individuals, Upanishadic narratives situate the transmission of knowledge in a number of specific social situations. Most generally, the dialogue form itself characterizes philosophy as a social practice. Rather than solitary Cartesian figures contemplating their own existence, or even practitioners of yoga in a deep state of meditation, Upanishadic philosophers are depicted interacting with other people. In the Upaniṣads, philosophy is something that is achieved through discussion and debate, confrontation and negotiation, with the dialogue form emphasizing intersubjectivity. Although many teachings address knowledge about the self, within the context of the narratives this knowledge is achieved only through dialogue with others.

Furthermore, the dialogues serve to outline to both brahmins and their dialogical partners which situations are appropriate for philosophical discussion and the proper techniques by which individuals should discuss philosophy, as each situation is connected to particular ways of speaking and behaving. There is an emphasis on real, concrete situations, with the specificity of the details of each scene and consistency of these details with other scenes suggesting that the dialogues represent a coherent portrayal of particular social situations, and that the Upaniṣads are as much about teaching etiquette and proper behavior as they are about personal transformation. Or, more precisely, personal transformation can only take place through strict adherence to the proper practices. In this way, the narratives establish the conditions under which philosophy should be discussed, describing four general social situations: education, debate, the negotiation of patronage, and the conducting of sexual relations. The dialogues establish the importance of these particular practices by connecting specific modes of address and behavior for each.

Another indication of the social context of the teachings is what kinds of rewards are promised to those who learn them. Unlike the later Upaniṣads, the early prose texts do not focus on the state of mind of those who seek to understand *ātman*, but rather make a number of claims as to what kinds of rewards this knowledge can bring, both in this world and the next. Throughout the texts there are passages, often marked by the words *ya evaṃ veda* (when a man knows this), that explicitly state the benefits of knowing either the text as a whole, or particular sections within the text. Although some of these passages promise immortality, others offer more immediate benefits such as cows, gold, and power over one's enemies, firmly rooting the teachings within the concerns of everyday life.

Another important feature of these passages is that they give us an indication, however oblique, of the anticipated audience of the composers and compilers of the texts. The principal audience is, of course, brahmin men. But, as we will see in chapter 3, references to the power to smash one's enemies to bits and to extend one's territory indicate that kings—and the *kṣatriya* class in general—were also part of the imagined audience. There are no such rewards that address women as explicitly, yet there are a number of teachings and instructions for performing rituals where their participation is required. As we will see in chapter 4, these sections are primarily concerned with procreation and aim to ensure male offspring. Nonetheless, these teachings and rituals require the involvement of the brahmin's wife both as sexual and ritual partner. As such, despite not being offered rewards for her own benefit, the brahmin wife emerges as another anticipated audience of the texts.

MYSTERY OR MYSTIQUE: THE CHARACTER OF KNOWLEDGE

One of the difficulties in approaching the Upaniṣads is how to understand a genre of literature that defines itself as secret. As we have seen, the notion of secrecy is intertwined with the meaning of the word *upaniṣad*. How do we go about studying texts that claim to contain secret teachings? How can we understand teachings that claim to be only meant for the initiated? How do we discuss texts whose teachings remain elusive? In his work on the Kartābhajā tradition of West Bengal and Bangladesh, Hugh Urban confronts similar issues regarding secrecy. Urban approaches this problem by concentrating more on the formal features of secrecy than on the secrets themselves. As he explains, "in most cases, the analysis of the strategies and forms of secrecy is both more *fruitful* . . . and more *interesting* than the search for the ever-elusive hidden content" (2001, 20). Urban points out that this does not mean that the content of secrets is meaningless or "semantically empty," but rather that there is often more to say about the "forms and the strategies through which secret information is concealed, revealed and exchanged" (2001, 20).

Similar to Urban, I will examine the formal features of the Upanishadic teachings, rather than attempt to "search for the ever-elusive hidden content." The Upaniṣads are not only traditionally regarded as esoteric texts, but on several occasions explicitly advertise themselves as secret. Teachers introduce their teaching by announcing that it has never reached certain ears before and conclude their instruction by outlining how this knowledge should remain restricted to students and sons. Knowledge is described as secret and opaque, and the path of learning is presented as difficult and dangerous. These details reinforce the secrecy and esoteric nature of the teachings and serve to create a mystique about the texts as a whole.

This esoteric atmosphere, established by the narrative frames, brings an increased importance and value to the teachings. As Charles Malamoud suggests in his discussion of esoteric language in Vedic discourses, "The gods' secret (at least when it claims to be grounded in language) is an artificial one: it proceeds, not from a will to protect a mystery, but rather, that of creating one" (1996, 206). Similarly, Urban comments, "Secrecy . . . is best understood as a strategy for concealing and revealing information. It is a tactic which functions to transform certain knowledge into a rare and valuable commodity, a scarce resource, which in turn enhances the status and prestige . . . of its possessor" (2001, 12).

Part of the particular mystique of the Upaniṣads is that the conversations themselves remain indirect and inconclusive. This lack of closure is crucial to how the brahmins depict themselves as experts in knowledge. Indeed, the Upanishadic narratives suggest that brahmins have a lot to gain by advertising themselves as possessors of secret knowledge. Brahmins command high rewards for their teachings, and there is always an exchange that takes place when knowledge is revealed. In fact, as we will discuss in chapter 3, brahmins get paid for their knowledge even if they are not the ones delivering the teaching. This emphasis on what the brahmins receive for their knowledge is reminiscent of what Lamont Lindstrom, in the context of his anthropological work in the South Pacific, calls a 'conversational economy'—a system of exchanges in which knowledge operates like a commodity that can be bought and sold. People 'swap or sell their secrets and/or knowledge' for money or other goods. 'By preserving patterns of ignorance in the information market, secrecy fuels talk between people who do not know and those who do . . . Knowledge that remains under discursive copyright is often, in fact, known by many people who merely lack the right to use this in serious talk' (1990, 119).

The indirect and inconclusive character of the Upanishadic dialogues also emphasizes that there is always more to be known, that despite profiting from their knowledge the brahmins give very little, if anything, away. These dialogues are as much stories about establishing the brahmins as the ones who know, as they are an expression of what they know. Because the teachings do not speak for themselves, brahmins are always needed to interpret them. In this way, the Upaniṣads continue to create their own mystique by claiming to contain secret teachings, yet at the same time suggesting that true knowledge remains hidden, that there is always more to be learned. Again, Lindstrom has made similar observations: 'A common discursive practice that protects secrets as they are told is budgeted revelation. Incremental revelation of knowledge serves to extend conversational exchange through time' (1990, 120).

It is important to point out, however, that an esoteric discourse is not new to the late Brāhmaṇas, Āraṇyakas, and early Upaniṣads. As Brereton (1999) has demonstrated, a number of hymns in the *Ṛgveda* actually pose a question that is left unanswered, the clues only apparent to those who know the discourse. Although there are a number of ways in which Upanishadic teachings are related to this Rigvedic tradition of riddles, the Upaniṣads are different in that they focus on the teaching of secrets, rather than on the secrets themselves.[29] Instead of actually posing esoteric questions, the Upaniṣads provide narratives about the transmission of esoteric knowledge. In the process, the Upaniṣads emphasize that a secret meaning is not something that is figured out, but rather something that is learned from the proper teacher. One can understand the meaning of the discourse only through someone else who knows.

An illustrative example of this shift from esoteric discourse to stories about individuals who engage in esoteric discourse can be seen in the *Chāndogya Upaniṣad*. In this episode a Vedic student (*brahmacārin*) approaches the brahmins Śaunaka Kāpeya and Abhiprātin Kākṣaseni asking for food. However, when they refuse him he poses a question:

> One god has swallowed four great ones (*mahātman*).
> Who is he, the guardian of the world?
> Him, Kāpeya, mortals do not see,
> Abhiprātin, he lives in many forms (4.3.6).[30]

Here the *brahmacārin* attempts to prove that he is worthy of eating with the two brahmins by showing that he has the proper knowledge. After he poses this question he announces that food has not been offered to whom it belongs. One of the brahmins, Śaunaka Kāpeya, replies with the following answer:

> He is the self (*ātman*) of the gods, the creator of creatures,
> With golden teeth, the devourer, truly wise.
> His greatness is truly great, they say,
> Because he eats what is not food without being eaten (4.3.7).[31]

After providing the answer to the riddle, Śaunaka offers the student some food, indicating that he accepts this student as an educated brahmin. Unlike in the riddle hymns of the *Ṛgveda*, the emphasis in this passage from the Upaniṣads is not on the answer to the riddle. In fact, the answer is provided for us in Śaunaka's response. Rather, this scene emphasizes the social context of posing a riddle, describing the interaction between the student and the two brahmins. The student proves he is a brahmin by showing that he knows the esoteric discourse; by posing a riddle himself, he shows that he is familiar with the secret language of the initiated.

More specifically, the *brahmacārin* in this episode shows that he knows the secret teaching of *ātman*, which despite its numerous meanings remains the most sought-after knowledge in the Upaniṣads. At first glance, the Upanishadic emphasis on teachings about *ātman* might appear similar to the Socratic dictum: know thyself. However, knowledge of the self in the Upaniṣads is quite different from how it appears in the works of Plato. As Alexander Nehemas suggests, "The Socratic dialogues demand of their audience what Socrates asks of his interlocutors: to examine their beliefs on any subject of importance to them, to determine to what other beliefs they are logically related, to accept only those that are compatible with one another, and to live their lives accordingly" (1998, 42). Thus, according to Nehemas, in Plato's dialogues knowledge of the self is achieved by means of introspection and self-examination. In contrast, the Upanishadic dialogues characterize knowledge about the self as an esoteric discourse that can be learned only from the proper teacher and in very specific social situations. Whereas the Socratic self is universalized and theoretically available to anyone, the Upanishadic self is largely restricted to brahmins, and as we will see, even when non-brahmin characters speak about the self, they are often symbolically granted the status of brahmin. Taken together, the dialogues tell brahmins how to receive a proper education, achieve fame, attract students, receive patronage, get married, and have male children, thus indicating that achieving selfhood is closely related to achieving the status of a brahmin.

CHAPTER ONE

Teachers and Students

The Emergence of Teaching as an Object of Discourse

INTRODUCTION

In this chapter we will look at a number of dialogues between teachers and students. These dialogues are significant both because they connect knowledge to particular individuals and because they situate knowledge within a particular social situation. We will focus our attention on prototypical teachers such as Śāṇḍilya and Uddālaka Āruṇi, as well as students such as Śvetaketu and Naciketas. Many of these individuals first appear in the late Brāhmaṇas merely as names mentioned to add authority to particular claims about the Vedic sacrifice. This marks a significant moment in the composition of the Brāhmaṇas, when suddenly it becomes important to link ideas with specific teachers and students, indicating that sacrificial knowledge begins to be authorized through a connection to specific individuals. By the time of the Upaniṣads, these individuals not only appear as authoritative names but also are represented as literary characters in extended narrative scenes.

In addition to describing a number of specific literary personae, these dialogues also present us with several more general character traits for social categories like teachers and students. Teachers show a reluctance to teach and often test pupils as a pedagogical exercise. Students are characterized by their honesty and eagerness to learn, addressing the teacher in respectful ways and offering to work for them.[1] Importantly, these character traits reflect the actions of teachers and students as described in the *upanayana*, the initiation ceremony of a brahmin student, as it is presented in the *Śatapatha Brāhmaṇa*. By looking at the dialogues alongside the *upanayana*, I will demonstrate that episodes about teachers and students reinforce the rules and regulations of teaching as a social practice.

The establishment of a proper code of behavior based on the activity of teaching is important because the Upaniṣads introduce new criteria for achieving the status of brahmin. A number of dialogues are critical of the *brahmabandhu*, the type of brahmin who is a brahmin only because of birth, and maintain that brahmins must also establish their credentials through knowledge and education. As such, the dialogues between teachers and students place more importance on the identity of one's teacher than on the identity of one's father.

One of the features that all of these dialogues have in common is that teachers instruct their students in discourses about the self. Different teachers reveal different understandings of *ātman*, but all present knowledge about the self as a fundamental part of their teachings. Śāṇḍilya identifies *ātman* with *brahman*, while Uddālaka Āruṇi describes *ātman* as the fundamental essence of life. Naciketas learns from Yama that the secret meaning of the sacrifice is to be found within himself, and Prajāpati presents *ātman* as the agent for sensing and cognizing. Although these teachers, as well as others, have different, and often contradicting understandings of *ātman*, they all present knowledge about the self as a new way of thinking that is opposed to Vedic ritualism and that is fundamental to the education of an Upanishadic student.

ŚĀṆḌILYA AND THE TEACHING OF *ĀTMAN* AND *BRAHMAN*

Śāṇḍilya is an appropriate character to begin our discussion with because he appears in some of the earliest narrative scenes in the Brāhmaṇas and is known as the composer of books six through ten of the *Śatapatha Brāhmaṇa*. In the early Upaniṣads, Śāṇḍilya appears four times, yet does not feature in any dialogues. He is mentioned in all three genealogical lists in the *Bṛhadāraṇyaka Upaniṣad*, and in the *Chāndogya Upaniṣad* he is named as the teacher of a discourse about *ātman* and *brahman*.[2] This teaching, that the self is equivalent to the underlying principle of reality, is one of the most important legacies of the early Upaniṣads.

Śāṇḍilya's teaching (CU 3.14.1–4) begins with *brahman*, stating that it is the entire world, and that what happens to people at the time of death is in accordance with their resolve in this world. He then turns his attention to *ātman*, which he describes in a number of different ways. He speaks of *ātman* as made of mind (*manas*), manifested in physical form as the *prāṇās*, and as dwelling within the heart (*hṛdaya*). Throughout his teaching, Śāṇḍilya describes *ātman* as something that defies definition and categorization: it is both smaller than a mustard seed and larger than all the worlds put together, smaller than a grain of rice, yet larger than the earth. As Brereton explains, Śāṇḍilya teaches about the extremes of reality through his use of paradox: "The self is the most intimate part of a person, the very center of one's being, and therefore it is the smallest of the small. Yet, at the same time, it surpasses everything. The paradox thus undercuts any exclusion or any separation of an individual from the rest of the world, for there is nothing beyond the self" (1990, 130).

After describing *ātman* in various ways, Śāṇḍilya then claims that *ātman* captured this whole world. This return to the subject of the whole world comes just before equating *ātman* with *brahman*. Knowledge of this equation, according to Śāṇḍilya, leads one to overcome death: "This self (*ātman*) of mine within the heart is *brahman*. On departing from here, I will enter into him" (3.14.4).[3] Brereton explains that the equivalence between *ātman* and *brahman* emphasizes that through knowledge of the universe, one can come to understand oneself: "Thus, in Upanishadic terms, the *brahman* is discovered within the *ātman*, or conversely, the secret of one's self lies in the root of all existence" (1990, 118).

The equivalence of *ātman* and *brahman* is the most well-known teaching in the Upaniṣads and is clearly the central message of Śāṇḍilya's instruction. Nevertheless, it is important to point out that this understanding of *ātman* is not shared by a number of other teachers. In most of the teachings that we will examine in this chapter the equivalence of *ātman* and *brahman* is not emphasized, or even mentioned. For example, Uddālaka Āruṇi, who imparts some of the most influential teachings of *ātman*, never mentions *brahman*.[4] Additionally, in several teachings where *ātman* is explicitly associated with *brahman*, the term *brahman* appears in a list with a number of other important terms. In the *Bṛhadāraṇyaka Upaniṣad* (1.6.3), for example, *ātman* is equated with the *uktha* (verses of the *Ṛgveda*), with the *sāman* (chants of the *Sāmaveda*) and with *brahman*.[5] A similar type of list appears in the *Aitareya Upaniṣad* (3.3), which equates *ātman* with *brahman*, Indra, Prajāpati, all the *devas* (gods), the five *mahābhūtas* (gross elements), and other things. These sections do not emphasize a specific correlation between *ātman* and *brahman*, but list *brahman* in the same way as they mention a number of other central ideas, such as Prajāpati and the *devas*, thus highlighting the importance of *ātman*.

It is also significant that there are many meanings of *brahman* throughout the Upaniṣads.[6] As Olivelle points out, "Brahman may mean a 'formulation of truth,' the Veda or the ultimate and basic essence of the cosmos" (1996, lvi).[7] As such, to identify something with *brahman* can be a way of bestowing a particular teaching with special significance. In this way, as Brereton suggests, in the Upaniṣads "*brahman* remains an open concept." *Brahman* is "the designation given to whatever principle or power a sage believes to be behind the world and to make the world explicable" (1990, 118).

It is not my intention to devalue the profundity of Śāṇḍilya's teaching, but rather to show that this is not the only teaching, nor the only understanding of *ātman*, contained in the Upaniṣads. According to the *Brahma Sūtra* and later Vedānta philosophers, the equivalence of *ātman* and *brahman* is the fundamental message of all the Upaniṣads. Additionally, a number of modern translators of the Upaniṣads, including Deussen, Hume, and Radhakrishnan, consider this the most important idea put forth by the texts. Deussen argues that the entire philosophy of the Upaniṣads revolves around *ātman* and *brahman*: "All thoughts of the Upanisads move around two fundamental ideas. They are ātman and Brahman" ([1919] 2000, 38). Hume characterizes the identification of *ātman* and *brahman* as a discovery that was waiting to happen since the early Vedic period, maintaining that the essential oneness of *ātman* and *brahman* was "hinted at" even before the Upaniṣads and that there was a "suspicion that these two theories were both of the same Being" ([1921] 1975, 31).[8]

Despite the fact that recent scholarship has expanded its considerations of the Upaniṣads to take into account their numerous and sometimes contradictory teachings, the equivalence of *ātman* and *brahman* remains the central doctrine associated with the texts. J. C. Heesterman, for example, sees the merging of these two ideas as already expected by the earlier Vedic material: "So fire, self [*ātman*], and *brahman* were already diffusely and shiftingly associated with each other in the visionary utterances of the Vedic poets and located in man, himself the solution of the cosmic riddle of life and death" (1993, 220). Brian Smith, in his studies of ritual ontology, also describes the *ātman/brahman* equivalence as a conclusion anticipated in discussions about the sacrifice:

> Taken together, then, the bandhus of ancient Indian ritualistic philosophy theoretically can account for and hook together everything in the universe. Such high ambitions can indeed be

> witnessed within Vedic texts, culminating perhaps in the Upanisads . . . and its ultimate product, the equation of the microcosm (*ātman*) and macrocosm (*brahman*). (1994, 12)

Although neither of these scholars concentrates specifically on the Upaniṣads, their assumptions illustrate how pervasive this reading continues to be in academic discourse. The importance of *ātman/brahman* has, in fact, been overemphasized, but more importantly, the focus on this teaching has taken attention away from other sections of the texts. Olivelle has pointed out this tendency among scholars:

> Even though this equation played a significant role in later developments of religion and theology in India and is the cornerstone of one of its major theological traditions, the Advaita Vedānta, it is incorrect to think that the single aim of all the Upaniṣads is to enunciate this simple truth. A close reader of these documents will note the diversity of goals that their authors pursue, chief among which are food, prosperity, power, fame, and a happy afterlife . . . Many scholars ignore these and similar passages in search for the 'philosophy' or 'the fundamental conception' of the Upaniṣads. (1996, lvi)[9]

As the equivalence of *ātman* and *brahman* is assumed to be the central philosophical position, or indeed, the underlying meaning of the texts, other sections have tended to be ignored or explained away. Hume is characteristic of this lack of consideration for the "non-philosophical" material: "In a few passages the Upanishads are sublime in their conception of the Infinite and of God, but more often they are puerile and groveling in trivialities and superstitions" ([1921] 1975, 70). As we turn our attention to the dialogues, as well as creation myths and procreation rites, we will see that rather than being extraneous, trivial material, these sections are central to the teachings of the texts.

ŚĀṆḌILYA: FROM RITUALIST TO TEACHER

One of the most fundamental aspects of the teaching of *ātman/brahman* is that it emphasizes Śāṇḍilya as its proponent. In addition to teaching the equivalence of *ātman* and *brahman* in the *Chāndogya Upaniṣad*, Śāṇḍilya also appears as the teacher of a similar discourse in the *Śatapatha Brāhmaṇa* (10.6.3.2). Thus, on the two occasions when this teaching is presented in the late Brāhmaṇas and early Upaniṣads,

Śāṇḍilya appears as the teacher. This represents an important trend in Vedic literature, as the truth of a teaching begins to be established by the authority of a specific individual.

Indeed, this trend coincides with the emergence of the dialogue form. In the late Brāhmaṇas and early Upaniṣads the dialogue is employed both to emphasize the authority of specific teachers and to recount the process of the transmission of knowledge. In these passages there are descriptions of a social situation new to Vedic literature: the teacher and student discussion. Of course, the dialogical nature of some of the poems of the *Ṛgveda* and the implicit instructions of the ritual texts suggest that the earlier Vedic material also was passed from teacher to student, and we would assume, especially in light of the accuracy with which the texts have been preserved, that strict modes of speech and behavior accompanied this transmission of knowledge.[10] What marks the pedagogical episodes from the late Brāhmaṇas and early Upaniṣads, however, is that the transmission of knowledge itself, as well as the relationship between the teacher and student, becomes a focus of the texts. Indeed, a number of stories are developed that glorify brahmins as teachers and that give details about how teachers and students interact with each other, thus placing these pedagogical situations as important activities through which individual brahmins derive authority. Priests are no longer praised for the sacrifices they perform, but rather their marks of authority are teaching, discussing, learning, and debating. As Romila Thapar explains, "The new teaching moved away from *brāhmaṇas* as priests to *kṣatriyas* and *brāhmaṇas* as teachers" (1994, 311).

Importantly, Śāṇḍilya is one of the first brahmins in Vedic literature who becomes known primarily as a teacher, rather than as a ritualist. Although he is never presented as participating in a full dialogue, it is significant that many of the times that his voice of authority is quoted it is from the context of teaching a particular student during a specific moment of instruction. In this way, he is portrayed both as a voice of authority and as someone who articulates his knowledge within conversations with students. On a number of the occasions in which his name is mentioned he is simply cited as an expert about ritual procedure. For example, at the end of the ninth book of the *Śatapatha Brāhmaṇa* (9.5.2.15–6), Śāṇḍilya is quoted about the ontological connection between the body of the sacrificer and the body of the sacrifice. Also, in a passage about the sacrificial bricks (*chandasya*), Śāṇḍilya's authority is invoked (7.5.2.43). In these cases, simply his name is mentioned and his status as a legendary figure is employed to give credence to this particular point of ritual action.

However, in a number of other passages, Śāṇḍilya is depicted in specific dialogical situations with students. Although these short exchanges are not the full dialogues that we see in the Upaniṣads, they are significant because they begin to show an interest in recounting the transmission of knowledge and in investing the act of teaching with a certain authority. For example, in the *Śatapatha Brāhmaṇa,* Śāṇḍilya is quoted as an authority on building the fire altar. On this occasion he is specifically named as a teacher, and he is depicted disputing with his student Sāptarathavāhani (10.1.4.10); on another occasion, Śāṇḍilya is described teaching the Kaṅkatīyas (ŚB 9.4.4.17). In these examples, not only is Śāṇḍilya named, but the narrative also gives us the identity of his students. Additionally, the text includes details about these distinct teaching encounters, telling us that at the end of his lesson to the Kaṅkatīyas, Śāṇḍilya "went on his way" saying that one should yoke day by day and unyoke day by day. Here, we see the inclusion of narrative details that connect the words of Śāṇḍilya to a particular event in space and time, thus grounding his authority in a specific moment of instruction. This is significant because at the same time that discursive knowledge is given importance over ritual activity, the act of teaching becomes an object of discourse. In these examples it is not merely the knowledge itself that is emphasized, but the process of teaching and the interaction between teacher and student.

These short episodes featuring Śāṇḍilya also show a tendency towards creating legends and stories about textual composers, emphasizing that texts and teachings have authors with names and life stories. Mahidāsa Aitareya is another famous teacher and textual composer who emerges as a voice of authority of esoteric teachings. According to Sāyaṇa, Mahidāsa authored the first three books of the *Aitareya Āraṇyaka,* as well as the entire *Aitareya Brāhmaṇa.* Like Śāṇḍilya, Mahidāsa not only is ascribed authorship to these texts, but also is cited within these texts as the teacher of a number of discourses (AĀ 2.1.8; 2.3.7).[11] Keith points out that he is most likely not the real author of these texts, although he could have been their editor or compiler ([1909] 1995, 16). Nevertheless, both Mahidāsa and Śāṇḍilya represent the kind of brahmin character portrayed in the Upaniṣads and illustrate that one of the most important literary innovations in the Brāhmaṇas, Āraṇyakas, and Upaniṣads is that these texts begin to recount legends about their own composers.[12]

By focusing on Śāṇḍilya and his development as a literary character, we can see that although the equivalence of *ātman* and *brahman* has often been represented as the essential teaching of the Upaniṣads, not enough attention has been paid to its teacher. The *ātman/brahman* teaching is specifically associated with Śāṇḍilya, and along with a number of short dialogues in the *Śatapatha Brāhmaṇa*, represents a focus on the authority of a specific individual, as well as an appeal to specific moments of instruction. In this context, Śāṇḍilya is one of several teachers who gives instructions about the self and who emphasizes the social practice of teaching.

UDDĀLAKA ĀRUṆI AND THE TEACHING OF *TAT TVAM ASI*

Uddālaka Āruṇi is another Upanishadic teacher known for his discourses on *ātman*. Whereas Śāṇḍilya teaches about the equivalence of *ātman* and *brahman*, Uddālaka describes *ātman* as the essence of life (CU 6.1–16). Indeed, in his teaching to his son Śvetaketu, Uddālaka describes the natural processes of a number of living organisms and claims that *ātman* is the common essence that gives life to all living things.[13] In order to make his point, Uddālaka uses many metaphors from the natural world. For example, he compares the *ātman* that exists in all living things to the nectar that, despite originating from different trees, when gathered together forms a homogenous whole. In the same way, argues Uddālaka, all living beings merge into the existent: "Whatever they are in this world, a tiger, a lion, a wolf, a boar, a worm, a fly, a gnat, or a mosquito, they all become that" (CU 6.9.3, 6.10.2).[14]

Throughout his instruction to his son, Uddālaka repeats one particular phrase on several occasions: *tat tvam asi*. The Vedānta tradition has rendered Uddālaka's refrain as "you are that," with philosophers such as Śaṅkara taking *tat tvam asi* to refer to the identity of *ātman* and *brahman*. As mentioned above, however, Uddālaka does not once use the word *brahman*. Furthermore, Brereton (1986) has cast doubt on the traditional rendering of this phrase, arguing that in Vedic grammar the pronoun *tat* (that) is neuter, and therefore cannot correspond with the masculine pronoun *tvam* (you). Thus, according to Brereton, if "you are that" was the intended meaning, then the passage should read *sa tvam asi*.[15] He concludes that *tat tvam asi* is better rendered as "that is how you are." Taken this way, Uddālaka uses this refrain to explain to Śvetaketu that he is made from the same essence as phenomena in the natural world. When Uddālaka points to the *nyagrodha* tree, for example, he tells Śvetaketu that he exists in the same way as the tree: the *nyagrodha* tree grows and lives because of an invisible essence and everything exists by means of such an essence. Accordingly, Uddālaka teaches that *ātman* is the essential life force in all living beings. At the end of his instruction, as Brereton explains, "Uddālaka personalizes the teaching. Śvetaketu should look upon himself in the same way. He, like the tree and the whole world, is pervaded by this essence, which is his final reality and true self" (1986, 109).

Crucially, this dialogue not only emphasizes what Uddālaka Āruṇi teaches, but also brings attention to his method of instruction. Throughout his lesson to Śvetaketu, Uddālaka points to observable phenomena and sets up repeatable experiments for the sake of leading Śvetaketu to a proper understanding. In order to show the subtlety of *ātman*, he instructs Śvetaketu to cut a banyan fruit and then to cut a seed within the fruit. When he has cut the seed, Śvetaketu proclaims that he cannot see anything inside it. Yet Uddālaka likens the fine essence within the seed that cannot even be seen to *ātman*. In order to show how *ātman* permeates everything but cannot be seen, he asks Śvetaketu to put a chunk of salt in water. A day later, Śvetaketu cannot locate the chunk of salt in the jug of water. However, he finds that even though he cannot see the salt it can be tasted in every part of the jug. Through this experiment Śvetaketu learns that, like salt in water, *ātman* permeates his entire body despite the fact that it is not immediately observable to the senses. In other examples, Uddālaka instructs his son about *ātman* by means of comparison with natural processes such as bees making honey, rivers flowing towards an ocean, and sap flowing out of a tree.[16]

Additionally, at one point Uddālaka instructs his son to refrain from eating for fifteen days. After this period he asks Śvetaketu to recite the verses from the *Ṛgveda*, the formulas from the *Yajurveda*, and the chants from the *Sāmaveda*. However, because he had fasted for fifteen days, Śvetaketu cannot remember any of this material. Uddālaka then compares Śvetaketu's inability to remember the Vedas to a sacrificial fire that goes out because it runs out of fuel. Uddālaka concludes, "Eat, then you will understand me" (CU 6.7.3). As opposed to traditional Vedic knowledge that is based upon the ontological connections that are made through ritual action, here Uddālaka explains the physiological connection between nourishment and memory.[17] Śvetaketu understands what his father is teaching because he actually experiences a memory loss when he goes for fifteen days without eating.

Although these may seem like quite simple experiments, they indicate a significant change in the means for attaining knowledge. As Thapar points out, the Upaniṣads do not construct merely a different ontological framework, but knowledge is established in different ways:

"The nature of the change was a shift from acceptance of the Vedas as revealed and as controlled by ritual to the possibility that knowledge could derive from intuition, observation, and analysis" (1994, 307). In this way, Uddālaka's teaching is important not only for the philosophical claims he makes, but also for the methods he prescribes for acquiring knowledge.

UDDĀLAKA AND ŚVETAKETU: ACTING OUT THE *UPANAYANA*

By far the most distinctive method for acquiring knowledge that is adopted throughout the Upanishadic dialogues, however, is the establishment of specific modes of address and behavior that accompany teaching. In this way, a significant aspect of the dialogue between Uddālaka and Śvetaketu is that it closely resembles the *upanayana*, as it is presented in the *Śatapatha Brāhmaṇa* (11.5.4.1–18).[18] The *upanayana* is the initiation ceremony through which one enters into the life of a Vedic student (*brahmacārin*). The first detailed description of the *upanayana* appears in the eleventh book of the *Śatapatha Brāhmaṇa*. As we will see, a number of the details in this presentation of the *upanayana* are featured in the dialogues between teachers and students throughout the early Upaniṣads.

The *upanayana* begins with the student approaching the teacher. The student announces, "I have come for *brahmacarya* . . . let me be a *brahmacārin*." The teacher responds with a question, in this case asking for the student's name. Importantly, the first action that the teacher performs is to take his student by the right hand and to make invocations to various gods. The *Śatapatha Brāhmaṇa* (11.5.4.12) later explains that by laying his right hand on the student, the teacher becomes pregnant with him. After these invocations, the teacher proclaims, "You are a *brahmacārin*." He then asks him to sip water, to do work, and to put fuel on the fire. The *Śatapatha Brāhmaṇa* account also describes a number of practices that are features of initiation in later literature: teaching the Sāvitrī *mantra*, giving the staff, the girdle, and garment to the student; and placing fuel on the fire.[19]

Walter Kaelber has argued that this presentation of the *upanayana* is of archaic origin: "Although the first extended literary reference to the student's initiation (*Upanayana*) is found in the Śatapatha Brāhmaṇa, there can be no question, as scholars have demonstrated, that this initiation as well as other activities of the *brahmacārin* are of archaic origin" (1989, 111).[20] Whether this description of teaching represents an older practice or not, it is significant that the *upanayana* is first described in the late Brāhmaṇas. As such, it is first presented as an object of discourse at the same time that dialogues between teachers and students begin to appear in the texts. Furthermore, the *upanayana* shares a number of details with these dialogues, together establishing the normative practices within which Upanishadic knowledge is learned.

The establishment of a proper code of behavior based on the activity of teaching is vital because education is a primary means of delimiting and controlling knowledge. Talal Asad makes this point in describing the importance of educational practices in establishing religious doctrine: "The connection between religious theory and practice is fundamentally a matter of intervention—of constructing religion in the world (and not in the mind) through definitional discourses, interpreting true meanings, excluding some utterances and practices and including others" (1993, 44). Similarly, the Upanishadic dialogues both outline particular modes of address and behavior, as well as connect these actions to specific teachings. Throughout the dialogues, the authority of knowledge is generated by the social practices of teaching.

The dialogue between Uddālaka Āruṇi and Śvetaketu, for example, not only emphasizes a new orientation of knowledge and a new way of attaining it, but also outlines the rules and regulations for a brahmin student. The dialogue begins when Uddālaka advises his son to become a *brahmacārin*. He explains that everyone in the family had received the traditional Vedic education and that no one of their clan is a *brahmabandhu*, one who is a brahmin only because of birth (CU 6.1.1). Here, Uddālaka distinguishes between two kinds of brahmins: those who are brahmins merely because of their birth and those brahmins who earn their status by means of their knowledge. Śvetaketu, although already a brahmin by birth, is encouraged to receive a proper education, and thus become a true brahmin like his father and grandfather.

Accordingly, Śvetaketu leaves his father and becomes a *brahmacārin* for twelve years, during which time he learns all the Vedas. The dialogue tells us that Śvetaketu's education begins when he is twelve and continues until he is twenty-four years old. These details about the number of years of a *brahmacarya* education are shared by other passages in the Upaniṣads.[21] For example, Upakosala Kāmalāyana lives as a Vedic student under Satyakāma for twelve years as well.

Like a number of teachings in the Upaniṣads, this dialogue criticizes traditional Vedic learning. Śvetaketu, after finishing his studies, returns arrogant (*mahāmanas*) and proud (*stabdha*), thinking that he is learned (CU 6.1.2–3). However, Śvetaketu's education proves to be incomplete, as he does not know his father's discourse about the rules of substitution. Even though Śvetaketu has studied for twelve years and has learned all the Vedas, he has not learned the type of knowledge that is characteristic of Upanishadic teachings.

In this dialogue Uddālaka Āruṇi represents the Upanishadic teacher who is familiar with knowledge about *ātman*, and he is contrasted with the eminent (*bhagavantas*) men who personify the traditional Vedic teacher. Although Uddālaka is Śvetaketu's father, the dialogue does not present him as his son's original teacher, as Śvetaketu initially goes away to receive his education. Rather, Uddālaka emerges as Śvetaketu's true teacher because he knows the true discourse, and not merely because he is supposed to be his son's teacher. In this dialogue he is presented favorably and contrasted to the official teachers, an important feature of this encounter because it is different from how their pedagogical relationship appears in other contexts. In a dialogue that immediately precedes this one in the *Chāndogya Upaniṣad* (CU 5.11–24), Uddālaka is cast as his son's original teacher, and Śvetaketu is again portrayed as an arrogant student who has received traditional Vedic teaching, but who has not learned the most fundamental knowledge. In this case, however, the king Pravāhaṇa Jaivali is characterized as knowledgeable, while Uddālaka Āruṇi is the ignorant and orthodox brahmin. We will examine this dialogue in more detail in chapter 3. In this discussion, however, it is noteworthy that this dialogue employs literary characters to present teachings about the self in contradistinction to traditional Vedic learning.

Nevertheless, this scene does not reject traditional Vedic knowledge completely, but rather suggests that Śvetaketu's teachers had lost touch with the teachings of Vedic antiquity. Indeed, Uddālaka connects his own teachings to the Vedic tradition when later in this dialogue he says that his discourse about the three appearances represents the knowledge of the great householders (*mahāśāla*) and great Vedic scholars (*mahāśrotriya*) of the past (CU 6.4.5). Thus, this dialogue rejects the authority of Śvetaketu's traditional teachers, while at the same time it authorizes Uddālaka's teaching by equating it with the Vedic tradition. This ambivalence is characteristic of the Upaniṣads in general, which firmly place themselves within the Vedic tradition, yet make a number of pointed critiques about Vedic ideas and practices. In the dialogues this ambivalence is played out through the interaction of particular characters, with Yājñavalkya, Naciketas, and Satyakāma often representing the ideal Upanishadic brahmins, while characters such as Śvetaketu's teachers and Yājñavalkya's opponents personify the traditional priests who are out of touch with the contemporary discourse.

INDRA AS THE PERSISTENT STUDENT

Another dialogue that depicts the student/teacher relationship features Prajāpati teaching both Indra and Virocana. In this episode, the Vedic myth of the battle between the *deva*s (gods) and *asura*s (demons) is recast as a competition over knowledge of *ātman* (CU 8.7.2).[22] This cosmic battle is repeated several times throughout the *Ṛgveda* and is a myth that continues in the Brāhmaṇas as well as in the *Mahābhārata* and Purāṇas.[23] As the textual and social contexts change, Indra's ability to defeat the *asura*s is attributed to different means. In the *Ṛgveda* it is *soma*—the sacrificial drink and food of the gods—that gives Indra the ability to conquer the *asura*s, while in the Brāhmaṇas the most important factor is the performance of the sacrifice. In the *Chāndogya Upaniṣad* Indra and Virocana attempt to establish their supremacy over one another by means of mastering Upanishadic teachings. Significantly, Prajāpati, the god most associated with the ontology of the sacrifice, appears as the teacher of this new knowledge.[24] In this telling of the cosmic battle, knowledge of the *ātman* replaces the sacrifice as that which is considered most important to the *deva*s. Moreover, Indra and Virocana are not interested in *ātman* merely for the sake of knowledge, but wish to obtain the worlds and have their desires fulfilled. In this way, like *soma* in the *Ṛgveda* and the sacrifice in the Brāhmaṇas, knowledge of *ātman* is directly linked to military and political power. The dialogue emphasizes this point by repeating that knowledge of *ātman* leads to obtaining all the worlds and fulfilling all desires (CU 8.7.2).

This dialogue also outlines a number of practices associated with the *upanayana*. When Indra and Virocana initially approach Prajāpati in order to learn about *ātman*, they arrive in the presence of their prospective teacher carrying firewood (CU 8.7.2). These two narrative details, the approach of the student and the offering of firewood, feature in the *Śatapatha Brāhmaṇa* account of the *upanayana*, and appear in a number of the teacher/student dialogues throughout the Upaniṣads. Together, these descriptions establish that it is up to students to seek out a teacher and that they should arrive willing to work for him. The usual tasks that students perform for teachers are tending the fires and taking care of the cows. The *Chāndogya Upaniṣad* (4.6.1), for example, describes Satyakāma working for his teacher by herding his cows, building a fire, and feeding the fire with wood. In the Upaniṣads carrying firewood is the most common trope for a student who offers to gather fuel and tend the fires for his teacher.

Throughout his encounter with Prajāpati, Indra is cast as a model pupil who is persistent in his search for knowledge. This is emphasized as he continues to return to Prajāpati in search of the true knowledge of *ātman*. Typically, Upanishadic teachers do not part with knowledge easily, so students such as Indra have to show that they are willing to work hard and be patient for the rewards of learning. Initially, both Indra and Virocana live as *brahmacārins* for twelve years before Prajāpati offers to give them instruction. This is not only a period of receiving instruction, but also a period when students may have to endure a number of tests to prove they are worthy of their teacher's knowledge. Even after thirty-two years, Prajāpati asks Indra and Virocana what they wanted when they came to him in the first place (CU 8.7.3). This question represents the teacher's characteristic aloofness and the importance for students to remain persistent in their quest for knowledge. Similarly, as we will see, Yama is reluctant to teach Naciketas (KaU 1.12) and Raikva does not impart his knowledge initially to Jānaśruti (CU 4.1). This reluctance to teach, at least initially, is one of the most common traits of the Upanishadic teacher, and is also reminiscent of knowledge exchanges observed by Lindstrom during his anthropological work in the South Pacific: 'Knowers, rather than destroying all their secrets in some impressive flow of information, carefully time their revelations so that these last from conversation to conversation. Here, secret tellers may indicate to auditors that they are holding back the real truths of their knowledge, although they communicate enough to convince people of the existence of their secrets to make these conversationally conspicuous" (1990, 120). As Prajāpati delivers his teaching in 'carefully timed' increments, Indra has to prove that he is both sufficiently intelligent and eager to learn.

When Prajāpati finally gets around to giving his first lesson, he imparts false knowledge, telling Indra and Virocana that the self that one sees in a mirror is the true *ātman*. He then orders them both to dress themselves beautifully, and he sends them on their way thinking that the external appearance of the self is the true *ātman*. However, Indra soon recognizes that this teaching cannot be correct. Before arriving back with the other gods, Indra returns to Prajāpati, again with firewood, and announces that he sees nothing worthwhile in this teaching, because he realizes that this kind of knowledge will not last: if the *ātman* is just the body, then the *ātman* would die when the body dies. Prajāpati tells him that if he stays for another thirty-two years he will teach him further.

Prajāpati's second teaching is that the true *ātman* goes happily about in a dream. Again, Indra leaves Prajāpati thinking that he has learned about *ātman*, but again he notices that Prajāpati has given him a false teaching. For a third time, Indra approaches Prajāpati, again carrying firewood and demanding further instruction. On this occasion, Prajāpati connects *ātman* with the state of dreamless sleep. In the following chapter we will see that this particular teaching is associated with Yājñavalkya. In this dialogue, however, this presentation of the self is not the true *ātman*, but rather is another false teaching that Prajāpati imparts to Indra. Yet once again Indra realizes that this is not the true *ātman* and he returns with firewood one more time finally to hear the true teaching. This time, Prajāpati demands that he stay for five more years, to bring his total number of years as a *brahmacārin* to 101. In his concluding lesson to Indra, Prajāpati explains that the true *ātman* is immortal because it leaves the body at the time of death.

Although *ātman* is the central idea of Prajāpati's teachings, his definition of *ātman* differs considerably from the teachings of both Śāṇḍilya and Uddālaka Āruṇi. Prajāpati describes *ātman* as the one who is aware behind the faculties of smell, sight, speech, hearing, and thinking. In this way, *ātman* is depicted as a consciousness that is the base of the faculties of sensing and cognizing. In order to make his point, Prajāpati first delivers a number of false teachings, which both represents potential rival positions and tests Indra's resolve as a student. Importantly, by challenging Indra's ability to distinguish the correct teaching from the false ones, Prajāpati prepares his student for the life of a brahmin teacher. As we will see in the following chapter, being a brahmin is a competitive occupation that includes elements of risk and deceit. Some brahmins do not know the meaning of the rituals they perform, while others challenge each other in debates with questions that they do not know themselves. When we look at Prajāpati's instructions in this context, we can see that a valuable aspect of imparting false teachings is preparing students for these situations. In this way, Prajāpati's deceit is not conducted out of spite, but out of pedagogy; by not telling Indra what he knows, he leads Indra towards the truth, in this case towards knowledge of the self.

In this dialogue, as Indra is a model of how to be a good Upanishadic student, Virocana is depicted as the superficial student who believes in false teachings. As such, Virocana serves to represent non-Vedic practices in a negative way. J. N. Mohanty suggests that Virocana's understanding of *ātman* as the material body represents the point of view of the Lokāyatas (2000, 3–4).[25] Indeed, this understanding of *ātman* as the body (*dehātmavāda*) is a central claim of the anti-Brahmanical materialism of the Lokāyata tradition. Whether or not this is a specific reference to the Lokāyatas, however, it is clear that Virocana's position represents a non-Vedic point of view. For example, Virocana is also depicted as following practices that are outside the Vedic tradition: he does not give gifts to brahmins, has no faith, and does not offer sacrifices. Furthermore, the narrative tells us that people who share this false understanding of *ātman* prepare a dead body with alms obtained by begging (*bhikṣa*), clothes (*vasana*), and adornments (*alaṃkāra*) (CU 8.8.5).[26] As in Uddālaka's teaching to Śvetaketu, this dialogue presents a situation in which an Upanishadic teaching is contrasted with rival positions and practices. Whereas Uddālaka's instruction is presented in contradistinction to traditional Vedic knowledge, Prajāpati's teaching of *ātman* is directly contrasted with a number of false doctrines of the self, some of which are explicitly non-Vedic.

NĀRADA AND SANATKUMĀRA: KNOWLEDGE OF *ĀTMAN* AS MORE IMPORTANT THAN THE VEDAS

In a dialogue between Nārada and Sanatkumāra, knowledge of *ātman* is directly contrasted with more traditional Vedic knowledge (CU 7.1). This encounter, which we have mentioned briefly at the beginning of the introduction, features the ancient sage Nārada as the student and Sanatkumāra, one of the mind-born sons of Brahmā, as the teacher. Nārada approaches his teacher having learned the entire Vedic curriculum, yet still acknowledging his ignorance of *ātman*, thus indicating that the entire corpus of Vedic knowledge is presented as inferior to Upanishadic teachings about the self. In addition to highlighting *ātman*, this dialogue also emphasizes several teaching practices that are mentioned in the *upanayana*, as well as in other dialogues. For example, Nārada is cast a persistent student, who, like Indra, shows an initiative to learn and on several occasions demands to know more from his teacher. In fact, throughout this dialogue Nārada repeats the same refrain on fourteen occasions, saying, "Sir, tell it to me" (CU 7.1–15). This is also a characteristic of Śvetaketu in his dialogue with his father Uddālaka Āruṇi, where he makes the same request nine different times (CU 6.5.1–6, 15.3). Although these refrains could be explained in terms of a literary convention, they also serve to characterize the speakers who say them. In these cases, students not only approach their teachers, but continue to display a desire to learn. If, like Virocana, they are satisfied with the initial utterances of their teacher, they are in danger of returning home with a false teaching.

As Nārada is portrayed as a model student, Sanatkumāra is typical of a number of teachers throughout the Upaniṣads, for whom an important part of their etiquette is to receive students with a question about who they are or what they already know. As we have seen in the *upanayana* in the *Śatapatha Brāhmaṇa*, the teacher greets his student by asking his name. Similarly, when Nārada asks him for a teaching, Sanatkumāra responds by asking him what he already knows (CU 7.1.1). Indeed, there are other examples that illustrate these common features between the *upanayana* and the pedagogical dialogues. In the *Śatapatha Brāhmaṇa* (10.3.3.1) Dhīra Sāptaparṇeya approaches Mahāsāla Jābāla asking him for a teaching and Jābāla greets him by asking him what he already knows; also, when King Pravāhaṇa receives Śvetaketu, he asks him if he has learned from his father (BU 6.2.1; CU 5.3.1). These situations indicate the close relationship between these dialogues and the *upanayana*, and reinforce the hierarchical relationship between teacher and student. As we will see in the context of debate, asking the first question is often associated with the position of power. In these dialogues asking the first question is equated with the superior status of the teacher.

Another salient feature of Sanatkumāra's instruction to Nārada is that he addresses how to speak well in a debate. As we have seen with Prajāpati's instruction to Indra, a vital aspect of education in the Upaniṣads is preparing students for the activities in a brahmin's life. In this case, Sanatkumāra prepares Nārada for debating against other brahmins by telling him how to respond if someone accuses him of being an *ativādin*, which throughout the Upaniṣads, refers to someone who debates well or "out-talks."[27] In some instances, this term is used negatively to suggest that one who argues well does not necessarily have true knowledge. For example, in the *brahmodya* in King Janaka's court, Śākalya accuses Yājñavalkya of being an *ativādin* when he doubts whether Yājñavalkya's debating skills are representative of true wisdom (BU 3.9.19). Sanatkumāra, however, describes an *ativādin* positively and suggests that this is a crucial aspect of his teaching to Nārada. He instructs Nārada that one should openly admit to being an *ativādin*, saying that if someone accuses him of out-talking, he should admit to out-talking and not deny it (CU 7.15.4). Yet Sanatkumāra specifies that one should out-talk correctly by knowing how to speak with truth. As Roebuck explains, to out-talk is "a doubtful quality in one without knowledge, but proper in one with knowledge beyond the normal limits" (2003, 425n.). In this dialogue Sanatkumāra not only imparts to Nārada a teaching of *ātman*, but he also reinforces the procedure of the *upanayana* and prepares Nārada for the crucial brahmin activity of debate.

NACIKETAS AND THE INITIATION OF AN UPANISHADIC BRAHMIN

One of the most well-known episodes between a student and teacher in the Upaniṣads features Naciketas and Yama. In this dialogue, Yama grants three wishes to Naciketas and eventually teaches him how to overcome death.[28] This story, as it appears in the *Kaṭha Upaniṣad*, is from an episode in the *Taittirīya Brāhmaṇa* (3.11.8) in which Yama explains to Naciketas the origin of the sacrificial fire altar.[29] As such, it richly employs symbolism pertaining to the *agnicayana* (altar-building ritual). Not only is *naciketas* one of the names associated with the fire altar in the *agnicayana*,[30] but also Naciketa's father, Vājaśravas, appears in the *Śatapatha Brāhmaṇa* as performing and teaching about the *agnicayana* (10.5.5.1).

In addition to Naciketas and his father, Yama is also connected to the imagery surrounding the fire altar. One of the numerous correspondences discussed in the *Śatapatha Brāhmaṇa* (10.5.2.1, 10.6.4.1) is the connection between the sun, the sacrificial altar, and the human body, with all three described as containing a *puruṣa* within them.[31] The gold man, which is buried under the first layer of bricks of the *agnicayana* fire altar, is the *puruṣa* within the body of the fire corresponding with the *puruṣa* in the sun, and with the *puruṣa* within the heart in the human body: "That man in yonder orb and that gold man are the same as this man in the right eye" (ŚB 10.5.2.7 tr. Eggeling). Significantly, the *Śatapatha Brāhmaṇa* states that "the man in yonder orb is no other than Death (Yama)" (ŚB 10.5.2.3 tr. Eggeling). Thus, the character of Yama not only is the personification of death, but also corresponds with the *puruṣa* within the sun.

In the *Kaṭha Upaniṣad*, Naciketas and Yama, who are already associated with aspects of the *agnicayana*, are presented as literary characters, thus shifting the emphasis away from the sacrifice itself, to Naciketas and Yama as individuals. Furthermore, this is consistent with the content of Yama's instruction. Yama teaches Naciketas that the knowledge of how to build the fire altar is more important than actually building it, proclaiming that the heavenly fires abide in the secret place, that the true fire dwells in the cave of the heart (1.14).

The episode begins when Naciketas observes that his father is giving milked and barren animals as a sacrifice. After he reflects to himself that his father's sacrifice is inadequate and not worthy of any rewards, he asks his father three times to whom his father will give him. After asking for the third time, his father declares that he will give him away to Yama. This incident articulates another sharp criticism of sacrifice, with Naciketas observing that his father's sacrifice is not truly giving anything meaningful away. We see a similar critique of sacrifice in the story of Uṣasti Cākrāyaṇa (aka Uṣasta Cākrāyaṇa) (CU 1.10–11).[32] In this episode, which we will explore in more detail in the following chapter, Uṣasti accuses a number of brahmins of performing a sacrifice without proper knowledge. In both examples, the criticism is not that sacrifices should not be performed, but that they are not being practiced correctly. In the case of Naciketas, his subsequent dialogue with Yama is presented in direct contrast to his father's poor attempt of performing a sacrifice.[33]

Indeed, Naciketas' entire encounter can be seen as a redefinition of sacrifice. Rather than offer milked and barren animals, Naciketas prompts his father into offering him in a ritual death before he is reborn again through the initiation ceremony. Similarly, James Helfer interprets the story of Naciketas and Yama as a model of the actual initiation of an *adhvaryu* priest: "The actual initiatory rite of an adhvaryu is used as the model or structure on the basis of which the dialogue between Naciketas and Yama is formed" (1968, 367). Naciketas has to go through the initiation ceremony, which is a ritual death, before he can emerge as a new person with new knowledge. According to Helfer, the sacrifice is not a literal offering, yet it is symbolically important for Naciketas as an initiate.

In this respect, it is significant that on other occasions the Upaniṣads compare the life of a *brahmacārin* with a sacrifice. The *Chāndogya Upaniṣad* states that what people usually call a sacrifice (*yajña*) is, in fact, the life of a celibate student (*brahmacarya*) (8.5.1). By means of a number of creative etymologies this passage goes on to connect several different aspects of the sacrifice with various dimensions of studentship.[34] In the case of Naciketas this metaphor is employed to present his sacrifice as favorable in contrast with his father's literal sacrifice, as he replaces the traditional Vedic sacrifice with his own sacrifice: becoming a *brahmacārin*.

After having been given to Yama by his father, Naciketas stays in Yama's house for three days and nights without food or water. This time period corresponds to the duration of the *upanayana* as presented in the *Śatapatha Brāhmaṇa*: "By laying his right hand on (the pupil), the teacher becomes pregnant (with him): in the third (night) he is born as a Brahmaṇa with the Sāvitrī" (11.5.4.12 tr. Eggeling).[35] Helfer's claim—that this period of three nights symbolizes a trial and consists of part of Naciketas' initiation—initially seems convincing, especially as it corresponds to other tests set by teachers in Upanishadic dialogues.[36] However, although it is clear that his teaching represents an initiation, it is significant that Yama's instruction to Naciketas is presented in direct contrast to the decaying practice of ritualism that Naciketas learns from his father. In this way, Naciketas is not educated to be an *adhvaryu* priest in the orthodox sense but rather is initiated into the new teachings of the Upaniṣads.

This point is further suggested by the apparent *varṇa* (class) distinction between Naciketas and Yama. When Naciketas enters his house Yama is not there, and when Yama returns a voice warns him that he should serve Naciketas food and water to appease him (KaU 1.7). Helfer interprets Yama's offering of water as part of the initiation ceremony, invoking Mircea Eliade to suggest that water is part of the universal structure for initiation (1968, 357). Indeed, offering water to a student is part of the *upanayana* as described in the *Śatapatha Brāhmaṇa*. In this instance, however, it seems more likely that Yama offers Naciketas water in order to show him the proper hospitality as a brahmin guest. In other Upanishadic dialogues water is offered only when a *kṣatriya* is teaching a brahmin, suggesting that there is a *varṇa* difference between Yama and Naciketas. This is further indicated in the *Bṛhāraṇyaka Upaniṣad*, which lists both Yama and Mṛtyu as the gods of *kṣatriya*s (1.4.11). If this is the case, then the hospitality that Yama shows Naciketas, even when he is the one doing the teaching, is similar to a number of dialogues where a *kṣatriya* offers gifts to brahmins, even though the *kṣatriya* delivers the discourse.

If this story were about the initiation of a Vedic ritualist, as Helfer suggests, we might assume that Naciketas would be initiated by an *adhvaryu* priest and that the building of the altar would be the most important aspect of the initiation. However, as opposed to learning from a brahmin with specific connections to the *Yajurveda*, Naciketas is instructed by Yama—who is cast in a role similar to that of a *kṣatriya* teacher—and he is initiated into a new kind of knowledge that is distinct from ritualism.

As with other teachers in the Upaniṣads, Yama's instruction is about the self. Although he does not discuss *ātman* directly, Yama focuses on typical Upanishadic themes such as the individual and how to overcome death. These ideas are presented in his responses to the three wishes of Naciketas. After the young brahmin's first wish, to reestablish connections with his father, Naciketas asks for the knowledge of how to construct the *naciketas* fire altar.[37] Yama explains every detail of the altar, the type of brick used, how many, and how they are to be placed, and he equates the *naciketas* altar with the beginning of the world. As in the *Śatapatha Brahmaṇa*, building the altar is ritually creating the world. However, Yama teaches that the importance of the *agnicayana* is in knowing it and not actually building it, that the knowledge of the *naciketas* fire altar lies hidden in the cave of the heart. As we have seen elsewhere, both *ātman* and *prāṇa* are represented as dwelling within the heart, and here Yama's teaching links knowledge of the fire altar with discourses about *ātman* and *prāṇa*.

After this explanation Yama names the altar after Naciketas. Although this is not specifically the initiation of an *adhvaryu* priest, it is, as Helfer points out, an aspect of many initiatory rites that the student receives a new name. In the *Kaṭha Upaniṣad*, Yama does not refer to Naciketas by name until he grants him the wish of knowing the fire altar, indicating that this could be a name only bestowed upon Naciketas after he has received instruction from Yama. More specifically, however, by naming the altar after Naciketas, Yama links the knowledge about the altar with Naciketas on an individual level. Thus, Yama instructs Naciketas that his knowledge of himself is more significant than performing the sacrifice, teaching him that with this knowledge he can build the eternal out of that which is fleeting (2.10).

Furthermore, this contrast between Upanishadic teachings and Vedic ritualism is emphasized in Naciketas' third and final wish, to understand death. In this context, death is both figuratively Naciketas' teacher, represented by the literary character Yama, as well as literally the subject of Yama's teaching. As Yama is personified as his teacher, Naciketas not only learns about death, but also comes to know Yama himself, and through knowing him both literally and figuratively becomes equipped with the possibility of overcoming death.

Throughout this dialogue, Naciketas displays the typical Upanishadic student's determination and eagerness to learn. When Naciketas asks to know about death, Yama refuses to teach him saying that this knowledge is too subtle and difficult to understand. Despite Yama's reluctance, Naciketas persists, saying that nothing could be equal to this knowledge. Yama continues to refuse and instead promises him sons and grandsons, livestock and elephants, horses and gold, and a lifespan as long as he chooses. Naciketas does not accept these material rewards, saying that these things cannot make one happy. In this exchange between teacher and student, Naciketas, like Indra and

Nārada, demonstrates that he understands the value of what his teacher knows, proving to Yama that he is worthy of learning this coveted knowledge. The remainder of this Upaniṣad consists of Yama's teaching to Naciketas.

THE GRADUATION OF A BRAHMIN STUDENT IN THE *TAITTIRĪYA UPANIṢAD*

Throughout this chapter we have seen that both the *upanayana* and the dialogues depicting teachers and students emphasize teaching, especially the initiation of a brahmin student. Whereas these accounts concentrate on how the student first approaches the teacher and asks for instructions, the *Taittirīya Upaniṣad* addresses the final words that a teacher should say to his student upon his graduation. According to the *Taittirīya Upaniṣad*, when a student has reached the completion of his Vedic studies, the teacher should say to him, "Speak the truth (*satya*). Practice *dharma*. Do not neglect reciting the Vedas aloud to yourself (*svādhyāya*). Having given a gift pleasing to the teacher, do not cut off your line of descendants" (1.11.1). As we discussed in the introduction, the Upanishadic dialogues not only present philosophical notions of the self, they also teach students how to be a particular kind of self, namely the brahmin householder. These instructions in the *Taittirīya Upaniṣad* make it clear that philosophical teachings are connected to particular ways of living one's life. In this case, the teacher emphasizes that a student must give gifts to his teacher and live the life of a householder.

The emphasis on giving gifts both reinforces the respectful etiquette with which a student should treat his teacher, and highlights the economic aspect of the teacher/student relationship. By means of giving gifts and doing work, students are important contributors to the income of their teachers. In a chant to Indra, the *Taittirīya Upaniṣad* further illustrates that brahmin teachers depend upon students for their livelihood: "May *brahmacārins* come to me, hail (*svāhā*). May *brahmacārins* gather around me, hail. May *brahmacārins* come forth to me, hail. May *brahmacārins* be self-controlled, hail. May *brahmacārins* be peaceful, hail" (1.4.2).[38] In the very next line, after these five requests for students, the speaker asks to be both famous and rich: "May I be famous among people, hail. May I be more wealthy than the very rich, hail" (1.4.3).[39] In the juxtaposition of these requests there is an explicit link between attracting students and accumulating wealth. Despite an apparent aloofness and reluctance to teach, these passages indicate that teachers are quite aware of their dependence upon students for their ability to make a living. Teachers never give away their knowledge for free, as there is always an exchange involved.

Additionally, the teacher's lesson to his student reinforces the authority of brahmins. As part of the graduation instructions in the *Taittirīya Upaniṣad,* the teacher tells his student that brahmins are always the ultimate authority for Vedic practices, that if there is ever any doubt about how to behave one should act in accordance with how brahmins behave. The teacher describes brahmins as competent to judge (*sammarśina*), proficient (*yukta*), devoted (*āyukta*), not harsh (*alukṣa*), and dedicated to *dharma*. Furthermore, the *Taittirīya Upaniṣad* emphasizes the importance of respecting teachers and other family members, as students are instructed to treat their mother, father, teacher, and guests like gods. The use of education to reinforce the superiority of brahmins is also employed by Sanatkumāra in his instruction to Nārada. He tells Nārada what to do if someone does not speak correctly to his father, mother, brother, sister, teacher, or a brahmin. Pravāhaṇa's teaching of the five fires, which we will explore in more detail in chapter 3, also concludes with an ethical instruction that includes the protection of brahmins and teachers.[40] These examples show that knowledge about *ātman, prāṇa,* and overcoming death is not abstracted from social practices, that an indelible aspect of these teachings is learning how properly to respect teachers, brahmins, and the family structure.

These instructions are not merely general advice that a teacher should give his students after they complete their studies, but rather these guidelines are presented as a fundamental part of a teacher's instruction. This point is emphasized at the end of the *Taittirīya Upaniṣad,* where the ethical rules and regulations are explicitly called *upaniṣads*: "This is the instruction (*ādeśa*). This is the teaching (*upadeśa*). This is the hidden connection (*upaniṣad*) of the Veda" (1.11.4). Through the use of the word *upaniṣad,* the social practices of giving gifts and respecting brahmins are equated with the esoteric discourses about the self. Similarly, the *Taittirīya Upaniṣad* describes knowledge about the relationship between teacher and students as an *upaniṣad,* thereby placing their relationship on a theoretical level. At the beginning of the *Taittirīya Upaniṣad,* there are explanations for the hidden connections (*upaniṣads*) for five topics: the worlds, the lights, knowledge, progeny, and the body (*ātman*). The *upaniṣad* for knowledge emphasizes the teacher/student relationship: "The teacher (*ācarya*) is the prior form. The student (*antesvāsin*) is the latter form. Knowledge (*vidyā*) is their union. Instruction (*pravacana*) is their connection" (1.3.2–3).[41] By using the word *upaniṣad*, this passage reinforces the fact that the relationship between teacher and student is intrinsic to discursive knowledge.

These passages from the *Taittirīya Upaniṣad* are representative of a general preoccupation with the transmission of knowledge. Not only do the dialogues develop stories about particular moments of instruction, but also they set out rules by which this knowledge should be conveyed in the future. This new attention to the transmission of knowledge is an essential aspects of the shift from Vedic ritualism to the kind of knowledge characteristic of the Upaniṣads, a point that is further emphasized by the numerous genealogies of teachers and students that appear throughout the texts. The *Bṛhadāraṇyaka Upaniṣad*, for example, is divided into three sections, all of which end with a genealogy (2.6.1–3, 4.6.1–3, 6.5.1–4). These genealogies are not family pedigrees, but rather are lineages of teachers and students, and like the dialogues, they focus attention on particular individuals, as well as the discursive activity of teaching. Genealogies also give a sense of history to the teachings. Even though a number of Upanishadic teachings present themselves as new or nontraditional, the genealogies trace particular teachings all the way back to mythological figures such as Āditya, Prajāpati, and Brahmā. Furthermore, the genealogies serve to reinforce the authority of a number of the same teachers that appear in the dialogues, as Śāṇḍilya, Uddālaka Āruṇi, and Yājñavalkya all are mentioned in genealogical lists.

This attention to the transmission of knowledge is also incorporated into the discourses themselves. At the end of a number of teachings there are instructions as to how knowledge should be passed. The *Aitareya Āraṇyaka*, for example, instructs that only those who live with a student and intend to become teachers should learn this knowledge: "These *saṃhitas* let no one tell to one who is not a resident pupil, who has not been with the teacher for one year, and who is not himself to become a teacher. Thus says the teacher" (3.2.6 tr. Keith). In the *Bṛhadāraṇyaka Upaniṣad*, at the end of a description of how to make a mixture for attaining greatness, the narrative records several moments of instruction as this teaching had been passed down from Uddālaka Āruṇi to Yājñavalkya, to Madhuka Paiṅgya, to Cūla Bhāgavitti, to Jānaki Āyasthūṇa, to Satyakāma, and to his students. After recording these moments of instruction the text warns that this knowledge should not be shared with anyone who is not a son (*putra*) or a student (*antevāsin*) (6.3.12).

The *Chāndogya Upaniṣad* (CU 3.11.4) also gives specific instructions for how knowledge should be transmitted. At the end of what is known as the honey doctrine, the narrative tells us that the genealogy of this teaching began with Brahmā, who instructed Prajāpati, who imparted it to Manu, who has passed it down to Uddālaka Āruṇi. As in the *Bṛhadāraṇyaka Upaniṣad*, the genealogy is followed by instructions that a father should only impart this teaching of *brahman* to his eldest son (*jyeṣṭha putra*) or a worthy pupil (*praṇāyya antesvāsin*), and never to anyone else.

These passages show that an integral aspect of Upanishadic teachings is how knowledge should be transmitted, with the genealogies indicating that the lineages from teacher to student become as important as family pedigrees. As we will see, this is true in the case of Yājñavalkya, who proves himself superior to his teacher's son Śvetaketu, and this is also illustrated in the story of Satyakāma, who, despite not knowing his family lineage, is able to establish himself as an authoritative brahmin. Indeed, throughout the dialogues between teachers and students, the institutional practices of the *upanayana* are considered more authoritative than one's family.

SATYAKĀMA AND THE BEGINNINGS OF A BRAHMIN HAGIOGRAPHY

In this chapter we have examined a number of dialogues featuring teachers and students. Most of these episodes appear in the texts as distinct scenes that are not drawn together to form a larger story. Although some characters, such as Uddālaka Āruṇi and Śvetaketu, feature in more than one dialogue, and maintain their literary personality from one scene to the next, the texts do not directly connect the events in one scene with what takes place in another scene. For example, Śvetaketu returns to his father after receiving a traditional education from orthodox brahmins in one dialogue (CU 6.1.16), while in another dialogue he is unable to answer any of the questions posed to him by King Pravāhaṇa (BU 6.2.1; CU 5.3; KṣU 1.1). As Olivelle (1999) demonstrates, there are a number of consistencies concerning Śvetaketu's character from one scene to the next, contributing to him being more or less the same literary personality throughout his appearances in the Upaniṣads. However, there is no logical or chronological connection linking the events of these stories that could be reconstructed to form an integrated story.

Satyakāma and Yājñvalkya, however, are two characters whose distinct appearances are collected together in a chronological order, and for whom we are presented with enough information to reconstruct a larger narrative. In both cases their lives are more of a sketch than a comprehensive biography, but in the way that the texts are edited, originally separate scenes are strung together to offer the outlines of a life story. It is not my intention here to argue that these distinct narrative incidents constitute hagiographies, but rather to suggest that, like hagiographies, the "life stories" of both Satyakāma and Yājñavalkya connect their teachings to particular ways of living. In this section we will explore the integrated episodes featuring Satyakāma as representing the model for a brahmin householder, while in the following chapter we will look at the "life story" of Yājñavalkya as representing a challenge to this ideal.

We first meet Satyakāma in one of the most well-known stories in the Upaniṣads, where he approaches his mother to ask about his lineage so that he can become a Vedic student (CU 4.4.1–5). His mother, however, replies that she is unable to determine who his father is because when she was younger she moved around a lot and had been with several men. She then instructs him to take her name, and to introduce himself as Satyakāma Jābāla. After this conversation with his mother, Satyakāma approaches the teacher Hāridrumata and asks to be admitted as his student. When Hāridrumata asks Satyakāma what his lineage is, the boy repeats the explanation that his mother told him and then introduces himself as Satyakāma Jābāla.

There have been two prevalent interpretations of this story offered by commentators and scholars.[42] The first is that Satyakāma is not a brahmin by birth and earns this status by impressing his teacher with his truthfulness, thus suggesting that the status of brahmin could be achieved by means of the proper behavior. The second explanation is that Satyakāma is a brahmin by birth, and that his truthfulness displays the kind of behavior that only a brahmin could have. This reading suggests a sort of biological determinism, whereby Satyakāma acts the way that he does because it is in his nature to do so. Despite arguments on both sides, the text remains wonderfully ambiguous.[43] Nevertheless, this story is central to our discussion in this chapter because it emphasizes the importance of the *upanayana* and the identity of Satyakāma's teacher: although Satyakāma's family identity remains unresolved, he is able to establish himself as a learned brahmin because of the identity of his teacher.

Both Satyakāma and Hāridrumata closely follow the script provided by the *upanayana*, with the young man approaching his prospective teacher exactly as outlined in the *Śatapatha Brāhmaṇa*: "Sir, I want to live as a vedic student (*brahmacārin*). I approach you, sir" (CU 4.4.3). Hāridrumata also acts out the *upanayana*, as he responds to Satyakāma's request by asking him about his lineage. After proclaiming that Satyakāma speaks like a brahmin, he then orders Satyakāma to bring him some firewood and he initiates him as his student.

Before Hāridrumata even begins to instruct him, Satyakāma establishes himself as a worthy student. After the initiation, Hāridrumata gives his student four hundred emaciated cows and asks him to look after them.[44] Satyakāma accepts them, promising not to return until he has a thousand cows. The dialogue suggests that this is a test set by Hāridrumata to see if Satyakāma could make emaciated and weak cows prosper, by recounting that Hāridrumata specifically picked out the weakest cows for Satyakāma to take care of. After a few years, however, Satyakāma fulfills his promise by increasing the number of cows to one thousand. That this is a test put to Satyakāma by his teacher is reinforced by the fact that soon after this a bull begins to instruct him about *brahman*. Subsequently, Satyakāma is taught by a fire, a goose, and a cormorant.[45] All of these instructions take place at sunset after he had completed his duties of building a fire, rounding up the cows, and fueling the fire. Here we see that immediately after completing the work that he had promised his teacher, he is rewarded with a number of teachings about *brahman*. In this way, the transmission of Upanishadic knowledge is directly connected with the tasks that a student performs for his teacher.[46]

When Satyakāma finally returns to his teacher's house, Hāridrumata notices that his student shines (*bhās*) like a man who knows *brahman* (CU 4.9.2). However, this dialogue emphasizes that despite his glow, the disciplinary practice of learning Upanishadic teachings is as important as the knowledge itself. When Hāridrumata questions Satyakāma about where he has learned about *brahman*, Satyakāma replies that it was not from humans. It is difficult to determine the exact symbolism relating to Satyakāma's unorthodox teachers. Do they represent other cultural traditions? Do they suggest that Satyakāma has learned about *brahman* by means of his own observations of natural phenomena? These questions remain unanswered. Nevertheless, it is clear that Satyakāma understands that if he is truly to be considered a brahmin, he must receive instruction from his official teacher.[47] After acknowledging that non-humans had taught him, Satyakāma adds that he wants to learn from Hāridrumata because he has heard from people that knowledge from one's teacher attains the best results.[48] The narrative emphasizes that this is the real teaching by adding that when Hāridrumata instructed him "nothing at all was left out, nothing was left out," suggesting that only a discursively sanctioned teacher knows the complete teaching (CU 4.9.3).[49] This episode illustrates that whereas the identity of Satyakāma's father proves unnecessary in establishing his lineage, the identity of his teacher is vital in establishing his knowledge.

Satyakāma reiterates this point when he later becomes a teacher himself. He receives Upakosala as his student, but then embarks on a journey before ever teaching him. When he is away, his student, like Satyakāma himself, receives instruction from unlikely sources. In this case, his teachers are the household fire, the southern fire, and the offertory fire. When Satyakāma returns he recognizes that now his own student shines like a man who knows *brahman*. However, when he learns that the fires taught Upakosala, he considers his student's knowledge incomplete and promises to teach him himself.[50] That both Satyakāma and Upakosala are described as shining like a man who knows *brahman* suggests that their knowledge led to a physical transformation that was discernible to their respective teachers. Nevertheless, in both cases even knowledge that led to this perceptible transformation was considered less valuable than instruction from a proper teacher.

These dialogues featuring Satyakāma both emphasize the proper mode of instruction and contribute to presenting an integrated biographical account of a particular brahmin life. Satyakāma is the only character in the Upaniṣads whom the narrative follows from his initiation as a student all the way to his becoming a teacher with his own students. The dialogues describe his adventures from his uncertain family origins, through to his tenure as a *brahmacārin*, and finally as an authoritative brahmin teacher who legitimizes Upanishadic teachings and who lives as a married householder supporting himself by taking on students. Taken together, the life of Satyakāma serves as a hagiographical model for the ideal brahmin life, as he is the embodiment of a number of discourses that advocate the life of the brahmin teacher. As I will develop further in the following chapters, there are general similarities among characters and dialogical situations among different Upaniṣads. Nevertheless, there are also important differences that point to competing agendas among the textual traditions. In this respect, it is pertinent that most of the dialogues about teaching that we have discussed in this chapter are taken from the *Chāndogya Upaniṣad*. This specific focus on teaching and the development of Satyakāma as a model for the Upanishadic teacher indicates that this particular ideal was part of the agenda of the *Chāndogya Upaniṣad*. In the following chapter we will see how the *Bṛhadāraṇyaka Upaniṣad* focuses on Satyakāma's rival, Yājñavalkya, who, rather than establishing himself through teaching, proves his authority through philosophical debate.

CONCLUSION

Throughout all the dialogues between teachers and students, the most important teachings are about the self. However, teachers have different understandings of *ātman* and they employ different teaching methods: Uddālaka teaches Śvetaketu by means of observation and experimentation; Prajāpati leads Indra to an understanding of *ātman* by imparting false knowledge and disclosing his discourse incrementally; Yama teaches Naciketas by making him endure a difficult initiation; and Satyakāma teaches by means of isolating his student. All these methods ultimately bring the student to knowledge of the self and, although different methods are used, all of them follow the script of the *upanayana* to some degree and reinforce the importance of a proper teacher and proper lineage.

One of the fundamental features of these dialogues is that they cast knowledge of *ātman* in opposition to traditional Vedic knowledge. The mythic battle between Indra and Virocana over control of the sacrifice is presented as a competition over knowledge of the self; Yama teaches Naciketas that the true knowledge of the sacrifice is to be found within the self; Nārada approaches Sanatkumāra claiming that despite his traditional Vedic education, he is ignorant about the self. This emphasis on the superiority of knowledge of the self over traditional Vedic knowledge is also connected to the Upanishadic redefinition of the status of brahmin. As Uddālaka Āruṇi comments, some are brahmins merely because of their birth, while others earn their status of brahmin through their knowledge (CU 6.1.1). Throughout, these dialogues present teachings about the self as the quintessential knowledge in defining the 'new' brahmin.

We began this chapter with Śāṇḍilya, who is most known for his teachings of *ātman* and *brahman*. As we have seen, this particular doctrine has been overemphasized, as it is often considered the fundamental teaching of all the Upaniṣads. Consequently, not enough attention has been paid to Śāṇḍilya as its teacher. Despite not appearing in any teacher/student dialogue in the Upaniṣads, Śāṇḍilya was one of the first authoritative names to appear in the narrative episodes about teaching in the Brāhmaṇas. Not only do these scenes indicate the emergence of the more detailed narratives we find in the Upaniṣads, but they also highlight the act of teaching itself, as well as the authority of teachers.

Indeed, the practice of teaching is further emphasized by the fact that the oldest extant description of the *upanayana* coincides with the development of narrative scenes about teaching. Both the *upanayana* and the pedagogical dialogues reinforce particular modes of address and behavior that accompany and control the transmission of knowledge. This focus on the transmission of knowledge is represented in the instructions that come at the end of a number of teachings, as well as in the genealogies in the *Bṛhadāraṇyaka Upaniṣad* and in the *Taittirīya Upaniṣad*'s account of a brahmin's graduation. By means of presenting important discourses in the form of conversations between teachers and students and outlining to whom this knowledge should be passed, brahmin composers establish hierarchies of authority, define appropriate philosophical positions, and establish normative practices through which knowledge can be disseminated.

This emphasis on how knowledge is transmitted is particularly stressed in stories about Satyakāma and his student, both of whom learn from unlikely sources the very discourses that their teachers eventually impart to them. In both cases, however, despite the fact that their own teachers recognize that their students "shine" like someone who knows, they instruct them anyway, thus reinforcing a common theme found throughout these dialogues: the authority of the teacher and the proper means of transmission are as important as the knowledge itself.

Finally, Satyakāma's story introduced us to one of the first integrated biographies of the life of a brahmin. As we followed his life from his departure from home in pursuit of an education to his becoming a teacher with a wife and his own students, Satyakāma's life story is the embodiment of the brahmin householder. As his biography illustrates, not only is it important that students learn particular teachings as part of their Upanishadic education, but it is crucial for them to learn how to use their knowledge to attract their own students and set up a household. In the next chapter we will see that in addition to teaching, one of the essential social practices for brahmins is the philosophical debate (*brahmodya*).

CHAPTER TWO

Debates between Brahmins

The Competitive Dynamics of the Brahmodya

INTRODUCTION

In this chapter we will look at dialogues that feature brahmins debating against other brahmins. Similar to the *upanayana,* these debates (*brahmodya*) are presented as a distinct practice, often in contrast to the performance of sacrifice. Yet unlike the dialogues about teaching, the *brahmodya* is characterized as competitive and aggressive, risking the reputations of brahmins and sometimes exhibiting political rivalries.

We will begin our discussion by tracing the literary presentation of the *brahmodya* from the Brāhmaṇas to the Upaniṣads, examining two types of these episodes: (1) private debates that are a competition between two priests and (2) public tournaments among several priests that usually take place in the presence of the king. We will look at two dialogues featuring Uddālaka Āruṇi as examples of the first type of *brahmodya,* and then turn our attention to Yājñavalkya, examing how he is particularly connected to the second type of *brahmodya,* those depicted as a philosophical tournament. In both types of debate we will pay particular attention to the participants and their debating tactics. As we will see, individuals often win arguments as much by their personal authority and how they debate, as by which arguments they put forth. We will closely examine a particular *brahmodya* where Yājñavalkya defeats a number of brahmins from Kuru-Pañcāla. This contest illustrates that in addition to competing for reputation, the debates of brahmin priests represent larger regional and political struggles. Finally, we will look at how Yājñavalkya exchanges his ideas for large amounts of material goods. Through the negotiations of Yājñavalkya, as well as other brahmins, we will see that setting an economic value for philosophical teachings is an important aspect of Upanishadic discourse.

THE *BRAHMODYA* AND THE SACRIFICE

As several scholars have noticed, verbal contests are reflected in Vedic literature as far back as the *Ṛgveda*, in hymns that pose a riddle or point to an esoteric meaning that can only become apparent with the proper understanding of ritual discourse.[1] Although the riddle hymns of the *Ṛgveda* share certain similarities with Upanishadic accounts of debate, the word *brahmodya* makes its initial appearance in the Brāhmaṇas (Thompson 1997, 22). This suggests that the emergence of the term *brahmodya* coincides with the appearance of numerous narrative descriptions of debates between two individuals, as well as philosophical tournaments featuring many priests. These literary scenes in the late Brāhmaṇas and early Upaniṣads that dramatize the contests of brahmins represent a change in focus from posing an enigmatic question to recounting the incident of debate itself. They also reveal an interest in the participants of philosophical debate and how they interact with each other. Even though they emerged out of a sacrificial context, the *brahmodyas*, as they appear in the late Brāhmaṇas and early Upaniṣads, no longer reflect a ritual situation. The participants often debate about topics relating to ritual, but the debate itself is described as a separate event which is often characterized in contradistinction to the practice of sacrifice. As Bodewitz argues, "There is no denying that the real *brahmodyas* (discussions with aggressive aspects in which often some issue is at stake) are found only in the late brāmaṇas such as the ŚB [*Śatapatha Brāhmaṇa*], JB [*Jaiminīya Brāhmaṇa*] and GB [*Gopatha Brāhmaṇa*]. This should warn us against drawing hasty conclusions as to the original nature of these verbal contests" (1976, 183). George Thompson agrees with this separation of the older discourse, which poses enigmatic questions, from the narrative accounts of the *brahmodya* that appear in the Upaniṣads. He describes the *brahmodya*s of the Vājasaneyi Saṃhitā as scripted for the performance within the Vedic ritual with memorized recitations. The *brahmodya*s of the Upaniṣads, however, were "unrehearsed, improvised performances, sometimes like examinations, but in any case *real* competitions—with the reputations, and perhaps even the heads, of the participants apparently very much at stake" (1997, 13). That the Upanishadic *brahmodya*s record real events remains speculative, nevertheless the literary presentation of the *brahmodya* establishes debate as a practice closely associated with Upanishadic teachings. Furthermore, these accounts outline the rules and tactics of the *brahmodya*, thus presenting debate as an indispensable activity for brahmins to use their knowledge in the social world.

Two of the first examples of *brahmodya*s in Vedic literature appear in the *Śatapatha Brāhmaṇa* where a verbal exchange is embedded within a royal ritual, in this case the *aśvamedha*.[2] These examples are illustrative because they serve as a model for understanding the structure of the Upanishadic *brahmodya*. However, these scripted exchanges also highlight important differences from the "unrehearsed" and "improvised" debates that appear in the Upaniṣads. In the first example, the *hotṛ* (invoker) and *brahman* (presider) priests each ask each other four questions:

> Brahman: Who is it that walketh singly?
>
> Hotṛ: It is yonder sun, doubtless, that walks singly, and he is spiritual lustre: spiritual lustre the two (priests) thus bestow on him.
>
> Brahman: Who is it that is born again?
>
> Hotṛ: It is the moon, doubtless, that is born again (and again): vitality they thus bestow on him.
>
> Brahman: What is the remedy for cold?
>
> Hotṛ: The remedy for cold, doubtless is Agni (fire): fiery spirit they thus bestow on him.
>
> Brahman: And what is the great vessel?
>
> Hotṛ: The great vessel, doubtless, is the (terrestrial) world: on this earth he thus establishes himself.
>
> Hotṛ: What was the first conception?
>
> Brahman: The first conception, doubtless, was the sky, rain: the sky, rain, he thus secures for himself.
>
> Hotṛ: Who was the great bird?
>
> Brahman: The great bird, doubtless, was the horse: vital power he thus secures for himself.

> Hotṛ: Who was the smooth one?
>
> Brahman: The smooth one (*pilippilā*), doubtless, was beauty (*śrī*): beauty he thus secures for himself.
>
> Hotṛ: Who was the tawny one?
>
> Brahman: The two tawny ones, doubtless, are the day and the night: in the day and night he thus establishes himself. (ŚB 13.2.6.9–17 tr. Eggeling)

In this example, which takes place prior to the binding of the sacrificial victims to the stakes, all of the questions are reminiscent of the kinds posed in the riddle hymns of the *Ṛgveda*; they are presented as a rehearsed exchange where both the questions and answers are known in advance, thus focusing on the ritualized verbal exchange itself and not on the individual participants.

Similarly, the second *brahmodya*, which occurs after the omenta have been roasted, features the four main priests, as well as the *yajamāna* (sacrificer) (ŚB 13.5.2.11–22). In this case, the *hotṛ* and *adhvaryu* (officiant) each trade one question and answer, followed by a similar exchange between the *udgātṛ* (chanter) and *brahman*. This format is then repeated a second time. As with the previous example, this *brahmodya* is scripted in the sense that there is a definite structure as to how and when the priests exchange questions. That the questions are part of a standard format is indicated by the fact that these two *brahmodya*s share three of the same questions and answers.[3]

These examples provide two alternative scenarios shared by the narrative accounts of the *brahmodya* throughout the late Brāhmaṇas and early Upaniṣads. The first is an example of the private debate that features only two brahmins with no official audience. The second example is a public debate that includes a number of contestants in the presence of the *yajamāna*. Despite these similarities in structure, however, there are some crucial differences between these verbal exchanges that are embedded within ritual actions and the narrative accounts of debates. Unlike the Upanishadic accounts that emphasize the individual literary personalities, these two examples from the *aśvamedha* refer to the priests generically according to their function. Accordingly, the verbal exchanges that take place within the ritual are not competitive: there are no winners or losers and nothing is at stake.

Additionally, as we will see with two dialogues featuring Uddālaka Āruṇi, the Upanishadic *brahmodya*s further develop the difference between the private and public debate: the private *brahmodya* becomes a contest of personal rivalry where the loser becomes the student of the winner, and the public debates are presented as philosophical tournaments with a number of contestants where the outcome has political implications. In both types of *brahmodya* there is always something at stake, whether it be the reputation of individual brahmins or material rewards, and on many occasions these debates are a forum in which brahmins compete for the patronage of kings. Unlike the *brahmodyas* that appear as part of the ritual, the accounts of the Upanishadic *brahmodya* focus on the individual participants and characterize debate as an important activity in establishing the authority of eminent brahmins such as Uddālaka Āruṇi and Yājñavalkya.

UDDĀLAKA ĀRUṆI AND THE *BRAHMODYA* IN THE *ŚATAPATHA BRĀHMAṆA*

In the *Śatapatha Brāhmaṇa*, Uddālaka Āruṇi participates in two private *brahmodyas*, both of which feature just one other opponent and no audience. As discussed in the previous chapter, Uddālaka Āruṇi appears in a dialogue with his son Śvetaketu in the *Chāndogya Upaniṣad*, where he is characterized as a wise teacher and a good father who is generally knowledgeable about Upanishadic teachings. Furthermore, his knowledge is given added authority as it is contrasted with what Śvetaketu has learned from more traditional teachers. This depiction of Uddālaka, however, is quite different from how he appears in the texts of the *Yajurveda*, the *Śatapatha Brāhmaṇa* and *Bṛhadāraṇyaka Upaniṣad*. Although he is respected, Uddālaka is the character who most often loses debates to both brahmins and *kṣatriyas* who are more familiar with typically Upanishadic teachings. This ambiguity in Uddālaka's character is shared throughout the late Brāhmaṇas and early Upaniṣads where he is both the respected, eminent Kuru-Pañcāla brahmin and the caricature of the orthodox priest who learns from non-traditional sources. In the following two dialogues, we will see both of these aspects of Uddālaka's literary personality. These episodes are significant because of Uddālaka Āruṇi's close association with the *brahmodya*, as well as the fact that both accounts contain a curious threat that is closely connected to verbal debate: the threat that the loser will lose his head.

In the first dialogue Śauceya Prācīnayogya challenges Uddālaka Āruṇi to a *brahmodya* about the *agnihotra* (twice-daily milk offering) (ŚB 11.5.3.1–13).[4] He proceeds to ask Uddālaka a number of questions regarding specific ritual actions: why wipe the spoon with grass after cleaning it the first time, why place the spoon in the southern part of the *vedi* (area between the sacrificial fires) after wiping it a second time, etc.[5] After each one of Uddālaka's answers, there is a refrain spoken by Śauceya where he acknowledges that he already knows what Uddālaka has told him, "This much, then reverend sir, we two know in common" (ŚB 11.5.3.7–11 tr. Eggeling). The repetition of this phrase indicates that Śauceya is testing Uddālaka's knowledge. As Bodewitz notes, before his final answer Uddālaka does not reveal any new teachings, yet Śauceya's last question is about what one should do when all the fires go out and there is no wind. Uddālaka instructs that in this case he would drink the oblation himself, saying that if one has proper knowledge of the *agnihotra*, it will belong to all deities and will be successful. In this dialogue, Uddālaka's teaching assumes a general understanding of *prāṇa* as the essence of life. Just as all the vital powers in the body depend on *prāṇa*, so all cosmic entities rely on the cosmic *prāṇa*. And at the time of death, the *prāṇa* in the body enters into the cosmic *prāṇa*. When Uddālaka offers this instruction, then Śauceya finally admits that this is something that he does not know. Consequently, Śauceya approaches Uddālaka with firewood and asks to be his student. Unlike the students we discussed in the previous chapter who approach their teachers with firewood at the beginning of the dialogue, Śauceya does not ask to be Uddālaka's student until after he has tested him, until after Uddālaka has proven that he can teach Śauceya something that he does not already know.

This dialogue is one of the first episodes to relate the famous threat of the shattering head to the practice of philosophical debate. Immediately after Śauceya asks to become his student, Uddālaka warns him: "If you had not responded thus, your head would have shattered apart (*yád evám̐ nāvākṣyo, mūrdhā́ te vyàpatiṣyat*)" (ŚB 11.5.3.13). The meaning of this phrase is debated among scholars. Witzel argues that it should be understood as a literal curse and that it therefore functions as a mortal threat (1987a). Taken this way, brahmins essentially risk their lives when they enter into a verbal debate. Stanley Insler, however, argues that the original meaning of this phrase was to lose one's presence of mind: "It means 'one's head flies off or away' in the sense of 'one loses self-possession or presence of mind, becomes confused,' precisely as the Oxford English Dictionary defines the English idiom 'to lose one's heads' " (1989–90: 113–14). We will return to this issue later in this chapter, but in this dialogue we will follow Insler's interpretation on the grounds that the narrative context does not give any indication that this is an actual curse of death. Rather, this encounter is primarily about authority and which brahmin has the higher position in relation to the other. When Uddālaka suggests that Śauceya would have lost his head, he is essentially saying that if Śauceya had not acknowledged Uddālaka's authority, he would have lost face and risked losing his reputation.

According to Insler there are two circumstances under which one disputant threatens another that their head will shatter apart: the first is when one opponent accuses the other of not knowing the answers to their own questions, and the second is when "one opponent concedes the superiority of the other and offers firewood as a gesture of asking to be the student of the opponent" (Insler 1989–90, 97–98).[6] For the first type, Insler gives the example of Yājñavalkya's warning to Gārgī, which we will discuss later in this chaper, as well as in chapter 4. The second type is illustrated by this debate between Uddālaka Āruṇi and Śauceya Prācīnayogya (ŚB 11.5.3.13). In this category of *brahmodya* the winner of the argument warns the loser after the fact, saying that if they had not admitted ignorance or defeat, their head would have shattered apart. In both situations "the parties involved lack the proper knowledge to continue the inquiry or the debate" (1989–90, 98–99). In this case Śauceya would have lost his head if he had claimed to have knowledge that he did not have. Uddālaka's ex post facto warning suggests that Śauceya asks to become Uddālaka's student not only because he wants to learn what Uddālaka knows, but also because he recognizes that if he had not obliged to become Uddālaka's student he would have lost his reputation.

In another dialogue from the *Śatapatha Brāhmaṇa*, Uddālaka Āruṇi is driving around in his chariot as an invited priest in the northern country of Madras (11.4.1.1–9).[7] Like a number of Upanishadic figures, Uddālaka is well traveled and has both taught and received teachings throughout ancient north India. The first thing Uddālaka does when he reaches the northern country is to challenge the local brahmins to a *brahmodya* by offering a gold coin. The *Śatapatha Brāhmaṇa* explains that in ancient times the gold coin was used to invite rival priests to a philosophical debate: "In the time of our forefathers a prize used to be offered by chosen (priests) when driving about, for the sake of calling out the timid to a disputation" (11.4.1.1 tr. Eggeling).[8] This suggests that it was a common practice for brahmins such as Uddālaka to travel around in their chariots and challenge local brahmins to disputes, with the gold coin illustrating the ritualized aspect of initiating such a disputation.

When Uddālaka offers the coin, the brahmins are fearful that he might take away their local authority. As Bodewitz points out, "Being a stranger he is not welcome as a rival and always runs the risk of being challenged to a *brahmodya* in which his prestige . . . will be at stake" (1974, 86). Consequently, the northern brahmins decide to challenge Uddālaka to a debate as a way to protect their local authority, electing Svaidāyana to represent them. Svaidāyana approaches him on his own and, after exchanging greetings, claims that although Uddālaka has been invited by a patron, he nevertheless needs to prove himself as superior to the local brahmins. Svaidāyana says that only those who know the new and full moon sacrifices are entitled to leave their own region and travel around as invited priests, or "free-lance" priests as Bodewitz suggests (1974, 85). Svaidāyana then repeats this phrase as a preface to each of his questions about the new and full moon sacrifices. Uddālaka is unable to answer any of the questions and finally responds to Svaidāyana by giving him the gold coin and praising him for his knowledge. By surrendering the coin, Uddālaka acknowledges that he has lost the debate and brings attention to the formal aspects of the *brahmodya*. Bodewitz further suggests that Uddālaka accepts defeat in private in order to avoid facing Svaidāyana again in a public debate (1974, 88). The narrative tells us that when Svaidāyana returns to the other brahmins he does not reveal to them that he defeated Uddālaka and won the gold coin. Thus, it seems that by admitting his defeat in private Uddālaka does not damage his reputation. Instead, Svaidāyana warns the other brahmins that anyone who would dare challenge Uddālaka would risk losing his head. Once again Uddālaka is linked with this threat and we are reminded that both brahmins are risking their reputation throughout this *brahmodya*.

Another important aspect of this debate concerns whether the winner should formally initiate the loser as his student. After Svaidāyana warns the other brahmins about the risks of encountering Uddālaka in a debate, Uddālaka returns to Svaidāyana, carrying firewood and asking to be his pupil. Svaidāyana responds by saying that he will teach him, but without initiating him. This qualification is a notable detail that figures in a number of dialogues that we will explore further in the next chapter. For now, however, it is important to distinguish this dialogue from the teacher/student dialogues that we explored last chapter. In the *upanayana* dialogues, where students approach teachers with firewood at the beginning of their discussion, it is always clear who is the teacher and who is the student. However, in this episode Uddālaka and Svaidāyana debate with each other first, and their encounter ends with Uddālaka asking to become his student. Indeed, one of the substantial features of the *brahmodyas* between two contestants is that the loser of the discussion asks to be the student of the victor after the argument. In these cases we see that the *brahmodya* serves as a negotiation process whereby brahmins establish their authority in relation to each other.

Furthermore, Svaidāyana's victory over Uddālaka represents a victory for the northern brahmins over the orthodox priests from Kuru-Pañcāla. Whereas in many dialogues Uddālaka's character functions as a foil to show the superior knowledge of prominent kings, in this episode Uddālaka is contrasted to the brahmins from the northern country. Accordingly, this debate not only concerns a rivalry between individual brahmins, but also represents a regional dynamic, perhaps indicating that the north was becoming an important center of Vedic learning.

These two dialogues with Uddālaka Āruṇi share a number of features that are characteristic of the private debate. In both episodes Uddālaka is cast as the senior brahmin who is challenged with a series of questions, with his personal authority the primary issue at stake. In the first case he maintains his superiority by answering all the questions successfully, and consequently wins over a new student. In the second dialogue he cannot answer the questions so he becomes a student himself. In this case, Uddālaka does not explicitly lose his reputation because the debate is in private and Svaidāyana—although his reasons remain unclear—does not reveal the outcome to others. Nevertheless, Svaidāyana establishes his own authority, at least in the eyes of Uddālaka, and has the gold coin if he ever needed to prove it to others. Additionally, both dialogues show the contestants playing by the rules of the debate, as both losers readily accept defeat and ask to become the student of the winner.

YĀJÑAVALKYA AND THE PHILOSOPHICAL TOURNAMENT

Whereas Uddālaka Āruṇi features in private debates, Yājñavalkya is the literary character most closely associated with the public *brahmodya*. Indeed, the emergence of Yājñavalkya as a literary character coincides with the development of the verbal contest as an important scenario in Upanishadic narrative. The *brahmodya* not only establishes Yājñavalkya as an authoritative figure, but also displays his knowledge as new and unorthodox.[9] Additionally, narrative accounts of Yājñavalkya and his interlocutors highlight the competitive dynamics of verbal debate and describe a number of underhanded debating tactics. In this way, these accounts show that Yājñavalkya establishes his superiority as much by how he conducts his arguments as by the particular discourses that he knows.

As in the case of Śāṇḍilya, in Yājñavalkya's first appearances in Vedic literature only his name is mentioned. He is presented as an authoritative figure who discusses the significance of ritual actions and is especially known for his expertise regarding the *agnihotra* (ŚB 11.3.1.2–8).[10] His name appears on several occasions in the *Śatapatha Brāhmaṇa*, but he is also mentioned in the *Śāṅkhāyana Āraṇyaka* (9.7, 13.1), and in the *Jaiminīya Brāhmaṇa* (1.19.23, 2.76) he is known by the name Vājasaneya, which reflects his connection to the Vājasaneyi *śākhā* of the White *Yajurveda*.[11] Fišer describes these quotations as "ad hoc" opinions about the sacrifice: "[They] are concise, brisk and totally unrelated pronouncements made (supposedly) by Yājñavalkya either alone or in the company of a few fellow-priests. None of these *dicta* contain anything but his name" (1984, 54).

Although these passages may seem unrelated in content, they contribute to establishing one of Yājñavalkya's most distinctive character traits: his superiority in verbal contests. Admittedly, none of these passages are explicitly described as a *brahmodya*, nevertheless they are similar in that they present controversies about ritual practice as a discussion among specific individuals, with a preference for one view over the others. Although there is no narrative description of the debate, these scenes are already different from the ritually embedded exchanges where there are no names of specific individuals and, crucially, no winners or losers. In most cases, Yājñavalkya's views are presented in direct contrast to the opinions of other brahmins, and he clearly emerges as superior. As Fišer argues, unless stated otherwise the text shows its preference for the views of Yājñavalkya by stating his words after those of his opponents.[12] For example, in a discussion about the offering of first fruits (*āgrayaṇeṣṭi*), Yājñavalkya is quoted directly after Kahoḍa Kauṣītaki indicating that his words are correct in contrast to the opinion of Kahoḍa (ŚB 2.4.3.1–2). This case is a clear example of the superior brahmin who gets in the last word.

In a passage about the offering of the omenta, the *Śatapatha Brāhmaṇa* casts Yājñavalkya in opposition to a number of other ritual specialists. Like later descriptions of the *brahmodya*, it presents the views of four different brahmins: Satyakāma Jābāla, Saumāpa Mānutantavyas, Śailāli Bhāllaveya, and Indrota Śaunaka. After recounting the positions of each priest, the text tells us that these opinions are only what these brahmins have said, but are not the accepted views, as the established practice is something different (13.5.3.5). The text then presents Yājñavalkya's opinion as the authorative view.

In a discussion about eating and fasting, Yājñavalkya has a different outlook from Aṣāḍha Sāvayasa and Barku Vārṣṇa (1.1.1.7–10). In this passage Yājñavalkya's opinions are not presented last, but the text nevertheless makes it clear that his ideas are accepted. In this case, it is Barku Vārṣṇa's views that are stated last, but the text clearly rejects his opinions, stating explicitly that his instructions should not be followed (1.1.1.10). In another example, there is a discussion about the pressing of *soma* (4.6.1). Here Yājñavalkya's views are contrasted with those of Rāma Aupatasvini and Buḍila Āśvatarāśvi. Again, Yājñavalkya's argument is presented last, and it is his opinion that is supported by the text. Interestingly, in this case Yājñavalkya appeals to the authority of a *ṛṣi* (seer) to substantiate his claim.[13]

Although these examples are not formally *brahmodyas*, they are descriptions of debates among brahmins where there is a clear winner to the argument. Taken together, these passages indicate that even before the more detailed accounts of the philosophical tournament, Yājñavalkya was already associated with disputes against other brahmins. This is different from Śāṇḍilya, for example, who is usually mentioned individually or in the context of teaching a specific student. In the five times Śāṇḍilya is mentioned in the *Śatapatha Brāhmaṇa*, his opinions are never presented in the format of a *brahmodya*.[14] Even when there are few narrative details, there is nevertheless a distinction between the two main figures of the *Śatapatha Brāhmaṇa*: whereas Śāṇḍilya is portrayed as a teacher, Yājñavalkya is mainly depicted as a disputant in philosophical debates.[15]

By the time of the *Bṛhadāraṇyaka Upaniṣad* (6.5.3), Yājñavalkya had become known as the founder of the Yajurvedic school and the author of parts of the *Śatapatha Brāhmaṇa*, as well as the *Bṛhadāraṇyaka Upaniṣad* itself. The examples of his verbal exchanges in this section have shown that even before he achieved the authoritative status as depicted in the *Bṛhadāraṇyaka Upaniṣad*, Yājñavalkya was known for his ability to defeat other brahmins in debate. In the *Bṛhadāraṇyaka Upaniṣad*, Yājñavalkya is featured in two *brahmodyas*, both of which take place in King Janaka's court. In the first episode, which is one of the most well-known scenes in the Upaniṣads, Yājñavalkya is challenged by seven brahmins from the Kuru-Pañcāla region. We will look at this *brahmodya* in more detail in the following three sections as we explore the significance of the participants, the tactics they employ, and the dramatic conclusion featured in this debate.[16]

The other *brahmodya* in the *Bṛhadāraṇyaka Upaniṣad* that involves Yājñavalkya is presented differently from accounts of other verbal disputes in the Brāhmaṇas and Upaniṣads. In this case, Yājñavalkya does not debate with his opponents directly, but rather counters the claims of other brahmins through Janaka's retelling of their arguments. Interestingly, this scenario is similar to a philosophical debate in the *Sāmaññaphala Sutta* (DN 2), where King Ajātasattu presents to the Buddha the views of six of his philosophical rivals. In this case the participants are: Pūraṇa Kassapa, Makhali Gosāla, Ajita Kesakambalī, Pakudha Kaccāyana, Nigaṇṭha Nāṭaputta, and Sañjaya Belaṭṭhaputta. In both the Upanishadic and Buddhist accounts, there is a similar literary paradigm at work. In the *Bṛhadāraṇyaka Upaniṣad*, the views of six brahmins are summarized by King Janaka and then refuted by the authoritative teacher Yājñavaḷkya; in the *Sāmaññaphala Sutta*, six rival positions are summarized by King Ajātasattu and then refuted by the authoritative teacher Guatama Buddha. This similarity between the Upanishadic and Buddhist presentation of philosophical debates indicates that the *brahmodya* became an important literary convention for presenting knowledge in subsequent narrative traditions. The literary presentation of the *brahmodya* is significant because the narrative details of these scenes are what distinguish them from the scripted exchanges that were nested within the Vedic ritual. More than merely serving as a narrative frame to record different teachings and opinions about the ritual, the literary details of the *brahmodya* highlight the social and interactive character of debate. In the following sections we will examine these dynamics of the public debate and identify three prominent literary features that develop both the personal and political implications of the *brahmodya*: (1) the identity of the individual participants, (2) the debating tactics the participants employ, and (3) the meaning and implications of the threat of head shattering.

YĀJÑAVALKYA'S INTERLOCUTORS: THE SOCIAL AND POLITICAL IMPLICATIONS OF DEBATE

In his study of verbal disputes in Homeric and Old English epic literature, Ward Parks comments on the importance of the individuals who participate in narrative accounts of debate: "The true subject of any verbal context is the contestants themselves; that this presupposition is embedded in the basic structure of the contests is borne out by the range of defensive or belligerent stances frequently adopted by the debators even when they are purportedly engaged in a 'purely intellectual inquiry' " (1990, 166). Similarly, the Upanishadic accounts of the *brahmodya* often emphasize the characters and their interactions with each other, as much as the discourses that they articulate. Nowhere is this more the case than in the well-known philosophical tournament in Janaka's court.[17] In this episode, Yājñavalkya and his opponents not only articulate opposing philosophical claims about the world, but also represent opposing political and cultural alliances. This aspect of the debate can be seen when we examine more closely the particular brahmins that Yājñavalkya argues against. Additionally, a number of Yājñavalkya's opponents appear in more than one verbal dispute against him.

In the philosophical tournament in Janaka's court, all of Yājñavalkya's opponents are from the western Kuru-Pañcāla region and all are representatives of the Rigvedic or Black Yajurvedic schools. Yājñavalkya's first opponent, the *hotṛ* priest Aśvala, is also a court brahmin of King Janaka. His name suggests that he is a member of the Āśvalāyana family, which is associated with the composition of a number of Vedic texts, including the Āśvalāyana recension of the *Ṛgveda*, as well as the *Āśvalāyana Gṛhyasūtra* and the *Āśvalāyana Śrautasūtra*. Another opponent, Kahola Kauṣītakeya, is the reputed author of the *Kauṣītaki Brāhmaṇa* and the *Kauṣītaki Āraṇyaka*. Yājñavalkya's final challenger, Vidagdha Śākalya, has been ascribed authorship of the *Padapāṭha*, which is the final editing of the *Ṛgveda* as we have it today. Throughout this episode not only is there a general connection between political power and Vedic schools, but the presence of these particular brahmins indicates that there is a specific rivalry between the *Yajurveda* and the *Ṛgveda*.[18] That both the political rivalries and canonical debates are linked together in the same event points to a close connection between regional superiority and a courtly alliance with a particular Vedic school. Additionally, the presence of these specific opponents suggests that there was a close association between those who composed Vedic texts and those who had direct contact with the king. Similar to other brahmin characters in the Upaniṣads, the participants in this debate are not depicted as conductors of the sacrifice, but rather as important figures in the king's court.

Many of Yājñavalkya's rivals in this debate also appear in other accounts of verbal contests. Of the eight challengers in Janaka's court, three of them appear in other *brahmodya*s with Yājñavalkya: Kahola Kauṣītakeya, Uddālaka Āruṇi and Vidagdha Śākalya. As we have seen,

Kahola Kauṣītakeya has opposing views to those of Yājñavalkya in the *Śatapatha Brāhmaṇa* (2.4.3.1), while Vidagdha Śākalya appears as a rival to Yājñavalkya in another *brahmodya* in the *Bṛhadāraṇyaka Upaniṣad* (4.1.7).

Uddālaka Āruṇi's appearance as one of Yājñavalkya's rivals in Janaka's court is of particular distinction because the two of them have a number of connections established in other literary contexts. The final genealogy in the *Bṛhadāraṇyaka Upaniṣad* states that Uddālaka is Yājñavalkya's teacher, and in most dialogues where they appear together Uddālaka is presented as the senior, and in some cases, the superior, of the two. For example, in one passage in the *Śatapatha Brāhmaṇa* (5.5.5.14) Yājñavalkya reports that Uddālaka once bewitched Bhadrasena Ājātaśatrava.[19] Here, there is no indication that Uddālaka instructed him, but the fact that Yājñavalkya reports Uddālaka's opinion suggests a hierarchical relationship. Another passage that places Uddālaka in a superior position concerns what to do if the cow in the *agnihotra* lies down while being milked (ŚB 12.4.1.9–11).[20] After stating Yājñavalkya's point of view, the text concludes with the words of (Uddālaka) Āruṇi. As we have seen, unless specifically stated otherwise, the brahmin who speaks last is usually presented as the most authoritative. Uddālaka's characterization as superior to Yājñavalkya from these other debating episodes highlights the dramatic effect of his participation in the dispute in Janaka's court and adds to the significance of Yājñavalkya defeating him in this contest.

Uddālaka Āruṇi also appears together with Yājñavalkya in the presence of Janaka in an account of a different *brahmodya* that appears in the *Jaiminīya Brāhmaṇa* (1.22–25). In this episode, five great brahmins approach King Janaka for a teaching about the *agnihotra*: Uddālaka Āruṇi, Yājñavalkya, Barku Vārṣṇa, Priya Anaśruteya, and Buḍila Āśvatarāśvi Vaiyāghrapadya.[21] In addition to Uddālaka Āruṇi, Barku Vārṣṇa is also a regular opponent of Yājñavalkya who is quoted in the *Śatapatha Brāhmaṇa* (1.1.1.10) as having a contrasting opinion about whether or not the *yajamāna* should fast after performing the *agnihotra*. Later in the dialogue in the *Jaiminīya Brāhmaṇa*, Barku is addressed as Agniveśya, a name that appears in two of the genealogies in the *Bṛhadāraṇyaka Upaniṣad* (BU 2.6.2, 4.6.2). Buḍila Āśvatarāśvi is another regular participant in debates, appearing in the *Chāndogya Upaniṣad* with Uddālaka Āruṇi as one of the five wealthy householders who discusses *ātman* (5.11.1, 5.11.16).[22] However, this is the only *brahmodya* where he is an opponent of Yājñavalkya.

We see some familiar names again in the *brahmodya* where Janaka reports the views of six brahmins to Yājñavalkya. The brahmins whose views Janaka recounts are Jitvan Śailini, Udaṅka Śaulbāyana, Barku Vārṣṇa, Gardhabhīvipīta Bhāradvāja, Satyakāma Jābāla, and Vidagdha Śākalya. In addition to Barku Vārṣṇa, Vidagdha Śākalya is once again cast as an opponent to Yājñavalkya, and similar to how he appears in Janaka's well-known tournament, he is again presented as Yājñavalkya's final opponent. Satyakāma Jābāla, who also features in this debate, is one of the most prominent brahmins in the *Chāndogya Upaniṣad*, and his personal rivalry with Yājñavalkya will be explored further in the final section of this chapter. Here, it is important to point out that in this episode three of the six opponents are known rivals of Yājñavalkya.

As we have seen, this *brahmodya* is notable also because it is different in style from other debates featured in the Brāhmaṇas and Upaniṣads, yet similar to a debate featuring the Buddha in the *Sāmaññaphala Sutta*. There is not only a similarity in presentation, as in both cases the rival positions are reported by the king, but also the Buddhist account places a similar emphasis on the individual participants. All the Buddha's rivals represent opposing religio-philosophical schools, most notably Nigaṇṭha Nātaputta (the name given throughout the Pāli Canon to refer to Vardhamāna Mahāvīra), who is known as the founder of Jainism, and Makhali Gosāla, who is known as the founder of the Ājīvikas. Their presence in this debate is noteworthy because it demonstrates that the Buddhists used a literary account of debate to play out real-world rivalries with other sects. It is well known that the Jains and Ājīvikas not only had different doctrinal positions from the Buddhists, but that they also competed with the Buddhists for the patronage of kings.[23] Similarly, although we know far less about some of the particular brahmin characters, it is clear that the Upanishadic *brahmodya*s use the literary presentation of debate to play out political and social rivalries.

In this section we have looked at the importance of the individual participants who appear in the *brahmodya*s. In both the tournament in King Janaka's court, as well as the example from the *Sāmaññaphala Sutta*, we have seen that many individuals represent specific regions or philosophical schools. In these cases the public debate not only is a contest about philosophy, but also has political and social implications. Additionally, we have seen that a number of the same characters make several appearances as Yājñavalkya's rivals. Some of these individuals, such as Satyakāma and Uddālaka Āruṇi, we know from other episodes, and thus we are able to understand, at least to a certain extent, the connotations of their particular rivalry with Yājñavalkya. Other figures, such as Bhadrasena Ājātaśatrava, do not appear anywhere else in the surviving literature, thus leaving us without the ability to interpret the significance of their particular presence. Yet taken together, Yājñavalkya's interlocutors, as well as the figure of Yājñavalkya himself, indicate that the identities of the individual participants play an important role in the literary presentation of the *brahmodya*. In addition to linking these verbal disputes to external rivalries, the individual identities of the characters also personalize these exchanges. As highlighted by the head-shattering motif, brahmins do not merely challenge each other's views, but question each other's personal authority.

YĀJÑAVALKYA AND THE TACTICS OF DEBATE

In addition to the specific individuals whom he opposes, these descriptions of the *brahmodya* emphasize how Yājñavalkya wins his arguments. Yājñavalkya's authority stems not only from his knowledge, but also from how he uses his knowledge in the context of debate. Yājñavalkya's tactical approach to verbal exchanges is closely connected to his unorthodox persona. This aspect of Yājñavalkya's character is present in some of his earliest appearances in the *Śatapatha Brāhmaṇa*, even in passages where his views are not supported by the text. As Fišer observes, "In spite of Yājñavalkya's doubtless fame and contrary to the current belief that his authority was conclusive, the texts show a variety of opinions. His views are, in fact, sometimes challenged, at other times doubted, and once or twice even rebuked" (1984, 57–58).

In one passage about Prajāpati's original creation, Yājñavalkya states that Prajāpati created two kinds of creatures, but the text disagrees and cites the views of ancient *ṛṣis* that there are three kinds of creatures (2.5.1.2). In another example, the text cites Yājñavalkya's opinion about the *āgnīdhrīya* fire (fire-shed fire). After stating his view, the *Śatapatha Brāhmaṇa* tells us that this is one way and there is also an alternative way (4.6.8.7).[24] On another occasion, in a discussion about the two cups of *soma* juice, the text quotes Yājñavalkya, but questions his opinion, suggesting that his views are too speculative: "Also Yājñavalkya said, 'Should we not rather draw them for the deities, since that is, as it were, the sign of conquest?' In this, however, he merely speculated, but he did not practice it" (4.2.1.7 tr. Eggeling). This passage is one of the first indications that Yājñavalkya's knowledge is unconventional.

In fact, throughout the *Śatapatha Brāhmaṇa*, Yājñavalkya's opinions emphasize newer Upanishadic ideals over and above orthodox opinions about the ritual. For example, on one occasion Yājñavalkya expresses the view that the brahmins themselves are the most important aspect of performing a sacrifice (3.1.1.4–5). Yājñavalkya recounts that when he, along with other priests, was choosing a place to conduct a sacrifice for Vārṣṇa, Sātyayajña expressed that any place where there are brahmins who have studied and are learned and wise, is a place appropriate for sacrifice. Here Yājñavalkya emphasizes that the individual participants are more essential than the ritual actions themselves, a viewpoint that anticipates one of the primary assumptions of the Upaniṣads: the authority of a particular teaching is vested within the person who articulates the teaching.

Although the *Śatapatha Brāhmaṇa* depicts Yājñavalkya as an innovative thinker, his views are primarily about the ritual. Yet whereas in the *Śatapatha Brāhmaṇa* he is presented as an expert on the *agnihotra*, in the Upaniṣads he generally rejects traditional ritualistic arguments that are based on homologies and etymologies. Rather, like a number of Upanishadic teachers, he focuses on teachings of the self, developing themes such as how the *prāṇā*s function in the body, how to overcome death, and the immortality of *ātman*. Throughout his teachings, the public *brahmodya*, as well as his private conversations with King Janaka, serves as a forum for him to articulate some of his most characteristic discourses. For example, in one of his dialogues with Janaka, his teaching begins when the king asks him to discuss where people go when they leave the world (BU 4.2.1). During his instruction he talks about the self, characteristically defining *ātman* by means of negation: "This self (*ātman*) is not this, not this (*neti neti*). It is ungraspable, as it cannot be grasped. It is indestructible, as it cannot be destroyed. It cannot be clung to, for it does not cling. It is unbound, not trembling, not able to be harmed" (BU 4.2.4).[25] In the second version of his dialogue with his wife Maitreyī (BU 4.5), Yājñavalkya imparts an identical teaching, where he again defines *ātman* by means of negation. Additionally, in Janaka's *brahmodya*, Yājñavalkya gives a version of the same discourse when arguing with Uddālaka and Gārgī. Similar to other teachers, Yājñavalkya often presents his ideas about the self in direct opposition to knowledge about the sacrifice.

However, the narrative accounts of the *brahmodya*s not only provide an opportunity for Yājñavalkya to present his views, but they also emphasize how he uses his knowledge to debate other brahmins. Comparable to Socrates in Plato's dialogues, Yājñavalkya does not always win because of the logic of his arguments or his overall knowledge.[26] Rather, Yājñavalkya claims his authority as much by how he makes his arguments, and by how he employs other means, such as humor, insult, and intimidation, to silence his opponents. In another similarity with Socrates, he does not always initially give his best answer to the questions put to him, but only reveals his more characteristic discourses when he is threatened by his opponents. In the following examples, we will see that Yājñavalkya's knowledge is to be found not merely in the consistency of his discourse, but also in his ability to out-talk his opponents. As such, Yājñavalkya's knowledge is often depicted as both situational and tactical.

One example of how Yājñavalkya offers his knowledge in a discriminating way is in his exchange with Jāratkārava Ārtabhāga (BU 3.2), the second rival to question him in Janaka's philosophical tournament. After asking Yājñavalkya about graspers (*graha*) and overgraspers (*atigraha*), Ārthabhāga begins to ask Yājñavalkya questions about the nature of death.[27] One of the questions that Ārtabhāga poses is whether the *prāṇā*s depart from a man when he dies. Yājñavalkya answers that they do not, that a dead man lies bloated (*ādhmāta*) because all the breaths gather together within the body, causing it to swell and to become inflated. Importantly, this answer contradicts one of Yājñavalkya's own teachings to Janaka.[28] Later in the *Bṛhadāraṇyaka Upaniṣad* (4.4.2) when Yājñavalkya is instructing Janaka, he says that when the *ātman* departs from the body, *prāṇa* departs with it; and when *prāṇa* departs, all the vital functions (*prāṇā*s) depart with it. Admittedly, it is possible that this contradiction has more to do with the editorial process of compiling the *Bṛhadāraṇyaka Upaniṣad*, rather than an inconsistency in Yājñavalkya's viewpoints. However, because throughout this exchange he is reluctant to share his knowledge with Ārtabhāga in public, it is also possible to interpret this as one of Yājñavalkya's debating tactics. In his final question Ārtabhāga returns to his earlier question: "When a man (*puruṣa*) dies, and his speech goes into fire, his breath into wind, his sight into the sun, his mind into the moon, his hearing into the cardinal directions, his body into the earth, his self (*ātman*) into space . . . then where is that man (*puruṣa*)" (3.2.13).[29] To this question Yājñavalkya does not answer, but rather replies, "Take my hand good man, Ārtabhāga. Only the two of us will know of this, it is not for us (to discuss) in public" (3.2.13).[30]

This is a curious response for a number of reasons. One possible explanation for why Yājñavalkya cannot discuss this in public is because he has not fooled Ārtabhāga with his first answer and does not want to contradict himself in public. As we have seen in Prajāpati's instruction to Indra, sometimes teachers would willfully teach an untrue doctrine to test the knowledge and humility of their students. Or, as we will see, Yājñavalkya does not always reveal his best answer at the beginning of his response. Considering that Yājñavalkya has different views on this subject in another dialogue, it is quite possible that Ārtabhāga has caught Yājñavalkya in a contradiction.

Another important detail is that Yājñavalkya takes Ārtabhāga's hand as they go outside. As we have seen, this is a gesture associated with the *upanayana* and the dialogues between teachers and students.[31] That Yājñavalkya takes Ārtabhāga by the hand suggests that he will discuss these matters with him only after he has formally initiated him as a student. Does this incident depict a behind-the-scenes initiation? Is Yājñavalkya's teaching so secret that he cannot discuss it in public? Does Yājñavalkya take Ārtabhāga out back to warn him more frankly? Has Ārtabhāga caught Yājñavalkya in a contradiction? The text remains ambiguous. Yet we are left with the curious fact that Yājñavalkya ushers his opponent to a private location and does not directly or publicly answer Ārtabhāga's question. Although we cannot say for certain what is going on in this scene, it is clear that Yājñavalkya employs a rather unusual method to silence his opponent. As we will see, the possibility that Yājñavalkya is not playing by the rules is implied in his exchanges with his other opponents, particularly Uṣasta Cākrāyana and Kahola Kauṣītakeya.

In addition to his sense of when to reveal and when to withhold his most coveted doctrines, Yājñavalkya makes use of humor in philosophical arguments. Not only does he make a number of witty remarks, but he employs his wit as a debating tactic to unsettle his opponents. Witzel explains that "he usually will give an unexpected, quick and undefeatable answer" (1987a, 400). One example of his use of humor occurs in the *Śatapatha Brāhmaṇa* when he is cursed by a group of wandering priests for following the ritual procedure of basting the omenta before the ghee. The priests warn him that if he does not perform the sacrifice according to their method that his breaths will leave his body. In response, Yājñavalkya points to his gray-haired arms and says, "These old arms—what in the world has become of that Brahmin's words!" (3.8.2.25 tr. Eggeling). In this case, rather than oppose the *adhvaryu* priests through argumentation, Yājñavalkya makes a joke about his gray hair, suggesting that since he has lived to be an old man already, the words of the priests cannot be correct. Similarly, in a passage about what an *adhvaryu* priest can eat during the sacrifice, the text warns against eating the flesh of a cow or an ox, stating that, in fact, the one who eats this meat is likely to be born as a strange being (3.1.2.21). However, Yājñavalkya responds that he will eat the meat, provided that it tastes good.[32] Once again, rather than answer with an opinion based on traditional discourse, Yājñavalkya retorts with a humorous remark, indicating a more pragmatic approach to ritual.[33] As we will see in the debate in Janaka's court, Yājñavalkya uses his humor on a number of occasions to literally outwit his opponents.

Another example of his humor is at the beginning of the debate at Janaka's court, when he attempts to unsettle his opponents before the debate even formally begins. When the brahmins gather in the presence of Janaka, the king challenges the most learned among them (*brahmiṣṭha*) to drive away one thousand cows, each with ten pieces of gold tied around their horns (BU 3.1.1–2).[34] Before any discussion takes place, however, Yājñavalkya claims to be the superior brahmin and instructs his pupil to take the cows and gold.[35] Thus, quite audaciously, Yājñavalkya shows his lack of respect for the Kuru-Pañcāla brahmins. In response, Aśvala, Janaka's *hotṛ* priest, questions Yājñavalkya's claim to be the most learned among them. Yājñavalkya sarcastically replies, "We do homage to the most learned brahmin. We just want the cows" (BU 3.1.2).[36] Again, rather than defend his claim through argumentation, Yājñavalkya displays his wit and sarcasm. It is this remark that provokes Aśvala to challenge Yājñavalkya to a series of questions. Indeed, this entire *brahmodya* is a series of challenges by the Kuru-Pañcāla priests to Yājñavalkya's claim of preeminence among them. Accordingly, this initial incident sets the competitive tone for the subsequent philosophical discussion. By claiming to be the most knowledgeable, Yājñavalkya puts himself in the position of having to defend himself. All the other brahmins ask questions while Yājñavalkya proves himself by displaying his ability to answer them. Yājñavalkya does not ask any questions himself until the climax when he goes on the offensive and interrogates Śākalya.

In addition to his use of humor, another recurring aspect of Yājñavalkya's debating style, especially with the Kuru-Pañcāla brahmins, is that he does not completely play by the rules. This is suggested by both Uṣasta Cākrāyana and Kahola Kauṣītakeya. Uṣasta Cākrāyana, the fourth brahmin to interrogate Yājñavalkya, is the first to show signs of dissatisfaction with Yājñavalkya's methods. Uṣasta begins his challenge with a criticism, asking Yājñavalkya to explain *brahman* in such a way that is evident (*sākṣād*) and perceptible (*aparokṣad*), and to reveal the *ātman* that is within everything. Yājñavalkya responds that the self (*ātman*) of the three breaths is the self (*ātman*) within all. Uṣasta, however, is not happy with this tautological explanation and replies sarcastically that defining the *ātman* as *ātman* is equivalent to calling a cow a cow, or a horse a horse (3.4.2). Not only does Uṣasta's sarcasm foreshadow Gārgī's mocking criticism of Yājñavalkya later in the debate, but also, like Gārgī does later, Uṣasta asks the same question twice, once again asking to hear about *brahman* in such a way that is evident (*sākṣād*) and perceptible (*aparokṣad*), and about the *ātman* that is within everything. By repeating his question, Uṣasta suggests that he is not satisfied with the quality of Yājñavalkya's answers. Yājñavalkya ultimately answers that the self cannot be known through the senses because it is the one doing the sensing. Because the *ātman* is always the perceiving subject, it can never be an object of thought or perception. This response is consistent with Yājñavalkya's discourses about *ātman* that he articulates to Uddālaka Āruṇi and Janaka. Here we see that only after Uṣasta's persistent questioning does Yājñavalkya disclose his real answer.

Kahola Kauṣītakeya, the next one to challenge Yājñavalkya's authority, also accuses him of not giving direct answers. Like Uṣasta, he asks Yājñavalkya to explain the *brahman* which is evident (*sākṣād*) and perceptible (*aparokṣad*), and to reveal the *ātman* that is within everything. That Kahola further repeats Uṣasta's question contributes to the dramatic tension developing as the *brahmodya* progresses. The Kuru-Pañcāla brahmins are clearly not happy with Yājñavalkya's answers, so they continue to ask the same questions and accuse Yājñavalkya of not being straight with his replies. In these cases, Yājñavalkya's enigmatic answers do not necessarily suggest that he does not know what he is talking about, but certainly these instances show that his interlocutors cast doubt on his explanations, if not also on his knowledge.

In the previous two sections we have seen that the narrative accounts of philosophical debates connect knowledge to specific individuals, describe the *brahmodya* as a social practice, and outline the modes of conduct by which a debate is conducted. Throughout these verbal contests, it is not only what is said that is important, but also who speaks and how they advance their arguments: debating tactics are recorded as much as the truth claims of the contestants. As Witzel observes, "The texts speak about a set of rules of discussions, rules of challenge and defeat" (1987a, 373). Every dialogue represents a particular event in the formal framework of debating, records the rules of the *brahmodya*, and points out possible tactics. Yājñavalkya, for example, does not necessarily win because of his wisdom, but because he knows the rules of the game, and how to break them. He knows how to convince people through his timing, humor, cryptic remarks, and as we shall see, intimidation and threats.

LOSING FACE OR LOSING ONE'S HEAD? THE MOTIF OF HEAD SHATTERING

Certainly, the most curious aspect of the *brahmodya* is the recurring warning: "your head will shatter apart!" (*mā te mūrdhā vyapaptat*). This threat appears in almost every significant *brahmodya*, both public and private, and is thus a vital characteristic of these exchanges. Additionally, this threat is one of the elements of the *brahmodya* that distinguishes these exchanges from dialogues between teachers and students, as well as dialogues between brahmins and kings. Whether this warning represents the loss of face or the curse of death, these words are employed as a threat to silence opponents and clearly point to the highly competitive character of these exchanges between brahmins. However, what this phrase actually means and its implications for the Upanishadic *brahmodya* are contested issues among scholars.

As we have seen, variations of this phrase occur a number of times in the *Śatapatha Brāhmaṇa* and tend to appear in debates that feature Uddālaka Āruṇi. This warning also occurs several times in the *Bṛhadāraṇyaka Upaniṣad* and the *Chāndogya Upaniṣad*, where it is most often expressed when one individual doubts the knowledge or philosophical claims of another.[37] When threatening Ayāsya Āṅgirasa, Brahmadatta Caikitāneya says that King Soma may make his head shatter apart if he does not sing the *udgītha* (the chant of the *Sāmaveda*) correctly (BU 1.3.24). In the *Chāndogya Upaniṣad*, Śilaka Śālāvatya accuses Caikitāyana Dālbhya of having an understanding of the *sāman* (a verse from the *Sāmaveda*) which lacks foundation, and threatens that if he continues to make such claims of knowledge he will lose his head (1.8.1–8). Not all of these occasions are within the context of a *brahmodya*, but this curse is generally associated with conversations about the significance of Vedic rituals rather than the performance of the ritual itself.[38] In fact, Insler argues that the threat of head shattering did not originate from incorrect performance of ritual actions but rather developed within the context of philosophical discussions: "Its original application concerned only theological discussions and debates" (1989–90, 102). This is a crucial observation because it suggests that this curse developed along with the emergence of the literary presentation of the *brahmodya*. The appearance of the threat of head shattering in these dialogues is significant because it is used to portray a tense atmosphere for philosophical discussions: participants are not merely stating different ontological claims about the world, but actually risking much more with their competing discourses. But what exactly are they risking? Are they risking just their reputations, or their lives?

The two scholars who most thoroughly pursue this issue are Witzel and Insler. Witzel's arguments begin from a philological premise: the phrase *mūrdha vi pat* has been mistranslated as "the head flies off" when it should be rendered as "the head flies apart" or "the head bursts" (1987a, 364).[39] Based on this literal rendering, Witzel concludes that passages containing this phrase imply a real threat of death. To further support this reading, Witzel cites a number of examples from other contexts where this phrase strongly suggests a literal reading. Two of these examples are worth mentioning, because both of them are significant to Insler's counterargument.

The first example comes from the *Ambaṭṭha Sutta* in the Pāli Canon.[40] In this scene, the Buddha demands to know the truth of Ambaṭṭha's ancestry, warning him that if he does not answer his question after three requests, Ambaṭṭha's head will split into seven pieces (DN 3.1.2).[41] At this moment, Vajirapāni, a *yakkha* (nature spirit; Sanskrit *yakṣa*) appears with a large hammer, hovering in the air above Ambaṭṭha. The *yakkha* thinks to himself, "If this young man Ambaṭṭha does not answer a proper question put to him by the Blessed Lord by the third time of asking, I'll split his head into seven pieces" (DN 3.1.21 tr. Walshe).[42] Upon seeing the *yakkha*, Ambaṭṭha answers the Buddha's question. In this case, as Witzel observes, head shattering constitutes a real threat, as indicated by the fact that Ambaṭṭha answers the Buddha's question because he actually sees the *yakkha* ready to strike him with a hammer, strongly indicating that Ambaṭṭha is not merely worried about his reputation, but in fact his very survival.[43]

Witzel also cites a story from the *Jaiminīya Brāhmaṇa* about Yavakrī, who was about to sleep with an *apsarā* (heavenly nymph) when a *gandharva* (heavenly being—the male counterpart to an *asparā*) appears with a metal hammer (2.269). As a punishment, the *gandharva* demands that Yavakrī cut off the heads of all the animals in the surrounding area. Before completing the slaughter, however, Yavakrī himself is killed by a deaf carpenter or woodsman. Curiously, the text states that when the other animals woke up, they assumed that Yavakrī had been killed by the *gandharva*. Although Yavakrī's death is not actually brought about by the *gandharva*'s blow, this story, like the Buddhist example, suggests that head shattering is a literal act that is conducted with a hammer. Witzel concludes from these examples, as well as others: "Obviously, in the late Vedic period and at the time when the Pāli texts were composed, someone to be punished by a supernatural being, like a Yakṣa, Gandharva, or a Ṛtu-devatā, is killed by a blow of a metal hammer and his head splits (into seven pieces, as the Buddhist texts say). In these passages killing is regarded as something quite real and is also described in [a] realistic way—shattering someone's head off with a hammer" (1987a, 384–85).

Insler agrees that in these cases the threat of a literal death is indeed implicit in the narrative, yet he argues that these examples are different in kind to the head-shattering episodes in verbal disputes. Insler maintains that in these two examples, head shattering is introduced as a punishment for specific crimes. Ambaṭṭha is threatened to be punished for falsifying his identity, while Yavakrī is punished for attempting to rape the *apsarā*: "Is it therefore not possible that head smashing at one time was equally a means of death for such instances of falsification? In short, it is my opinion that there were some crimes whose original punishment entailed the smashing of the violator's head by some type of blunt instrument" (1989–90, 107). In his analysis of these stories Insler makes an important point: merely because head shattering is considered real in some literary episodes, it is not necessarily considered real in others. As he explains, the Yavakrī story, in particular, is quite different from the *brahmodya* episodes, not only in terms of what the story is about, but also in its language and specifically in its ways of expressing head shattering.[44] Thus, by establishing the differences in the kinds of stories that feature head shattering, Insler interprets *mūrdha vi pat* as losing one's head or making a fool of oneself, concluding that if this meaning is correct "then it must also be true that no one ever died within the context of a Brahmanic debate" (1989–90, 115).[45]

Both Witzel and Insler bring up important points and cite examples that shed light on this issue, but with their diametrically opposed conclusions, where does this leave us in understanding the threat of head shattering in the Upanishadic *brahmodya*? Thus far, we have followed Insler's rendering of this phrase on the grounds that in the episodes we have considered there have been no explicit suggestions of a death threat. For example, just because a *yakkha* hovers above Ambaṭṭha with a hammer in the Pāli Canon, we cannot assume that one is hovering over Śauceya Prācīnayogya or Uddālaka Āruṇi when they are faced with this threat. Rather, it is significant that in the episodes that we have looked at thus far, namely the private debates featuring Uddālaka Āruṇi, there is nothing in the narrative to suggest losing one's head is a literal threat. These episodes are primarily about a competition for personal authority, where losing one's reputation would be considered a terrible consequence. As Insler expresses, "The learned man simply is warning the other person that he is on the point of making a fool of himself before the others. What greater blow to one's prestige could happen among those who especially consider themselves learned?" (1989–90, 114–15).

Nevertheless, although Insler is correct in challenging Witzel's tendency to interpret all of these incidents as a mortal threat, he goes too far in the opposite direction in concluding that no actual deaths are recounted in the context of philosophical debates. As we will see, the narrative context strongly suggests that in the case of Śākalya the threat of head shattering should be taken literally. To say that this should be taken literally does not imply that this scene records a real historic event. Rather, Śākalya's head really shatters apart in the context of the story. It is important to remember that the Upanishadic narratives are stories, perhaps based on real-world activities, but not necessarily actual records of real-life incidents. It is not surprising therefore, that brahmins would want to embellish these tales to attribute to themselves powers that they did not actually have in real life. In this way, Insler is probably correct in assuming that no real death actually took place in a Brahmanical debate, but that is not the same thing as saying that a real death did not take place in an ancient Indian story about a debate.

In the remainder of this section we will return to the tournament in Janaka's court and examine the events that lead up to its dramatic conclusion. As we will see, there are compelling reasons to suggest that Śākalya does actually lose his head at the end of this *brahmodya*. This is not to suggest that all such incidents should be taken literally in this way, but rather that this conclusion is specific to the debate in Janaka's court and separates this *brahmodya* from other similar episodes. As Olivelle suggests, "[Head shattering] may have been used metaphorically at first to mean something like our colloquial use 'blow your mind,' or 'go nuts' . . . The metaphor may have been turned into a threat and a curse with fatal consequences later on, and the myth of the shattering of Śākalya's head may have been the basis of this transformation" (1996, 295n).

The most compelling reason to assume that Śākalya's head shattering is meant to be a real death is because his death is also reported in a similar incident in the *Śatapatha Brāhmaṇa* (11.6.3.11).[46] In the

Śatapatha Brāhmaṇa version, there is also a debate sponsored by Janaka, but in this case the verbal exchange features Śākalya as Yājñavalkya's only challenger. Importantly, in this encounter Yājñavalkya accuses Śākalya of asking questions beyond his knowledge and predicts that he will die as a consequence. The *Śatapatha Brāhmaṇa* then confirms that Śākalya died, although it does not specify when or how he dies. Because Śākalya's death is clearly reported in the *Śatapatha Brāhmaṇa*, it is highly unlikely that the reference to his head shattering in the *Bṛhadāraṇyaka Upaniṣad* merely refers to Śākalya losing face or his reputation. Rather than change his fate, the *Bṛhadāraṇyaka Upaniṣad* version of this incident attributes Śākalya's death to a different cause. Whereas in the *Śatapatha Brāhmaṇa* he dies after Yājñavalkya predicts his death, in the *Bṛhadāraṇyaka Upaniṣad* he dies after Yājñavalkya warns him that his head will shatter apart. We will look at the implications of this change in the narrative at the end of this section; for now, however, it is important to show that the narrative context suggests that this case of head shattering should be taken literally.

Let us now examine the events leading up to the dramatic conclusion of this debate. A good place to start is Yājñavalkya's encounter with Gārgī Vācaknavī, because it is in response to Gārgī's line of questioning that Yājñavalkya first invokes the threat of head shattering. With this challenge the atmosphere of the debate rises in intensity. By means of this threat, Yājñavalkya accuses Gārgī of asking beyond her own knowledge. Although Gārgī proves otherwise, Yājñavalkya seems to assume that he is picking on an easy target. As we will see in chapter 4, throughout the Upaniṣads the knowledge of women is not sanctioned with discursive authority, even when women make the same philosophical claims as eminent brahmins. In light of this, it is not surprising that Yājñavalkya chooses to call Gārgī's bluff by questioning her knowledge, rather than to try to answer her question. This incident highlights Yājñavalkya's aggressive style of argumentation, yet the fact that Gārgī challenges him again after Uddālaka Āruṇi, suggests that she is confident that she is not speaking beyond her knowledge, and that, consequently, Yājñavalkya's threat cannot harm her.

After Yājñavalkya threatens Gārgī, Uddālaka Āruṇi steps in to make a challenge. As we have seen, Uddālaka Āruṇi is Yājñavalkya's superior and is sometimes considered his teacher. Additionally, in the *Śatapatha Brāhmaṇa* it is Uddālaka who is most closely associated with the threat of head shattering. Uddālaka begins his questions by recounting an almost identical frame story as Bhujyu Lāhyāyani did earlier in the debate. Similar to Bhujyu, Uddālaka was also a student when he visited Patañcala Kāpya, and received a teaching from Patañcala's wife, who was possessed by the *gandharva* Kabandha Ārthavaṇa.[47] As he is speaking to Yājñavalkya, Uddālaka emphasizes that he knows the discourse that the *gandharva* has taught him: a teaching about the string on which this world and the next are strung together. Uddālaka's outright assertion that he knows this teaching is a response to how Yājñavalkya has handled Gārgī's question. Surely, Yājñavalkya is not about to question the knowledge of his superior, especially when Uddālaka makes a point to claim that he knows the discourse.

Furthermore, Uddālaka preemptively challenges Yājñavalkya by warning that his head will shatter apart if he, who has claimed authority over the other brahmins, does not know this teaching: "If you, Yājñavalkya, drive out those cows meant for the brahmins without knowing the thread and the inner controller, your head will shatter apart" (BU 3.7.1).[48] Uddālaka's use of this threat at this moment of the *brahmodya* suggests that Uddālaka shares a similar concern with the other Kuru-Pañcāla brahmins: that Yājñavalkya is not playing by the rules. By emphasizing what will happen if he does not answer properly, Uddālaka forces Yājñavalkya to answer his questions directly.

In addition to the fact that he employs the same threat against Yājñavalkya that was used against Gārgī, Uddālaka's question is similar to Gārgī's. Whereas Gārgī's first question is about the foundation on which the world of *brahman* is woven, like a warp and weft, Uddālaka uses similar weaving imagery as he asks about the string (*sūtra*) with which this world, the other world, and all beings are strung together. It is significant that the challenges of Gārgī and Uddālaka are threaded together through metaphor, because it is after Uddālaka offers his counterchallenge to Yājñavalkya that Gārgī rejoins the debate and continues to question Yājñavalkya, suggesting that Uddālaka has stepped in to defend her.

Yājñavalkya responds with a long discourse about *ātman*, arguing that *ātman* is the inner controller, the immortal (*amṛta*), and that it is distinct from the *prāṇā*s and the physical and mental capacities of the body. He concludes with a similar teaching that he had offered Uṣasta and Kahola: that the *ātman* is the perceiver of all the senses and that it therefore cannot be perceived by the senses. Here we see that when Yājñavalkya is threatened he reveals his more characteristic teaching, and it is this discourse that finally silences Uddālaka.

The tension in this *brahmodya* continues to build as Gārgī enters the debate for the second time. She begins by addressing all the brahmins present and then predicts that if Yājñavalkya can answer her two questions, then none of them will be able to defeat him. She then frames her first question with a martial metaphor comparing herself to a fierce warrior who is stringing her bow with two deadly arrows and rising to challenge her enemy. She demands, "Answer them for me" (3.8.2). This battle analogy not only points to the political and regional rivalries that are at stake, but also foreshadows the fatal conclusions of this debate. We will discuss this encounter between Gārgī and Yājñavalkya in greater detail in chapter 4. For now, let us skip to the end of their exchange when Gārgī again anticipates the outcome of the *brahmodya*. For the second time, she addresses all the brahmins and predicts that something dramatic is about to occur: "Eminent brahmins. You should consider it great if you escape from him by (merely) paying him respect" (3.8.12).[49]

After Gārgī's warning, Vidagdha Śākalya, the final opponent, challenges Yājñavalkya.[50] In the *Śatapatha Brāhmaṇa* version of this dialogue, Śākalya is the only opponent of Yājñavalkya, and the fact that he is the last one to challenge Yājñavalkya in this *brahmodya* and that his encounter with him is the longest, suggests that despite Yājñavalkya's insults, Śākalya poses the biggest threat to him. As in the *Śatapatha Brāhmaṇa* version, Śākalya begins his interrogation by asking Yājñavalkya how many gods there are. In fact, the first section of their debate in the *Bṛhadāraṇyaka Upaniṣad* is almost exactly the same as it appears in the *Śatapatha Brāhmaṇa*. In the *Śatapatha Brāhmaṇa*, however, Yājñavalkya accuses Śākalya of questioning beyond his knowledge after he asks: who is the one god? In both versions Yājñavalkya answers: breath (*prāṇa*). Whereas in the *Śatapatha Brāhmaṇa* Yājñavalkya terminates the discussion with this answer, in the *Bṛhadāraṇyaka Upaniṣad*, Yājñavalkya reverses the challenge and begins to question Śākalya, the first time in this entire *brahmodya* that Yājñavalkya assumes the role of the interrogator.

Śākalya has a number of responses as Yājñavalkya continues to test him, however, when Śākalya answers that Prajāpati is the god of the person (*puruṣa*), Yājñavalkya condescendingly exclaims, "Śākalya, have the brahmins made you their instrument for removing burning coals (*aṅgārāvaksayaṇa*)" (3.9.18).[51] After this remark, Śākalya again takes up the questioning, this time asking Yājñavalkya how he is able to out-talk (*ati-vad*) the other brahmins. Śākalya's use of the verb *ati-vad*, related to the word *ativādin*, implies that in his opinion Yājñavalkya's success against the other brahmins has more to do with his oratory skills than his knowledge.

Later, after Śākalya asks about what the heart is founded upon, Yājñavalkya again insults Śākalya, saying that he is an idiot (*ahallika*) for thinking that the heart could be founded any place other than in ourselves (3.9.25). It is noteworthy that this is the second time that Yājñavalkya has answered that something has been founded upon the heart. Earlier, Yājñavalkya had answered that semen was founded upon the heart. When Yājñavalkya had delivered this answer, Śākalya did not continue in the same line of questioning, but rather asked him about the god of the northern quarter. In this case, however, Śākalya continues in the same line of questioning and Yājñavalkya accuses him of being stupid. Śākalya questions Yājñavalkya for much longer than his other opponents and this could be seen as his relative success in arguing with Yājñavalkya. Yet, as in his encounter with Gārgī, when Yājñavalkya is not convincing his opponents with his knowledge, he relies on threats and insults to intimidate them.

After Śākalya asks who the up-breath (*prāṇa*) is founded upon, Yājñavalkya answers the link-breath (*apāna*) and then begins a brief discourse about *ātman*. Yājñavalkya reveals that *ātman* is the perceiving subject and not an object of thought or perception, again disclosing his more characteristic teaching at the end of their encounter. Then Yājñavalkya assumes the role of the interrogator again and returns to a set of questions about the *puruṣa* discussed earlier in their encounter: "I ask you about the dominant reality (*upaniṣad*) of the *puruṣa*. If you do not explain that to me, your head will shatter apart" (BU 3.9.26).[52] Śākalya does not know the answer and his head does indeed shatter apart.[53]

The implications of this head-shattering episode can be further explored by comparing it with the encounter between Yājñavalkya and Śākalya in the *Śatapatha Brāhmaṇa*, where, as we have seen, Śākalya dies at the end of the dialogue, but his head does not shatter apart. Additionally, in the earlier account Śākalya's death is not brought about by his inability to answer questions (Yājñavalkya does not assume the role of the interrogator), but rather because he questions beyond his own knowledge. Thus, in the *Śatapatha Brāhmaṇa*, Yājñavalkya merely predicts Śākalya's death. In the *Bṛhadāraṇyaka Upaniṣad*, however, Śākalya does not ask beyond his knowledge, but is confronted with Yājñavalkya's direct question about the *upaniṣad* (dominant reality) of the *puruṣa*. These changes in the narrative are significant because by pressuring Śākalya to answer his question and then by explicitly threatening him, Yājñavalkya is more connected as an agent to Śākalya's death. Whereas in the *Śatapatha Brāhmaṇa* Yājñavalkya has the ability to foresee Śākalya's death, the *Bṛhadāraṇyaka Upaniṣad* implies that he has the power to kill him. As Witzel points out, in the *Śatapatha Brāhmaṇa* Śākalya's death is merely reported, whereas in the *Bṛhadāraṇyaka Upaniṣad* it is intended as the climax of the discussion (1987a, 406).

After Śākalya's head shatters apart, Yājñavalkya challenges all the brahmins at once. He declares that he is ready to answer any of their individual or collective questions or he is willing to ask them questions, either individually or collectively. Not surprisingly, none of the brahmins dare to challenge him further and Yājñavalkya emerges unanimously as the victor.

As we have seen, this entire episode records far more than who wins and who loses, but draws attention to the personal dynamics among the various participants, with the competitive and potentially violent nature of this *brahmodya* illustrating the high stakes of philosophical discussion. Despite winning the debate, Yājñavalkya's methods are clearly unorthodox, as he is accused of speaking obscurely on several occasions and a number of his opponents ask questions in such a way that show that they are not satisfied with his answers. Moreover, Yājñavalkya twice uses threats to silence his opponents, the second occasion ending fatally for Śākalya. As Brereton comments, "Initially this is a contest for cows, but becomes a life and death struggle" (1997, 2).

UPANISHADIC TEACHINGS AND MATERIAL WEALTH

Thus far, we have looked at the personal and political consequences at stake in the *brahmodya*. However, in addition to competing for their own reputations and on the behalf of the kings who sponsored them, brahmins also competed for large amounts of material goods. As we will see, the descriptions of the wealth accumulated by brahmins are crucial details that are employed both to characterize the value of Upanishadic teachings and to criticize Vedic ritualism.[54] Indeed, the *brahmodya* eclipses ritual performance as the activity through which brahmins have the opportunity to secure the most wealth. The growing importance of the *brahmodya* in relation to the sacrifice is clear from the competition in Janaka's court. At the beginning of this episode, the narrative tells us that brahmins were gathered together because Janaka was about to sponsor a sacrifice at which he would give generously to the officiating priests (BU 3.1.1). Although the *brahmodya* is clearly connected to sacrifice, the narrative never returns to the issue of sacrifice, as the *brahmodya* itself is the focus of the story. As opposed to the earlier accounts where the *brahmodya* is embedded within ritual actions, the debate in Janaka's court is not presented as merely a part of the sacrifice. Rather, the *brahmodya* emerges as a distinct practice, as demonstrated by the fact that the authority claimed by Yājñavalkya at the end of the debate is completely based on his performance in the *brahmodya* itself.

Another episode that clearly distinguishes philosophical discussion from sacrificial performance features Uṣasti Cākrāyaṇa, who is described as a pauper living in the village of a rich man (CU 1.10.1). He has to resort to begging from the rich man, but refuses to take more than he needs to survive. The next morning Uṣasti arrives at a sacrifice where the officiating priests do not know the esoteric significance of the ritual actions they are performing. Uṣasti criticizes them, warning that if they continue to perform the Vedic chants without the proper knowledge, their heads will shatter apart. This warning attracts the attention of the *yajamāna* (sacrificer) who then asks Uṣasti to perform all the priestly duties. Before agreeing, however, Uṣasti demands that he earn the same amount as all the other priests combined.

In this story teachings are contrasted with the practice of sacrifice, as Uṣasti, who is a specialist in the discursive knowledge characteristic of the Upaniṣads, is presented favorably in comparison with the ritual specialists. Although the text suggests that a sacrifice was performed, this episode ends with the ritualists asking Uṣasti to teach them what he knows; despite the fact that the sacrifice is mentioned and serves as a backdrop to this incident, the narrative emphasizes Uṣasti's teaching. In this way, both the story of Uṣasti and the *brahmodya* in Janaka's court begin with a sacrifice, but instead focus on a teaching or a debate in which one brahmin proves his authority over more traditional priests who are ritual specialists.

The complex relationship between the early Upaniṣads and the practice of sacrifice has been discussed on a number of occasions. Some scholars have attempted to explain this relationship as an internalization of the ritual, suggesting that the sacrifice became a symbolic construct that was performed mentally; others have argued that economic factors led to the decline in the practice of sacrifice.[55] In the examples of Yājñavalkya and Uṣasti, although they prove their authority through practices set in contradistinction to sacrifice, one of their rewards for proving their knowledge is the role of performing a sacrifice. As such, these cases do not point to a complete rejection of sacrifice, but rather to a focus on other practices such as teaching and debating.

As the sacrifice is no longer the central concern, many narratives tell the story of brahmins who are looking for new ways to make a living in a changing world. Brahmins who are specialists in the new teachings about the self can sell their ideas for material goods such as gold, cows, and land, often taking home much more wealth than brahmin ritualists. Such stories establish teaching and debating, over and above ritual expertise, as the currency by which brahmins survive, and indeed claim power. The economic value of Upanishadic teachings is highlighted on numerous occasions, with the high financial stakes of debates between brahmins adding to the competitive atmosphere of verbal contests.

Many of the brahmins who are depicted as knowledgeable are described teaching and debating in a number of regions throughout ancient north India, with the traveling brahmin serving as a typical epithet for the knowledgeable Upanishadic teacher. Yājñavalkya, Uddālaka, and Śvetaketu are all described in the *Śatapatha Brāhmaṇa* as traveling around on their chariots. Uddālaka Āruṇi travels throughout all of north India trading in ideas, not only appearing with Yājñavalkya in Videha (BU 3.7.1), but also driving his chariot in the northern region of Madras (ŚB 11.4.1.1–9) and learning from Pravāhaṇa in Pañcāla (CU 5.3.1). Additionally, the *Kauṣītaki Upaniṣad* (4.1) describes Gārgya as a learned man from Uśinara, who had traveled widely in Satvan and Matsya, Kuru and Pañcāla, and Kāśi and Videha. These examples indicate that travel and familiarity with a number of the different regions function as important qualifications for an Upanishadic teacher.

Of all the brahmins who travel about seeking patronage, Yājñavalkya by far emerges as the wealthiest. Indeed, on a number of occasions he jokes about his pursuit of material possessions. Before his debate with the Kuru-Pañcāla brahmins, Yājñavalkya cynically claims that the economic prize of cows and gold outweighs the honor of being declared the most learned brahmin.[56] Although this quip is intended as a joke, and quite likely is a debating tactic employed to disarm his opponents, this remark also indicates that Yājñavalkya is well aware of the considerable financial gain to be won from philosophical tournaments. In a later discussion with Janaka, the king asks him, "Yājñavalkya, for what purpose have you come? Do you want cows or subtle disputations? (*aṇvanta*)" (BU 4.1.1).[57] Yājñavalkya confirms Janaka's comment by answering, "Both, your majesty." This exchange is illustrative of the friendly banter between the brahmin and king, yet these remarks also bring attention to Yājñavalkya's reputation for pursuing material gain. In fact, in every one of Yājñavalkya's dialogues in the Upaniṣads an economic transaction takes place: he claims the prize at Janaka's tournament, he wins thousands of cows from Janaka for his private instructions, and his dialogue with Maitreyī takes place within the context of dividing his inheritance.

As Upanishadic teachings begin to compete with sacrifice in terms of their claims to bring desired rewards, they also begin to be considered more valuable. For example, Yājñavalkya earns more from his debate in Janaka's court as it appears in the *Bṛhadāraṇyaka Upaniṣad* than he does in the frame narrative in the *Śatapatha Brāhmaṇa*. In the *Śatapatha Brāhmaṇa* (9.6.3.1) Janaka gives away a hundred cows and numerous gifts, yet in the *Bṛhadāraṇyaka Upaniṣad* (3.3.1) Janaka gives away the more lavish prize of one thousand cows, each with ten pieces of gold attached. Although these figures are likely to be exaggerations, the inflated value of winning a *brahmodya* in the Upaniṣads reflects its emerging importance.

A number of other dialogues further highlight the economic aspect of Upanishadic knowledge. One example features Jānaśruti Pautrāyana and Raikva (CU 4.1–2). Jānaśruti, presumably a king, is described as a man who is devoted to giving and who built numerous hospices. One day, he overhears two geese talking about a famous teacher known as Raikva the gatherer. Jānaśruti sends his steward to find Raikva because he wants to learn what Raikva knows.[58] After his steward has located him, Jānaśruti approaches Raikva with six hundred cows, a gold necklace (*niṣka*), and a chariot (*ratha*) drawn by she-mules. At first Raikva refuses this material wealth and rudely calls Jānaśruti a *śūdra* (one from the lowest class), ordering him to leave and take his wealth with him. Jānaśruti, however, returns to Raikva, offering him the same necklace and chariot, but this time one thousand cows (*sahasra gava*), as well as his daughter (*duhitā*) and a village (*grāma*).[59] This time, charmed by the face of Jānaśruti's daughter, Raikva accepts his offer. The text then relates that the village is now named after Raikva.

Returning to Uṣasti Cākrāyaṇa, in addition to displaying a critique of the sacrifice, his story also illustrates how brahmins competed among each other for patronage. Before arriving at the sacrifice Uṣasti had no food and lived like a pauper (CU 1.10–11). Yet by displaying his knowledge in front of the *yajamāna*, Uṣasti earns himself the position of carrying out the sacrifice. Significantly, he demands a fee equal to the total of all the other brahmins. Here we see that in the marketplace of Upanishadic ideas, brahmins are pitted against each other as individuals rather than collectively performing rituals together. One brahmin such as Uṣasti can perform the jobs of all the other priests combined, suggesting that an important incentive for brahmins to learn

Upanishadic teachings is that they reap the same economic rewards as the collective payment for the sacrifice.[60]

Two of the most explicit examples where wealth is directly compared to Upanishadic teachings feature Uddālaka Āruṇi and Naciketas. In the *Bṛhadāraṇyaka Upaniṣad* (6.2.7) version of Uddālaka's dialogue with Pravāhaṇa, the brahmin claims to have plenty of gold, cows, horses, female slaves, cloths, and clothing, and thus prefers to learn the king's teaching over receiving more wealth. Similarly, in the *Kaṭha Upaniṣad* (1.26–27), Naciketas refuses the material wealth offered by Yama, telling him that wealth does not lead to happiness and will be of no use after one has died. On the one hand, these details contrast knowledge with material wealth and consistently present knowledge as more valuable than worldly possessions. Yet on the other hand, these stories emphasize that a payment to brahmins is inextricably connected to Upanishadic teachings. Although both Uddālaka and Naciketas refuse wealth for the sake of receiving a teaching, they are not necessarily choosing the spiritual over the material, as neither Uddālaka nor Naciketas are opting for a life without wealth or possessions. Rather, they recognize that with the rewards promised by Upanishadic teachings, ultimately the knowledge they receive will be more valuable than the wealth that they refuse. In fact, Uddālaka's inventory of possessions is a good indication of how much more he can collect if he learns the knowledge of the five fires from Pravāhaṇa.

In this section we have looked at the importance of wealth in Upanishadic dialogues. The economic worth of teachings is highlighted on numerous occasions and all the dialogues make it clear that when brahmins share their knowledge they always receive something in return. As we saw in the preceding chapter, when brahmins take on a student they have someone to tend their fires and look after their cows; in this chapter we have seen that when brahmins debate in front of or teach kings they take home large amounts of material goods, including gold and cows. Yājñavalkya emerges as the wealthiest of all the brahmins depicted in the Upaniṣads, but Uṣasti Cākrāyaṇa and Uddālaka Āruṇi become quite rich as well. Taken together, these narrative episodes illustrate that the brahmins in the Upaniṣads are wily negotiators who demand high rewards for their teachings.

YĀJÑAVALKYA AND RENUNCIATION

The characterization of brahmins as accumulating enormous amounts of material possessions and aggressively competing for patronage and power is significant because scholars have often assumed that the

Upaniṣads represent the expressions of mendicants who abstain from the affairs of everyday life. In this section we will look at the two main scholarly trajectories that have presented the Upaniṣads as renunciatory texts: those who consider renunciation as the natural outgrowth of Vedic ritualism and those who suggest that central ideas in the Upaniṣads originated from non-Vedic traditions. We will also examine those passages in the Upaniṣads that clearly advocate renunciation, considering them within the context of dialogues that emphasize wealth and competition.

Heesterman has famously argued that the Upaniṣads represent a natural shift from ritualism to renunciation, claiming that the emergence of Upanishadic teachings marks the beginning of the figure of the world-renouncer:[61] "It would seem to me that here we touch the principle of world renunciation, the emergence of which has been of crucial importance in the development of Indian religious thinking. The renouncer can turn his back on the world because he is emancipated from the relations which govern it" (1985, 38–44). For Heesterman, not only do the discourses of the Upaniṣads follow naturally from speculation about the sacrifice, but the practice of world renunciation is the logical and inevitable outgrowth of ritual activity. In this context Heesterman sees the role of the brahmin as primarily one of detachment from the world: "The real brahmin is not the officiating priest or purohita, but the brahmin who keeps aloof from occupations that would enclose him in the web of relations and tie him to the others" (1985, 42). He defines the dynamic between the renunciation-oriented brahmin and the this-worldly king as the "inner conflict of tradition" (see 1985, 26–44).

As Heesterman's interpretative framework is called the orthogenetic model, Kaelber terms the alternative interpretive trajectory, represented by scholars such as Eliade and Louis Dumont, as "challenge and assimilation" (1989, 101–24). Dumont understands the history of Indian religion and society in terms of the dichotomy between "man-in-the-world" and "individual-outside-the-world," ascribing all religio-philosophical innovation to those outside the world (1966, 185). In this way, Dumont does not assign authorship to either brahmins or *kṣatriyas*, but rather he sees the Upaniṣads as the products of both those brahmins and *kṣatriyas* who had become renunciates: "At the end of the Vedic period, in the Upanishads, one can see the development of philosophical speculation bearing first and foremost on the universal being. This speculation is the work of Brahmans and Kshatriyas who withdrew in order to devote themselves to it" (1966, 186).

Although these two trajectories in the scholarship attribute the authorship of new ideas to different sources, both the orthogenetic and the assimilation arguments agree in assuming that the teachings of the early Upaniṣads are connected to renunciation. Within the context of the dialogues that we have looked at so far, where brahmins are depicted in interactive social situations such as teaching, learning, and debating, it is difficult to see why so many scholars associate these texts with a renunciate movement. What is the evidence for renunciation within the Upaniṣads?

It is well accepted that by the time of the Buddha there was quite a large population of wandering mendicants, and indeed there are some references that suggest renunciation in the early Upaniṣads (BU 3.5, 4.4.22, 4.5.1).[62] In one of his teachings to Janaka, for example, Yājñavalkya explicitly advocates the life of mendicancy, explaining that brahmins seek to know *ātman* through Vedic recitation, sacrifice, gift-giving, austerity, and fasting. However, those who come to know *ātman* live a life of wandering: "Upon knowing it, one becomes an ascetic (*muni*). Desiring it as their world, renouncers (*pravrājina*) wander forth (*pra + vraj*)" (BU 4.4.22).[63]

If Yājñavalkya's teaching had stopped here, there would be nothing that necessarily contradicted the lifestyle of the brahmin characters portrayed throughout the Upanishadic dialogues, not to mention Yājñavalkya's own life. As we have seen in the previous chapter, many brahmin teachers are both householders and wanderers. Satyakāma, for example, has a wife and has taken on a number of students, yet he still leaves his household for a period of time, presumably to learn more discourses, participate in debates, or to attract more students. Additionally, Uddālaka Āruṇi, whose travels are recorded more than any other character, maintains his important duty as a householder by having a son.

However, the next part of Yājñavalkya's instruction clearly contradicts the views of other Upanishadic teachers. Here, Yājñavalkya explains to Janaka that when one knows *ātman*, there is no need for offspring. In fact, Yājñavalkya relates that sages in former times who had come to know *ātman* "abandoned the desire for sons, the desire for wealth, and the desire for worlds, and took up a life of mendicancy" (BU 4.4.22).[64] Similarly, he reveals this same discourse to Kahola Kauṣītakeya during the *brahmodya* in Janaka's court, indicating that this instruction is specifically associated with Yājñavalkya (BU 3.5). In these examples, Yājñavalkya clearly challenges the importance of having sons, which, as we will examine further, is considered a fundamental link to immortality in many Upanishadic teachings. In addition to teaching about giving up the desire for sons, Yājñavalkya seems to follow his own advice, as he apparently has no sons and in one version of his dialogue with Maitreyī specifically states that he leaves his household for the life of a wandering mendicant (BU 4.5.1). Yājñavalkya's association with these ideals contributes to setting him apart from Kuru-Pañcāla brahmins, as well as other Upanishadic teachers, and further develops his innovative literary personality.

These articulations of renunciation are significant both in terms of our understanding of the historical developments of renunciation in ancient India and our understanding of Yājñavalkya as a literary figure. These are the first textual expressions of renunciation as a way of life, and Yājñavalkya is the first individual who is depicted as taking up this way of life. Nevertheless, it is important to emphasize that Yājñavalkya is the only brahmin in the early Upaniṣads who advocates a life of mendicancy and none of the other brahmins are depicted as living as renunciates or talking about renunciation. In fact, Yājñavalkya's own adherence to this way of life is not at all straightforward. Despite teaching about renunciation, Yājñavalkya amasses more wealth than any other Upanishadic teacher and is connected to both the court and the household. Additionally, in both instances where Yājñavalkya teaches that wealth is not important, he wins a sizeable amount of material possessions. In Janaka's *brahmodya* Yājñavalkya takes home the gold and cows. Similarly, after his instruction to Janaka, the king offers both himself and the people of Videha to be his slaves. In this case, the concluding section of the narrative promises that one who knows this discourse about *ātman* finds wealth (*vasu*) (4.4.24). These examples clearly illustrate that even when Yājñavalkya teaches about mendicancy, he is speaking within a context where his knowledge gains him tremendous wealth.

Furthermore, Yājñavalkya's knowledge is displayed within the context of discussion and debate. As we have seen, the kind of knowledge that Yājñavalkya displays to argue successfully against other brahmins is not based exclusively on the truth of his teachings, but also on his understanding of the rules of game of debate. He emerges victorious, because of his use of sarcasm, insults, and threats, hardly gestures that we would expect from a mendicant.

In these ways, despite discussing mendicancy, Yājñavalkya establishes his reputation in situations that are more connected to the competitive practice of the *brahmodya* than to the renunciate life. It is only in the later Upaniṣads where knowledge is explicitly connected to renunciation, or at least the meditative and yogic practices often associated with this lifestyle. Similar to how the early Upaniṣads outline practices of teaching and debating, the later Upaniṣads directly connect their discourses with techniques for how to concentrate and meditate. The *Kaṭha Upaniṣad* (6.10–11) describes yogic practices such as making the perceptions still and reining in the senses, while the *Śvetāśvatara Upaniṣad* (2.8–9) is more explicit by describing bodily postures and the controlling of the breath. Also the *Śvetāśvatara Upaniṣad* explains exactly where and under what conditions one should engage in yogic practices: "In a place level and clean, free from gravel, fire and sand; near soundless water, a hut, and so on. Pleasing to the mind, but not disturbing to the eye; hidden and protected from the wind; one should practice *yoga*" (2.10).[65] Although some of the teachings in the early Upaniṣads are later developed by yogic and renunciate traditions, these practices are not described in the dialogues.

When we look at the early Upaniṣads as a whole, it is clear that renunciation is not the main practice. Rather, far from achieving a distance from social relations, the brahmins are depicted as active participants in their social world: they are shown in interactive social situations such as teaching, learning, and debating, while Upanishadic ideas are presented firmly within the contexts of personal, regional, and political rivalries.

THE LIFE STORY OF YĀJÑAVALKYA

Throughout this chapter, we have returned to the figure of Yājñavalkya. He is the persona most associated with the *brahmodya*, and he appears in more narrative episodes than any other figure in the Yajurvedic tradition. Additionally, similar to the *Chāndogya Upaniṣad*'s portrayal of Satyakāma, the *Bṛhadāraṇyaka Upaniṣad* presents an integrated biographical sketch of the life of Yājñavalkya. As we have seen, in the *Śatapatha Brāhmaṇa* Yājñavalkya is often presented as merely an authoritative name, but by the time of the *Bṛhadāraṇyaka Upaniṣad* he has become a well-developed literary personality. He is consistently portrayed as a great knower of Upanishadic teachings, especially about *ātman* and *prāṇa*, and he teaches these discourses as a court brahmin under the patronage of King Janaka of Videha. As we will examine further in the next chapter, the *Bṛhadāraṇyaka Upaniṣad* explains Yājñavalkya's presence in Janaka's court by means of referring to an encounter between the two of them on chariots that is described in the *Śatapatha Brāhmaṇa*. The entirety of books three and four in the *Bṛhadāraṇyaka Upaniṣad* consists of dialogues featuring Yājñavalkya, and most of them assume that he is the court priest of Janaka. His first appearance in the third book is his debate against the Kuru-Pañcāla brahmins, and subsequently he has three short dialogues with Janaka, the last of which describes his release from serving the king. In the very next dialogue he appears at home with his two wives about to settle his inheritance and to embark on the life of a mendicant. Although alternative versions of some of these dialogues suggest that books three and four consist of distinct textual components that are only brought together through editing, their presentation within the *Bṛhadāraṇyaka Upaniṣad* forms a rough sketch of a life story of Yājñavalkya: the wealthy court priest who gives up both the court and the household to pursue the mendicant way of life.

Throughout these dialogues Yājñavalkya embodies a number of teachings that are central to the *Bṛhadāraṇyaka Upaniṣad*. For example, more than the *Chāndogya Upaniṣad* or the *Kauṣītaki Upaniṣad*, the *Bṛhadāraṇyaka Upaniṣad* emphasizes the competitive nature of Upanishadic teachings and makes more explicit links between the debates of the brahmins and the political rivalries of kings. As we have seen, the debate in King Janaka's court is presented as a competition between Videha and Kuru-Pañcāla, and Gārgī's challenge to Yājñavalkya is compared to a military battle between Videha and Kāśi. In these cases, Yājñavalkya is the reference point that places Videha at the center, and presents Kuru-Pañcāla and Kāśi as military and political threats. In contrast, the *Chāndogya Upaniṣad* and the *Kauṣītaki Upaniṣad* do not focus on one particular individual. For example, Satyakāma does not dominate the *Chāndogya Upaniṣad* to the degree that Yājñavalkya does in the *Bṛhadāraṇyaka Upaniṣad*, nor are there any details that link Satyakāma to any specific geographical location. Other brahmins who figure prominently in the *Chāndogya Upaniṣad*, for example Śāṇḍilya and Uddālaka Āruṇi, are generally associated with Kuru-Pañcāla, but the *Chāndogya Upaniṣad* does not emphasize these details.

In regards to the *Kauṣītaki Upaniṣad*, the text takes its name from its alleged composer, Sarvajit Kauṣītaki. Kauṣītaki, however, is only mentioned once in the text (2.7), and there are no narrative details about his character. Of the other characters described in this Upaniṣad, only Ajātaśatru, king of Kāśi, is linked to a specific place, but this detail is shared with the *Bṛhadāraṇyaka Upaniṣad*, and the *Kauṣītaki Upaniṣad* does not generally favor Kāśi or any other particular region. Although both the *Chāndogya Upaniṣad* and the *Kauṣītaki Upaniṣad* characterize knowledge as competitive, with political and military implications, neither text presents knowledge within the context of any particular conflict. By contrast, it is through its depiction of Yājñavalkya, as well as King Janaka, that the *Bṛhadāraṇyaka Upaniṣad* makes specific political claims and aligns itself with the region of Videha.

In addition to highlighting political and military rivalries, the *Bṛhadāraṇyaka Upaniṣad* portrays a personal rivalry between Yājñavalkya and Satyakāma. The particular rivalry between these two brahmins is traceable to the *Śatapatha Brāhmaṇa* (13.5.3.1–7), which presents Satyakāma as one of several brahmins with opposing views to Yājñavalkya. Although Yājñavalkya does not appear at all in the *Chāndogya Upaniṣad,* Satyakāma is mentioned twice in the *Bṛhadāraṇyaka Upaniṣad,* with both instances pointing further to a personal rivalry between them. On one occasion Satyakāma is one of the six priests whose arguments are summarized by Janaka before being rejected by Yājñavalkya. Here, Satyakāma is clearly depicted as a rival to Yājñavalkya. On another occasion Satyakāma is quoted as one of six priests who are authorities on a rite for achieving greatness (BU 6.3.7–12). In a parallel passage in the *Chāndogya Upaniṣad,* however, Satyakāma is the only name quoted (5.2.3).[66] Thus, while the *Chāndogya Upaniṣad* attributes exclusive authority of this teaching to Satyakāma, in the *Bṛhadāraṇyaka Upaniṣad* he is merely one of six priests associated with this discourse. Furthermore, two of the other priests mentioned are Uddālaka Āruṇi and Yājñavalkya, where Uddālaka marks the beginning of the genealogy and Yājñavalkya is depicted as his student. In this case, not only does Satyakāma share authority, but he is placed as subordinate to both Uddālaka Āruṇi and Yājñavalkya.

In addition to their historic rivalry, Satyakāma and Yājñavalkya represent competing portrayals of the ideal Upanishadic priest. The lifestories of both Satyakāma and Yājñavalkya remain sketches and are clearly not well-developed biographies or hagiographies, yet both literary personae are presented as paradigmatic figures, whose actions embody central teachings of their respective texts. Whereas Satyakāma is associated with the practice of teaching and the social location of the household, Yājñavalkya's character is most closely connected to the court and develops through his performance in the *brahmodya* as he competes against other brahmins and wins the patronage of kings.

CONCLUSION

In this chapter we have examined dialogues between brahmins and other brahmins. We began by examining the distinction between the ritually-embedded verbal exchanges and the narrative descriptions of the *brahmodya*. On the one hand, the verbal exchanges that are part of the Vedic sacrifice serve as models for the two types of Upanishadic debate. Yet when the *brahmodya* becomes a narrative scene, a number of aspects of debating are highlighted, particularly the literary characters and the debating tactics they employ, with both of these features drawing attention to the interactive and competitive nature of the *brahmodya*. In this way, the Upanishadic *brahmodya* is not merely a display of different philosophical positions, but an exploration of what is at stake in verbal competitions. The individual participants, especially the Kuru-Pañcāla brahmins, link the philosophical competition to regional and political rivalries, suggesting that kings could establish their reputations partly through aligning themselves with particular priests. The narratives also highlight the tactical dimension of debate, indicating that, especially with such high stakes involved, philosophers such as Yājñavalkya could employ his humor, as well as tricks and intimidation, to unsettle his opponents and emerge victorious in debate.

One of the features that particularly is connected with the *brahmodya* is the motif of head shattering. As we have seen, there is disagreement among scholars as to its exact implications, but whether this phrase is taken figuratively or literally, it undoubtedly constitutes a threat, often used by brahmins to unsettle their opponents. In this chapter we have taken head shattering as predominantly an attack on personal authority, without physical consequences. On such occasions this threat is mostly used as a warning that one brahmin is about to lose his or her reputation or "lose face" if he or she does not recognize the authority of the other. However, I have also argued that in one particular episode this threat is quite literal and that it is invoked with fatal consequences. This reading is supported by the fact that, in an earlier version of this debate, Śākalya, the victim of Yājñavalkya's warning, is already known to have died. Additionally, it is not out of context that this *brahmodya*, which most develops the regional and political struggles involved in philosophical tournaments, would also show that there is more at stake in verbal debate than merely the reputation of brahmins.

In addition to the political and regional rivalries, we have also explored the economic dimensions of the *brahmodya*. In every description of a *brahmodya* there is some sort of material reward at stake. Additionally, a number of stories explicitly point out that there is more wealth to be gained through debating than performing a Vedic sacrifice. In these episodes the Upanishadic narratives present the *brahmodya* as eclipsing the sacrifice and becoming the activity by which brahmins establish both their authority and their wealth.

The personal, political, and economic dimensions of the *brahmodya* all point to the interactive and competitive nature of Upanishadic philosophy. These features are especially important to keep in mind when we remember that many of the prevailing interpretations of these texts characterize the brahmins as solitary knowledge-seekers, aloof from the affairs of everyday life. As is clear from the narrative descriptions of debate, the brahmins that feature in the Upaniṣads are not renunciates, but tactical orators and wily negotiators who are active participants in personal, regional, and political rivalries.

Yājñavalkya is the character who most personifies these social aspects of Upanishadic philosophy. Despite teaching about renunciation and opting to live as a renunciate in his later years, he establishes his reputation by means of the debates that he wins and the wealth he accumulates. Additionally, one of Yājñavalkya's most distinctive characteristics is his close friendship with King Janaka. We will explore this relationship further in the following chapter as we examine how brahmins interact with kings to win their patronage.

CHAPTER THREE

Kings and Brahmins

The Political Dimensions of the Upaniṣads

INTRODUCTION

We will now turn our attention to a number of dialogues between brahmins and *kṣatriyas*. Some of these encounters feature a brahmin giving a king a private instruction, while others depict the king teaching the brahmin. Indeed, the king teaching a brahmin is a prominent motif throughout the late Brāhmaṇas and early Upaniṣads, with some of the dialogues not only featuring the king as teacher, but overtly claiming that particular teachings actually originated among the *kṣatriyas*. In both the *Bṛhadāraṇyaka Upaniṣad* and the *Chāndogya Upaniṣad*, King Pravāhaṇa Jaivali explicitly asserts that his knowledge had never reached the brahmins before. The *Chāndogya Upaniṣad* account makes an even stronger claim, maintaining that the *kṣatriya* monopoly on political power is founded on an exclusive possession of this knowledge: "Prior to you, this knowledge has not gone to the brahmins. Therefore, in all the worlds government has belonged only to the *kṣatriyas*" (5.3.7).[1]

These words spoken by Pravāhaṇa have led many scholars to believe that the knowledge of the five fires (*pañcāgnividyā*) was literally authored by *kṣatriyas*. However, as Bodewitz illustrates, many of the teachings spoken by *kṣatriyas* had appeared earlier in Vedic literature, but then were presented again as the speech of a *kṣatriya* in the Upaniṣads (1974, 216).[2] For example, Pravāhaṇa's teaching also appears in the *Jaiminīya Brāhmaṇa* (1.45–46), but without the context of a dialogue between a *kṣatriya* and a brahmin. Also, alternative versions of this discourse appear in the *Aitareya Āraṇyaka* and the *Śatapatha Brāhmaṇa*.[3] Taking this into account, Pravāhaṇa's claims that this teaching is known only by *kṣatriyas* is clearly not a factual representation of the origins of the discourse, but rather part of the literary presentation of teachings in the Upaniṣads.[4] In this chapter we will consider Pravāhaṇa's claim within the context of other dialogues that feature brahmins and kings.

As we have seen in accounts of the *brahmodya*, Upanishadic teachings are presented against the background of regional and political rivalries, with a number of teachings making promises specifically connected to the goals of the king. In this chapter we will see that even though many dialogues depict kings teaching brahmins, indicating that kings are not dependent upon brahmins for their knowledge, the Upaniṣads nevertheless emphasize that the presence of brahmins is essential for kings to be successful. Throughout these dialogues, receiving brahmins as esteemed guests by offering food and accommodation is an integral aspect of the ideal king. Seen in this context, the narrative scenes featuring kings claiming to have authored particular discourses are part of a more general *kṣatriya* orientation that is present in a number of teachings throughout the early Upaniṣads. As we will see, dialogues between brahmins and kings characterize Upanishadic teachings as indispensable to the king's political power and reflect an attempt by brahmins to secure patronage from kings.

Of course, the king also had a central role in the sacrifice, as indicated in the ritual texts where there are a number of passages that praise kings for the specific sacrifices they sponsor. The *Śatapatha Brāhmaṇa* (13.5.4.1–22), for example, contains a list of kings who had sponsored *aśvamedha* sacrifices and describes a great *aśvamedha* hosted by Bharata Duḥṣanti where seventy-eight horses are bound near the Yamunā and fifty-five near the Gaṅgā. His descendant King Bharata conquered the earth and brought more than one thousand horses for Indra. Additionally, an important aspect of the mythology of the Brāhmaṇas is making an equivalence between the king, as *yajamāna*, and Prajāpati, suggesting a perceived divinity of the king. Like Prajāpati, the king is portrayed as lord of creatures, and the sacrifice is an integral aspect of displaying his divine power. However, in the late Brāhmaṇas and early Upaniṣads, as the emphasis of the discourse moves away from the performance of the sacrifice, the king is no longer depicted as the *yajamāna* who sponsors great sacrifices. Rather, the ideal Upanishadic king hosts philosophical tournaments and participates in philosophical discussions. Moreover, these activities are linked to a number of new theorizations about the king and the source of his power.

The kings who are the most prominent in the early Upaniṣads are Janaka, Ajātaśatru, Aśvapati, and Pravāhaṇa. Janaka is known for both his knowledge and generosity, yet in the *Bṛhadāraṇyaka Upaniṣad* his political authority is increasingly attributed not to his own knowledge, but to his affiliation with his court priest, Yājñavalkya. Ajātaśatru, the king of Kāśi, teaches about the vital functions in an attempt to compete with Janaka, his political rival. His teaching is characteristic of the knowledge attributed to kings throughout the Upaniṣads and is presented in direct contrast to the ritual knowledge of the brahmin Gārgya. Aśvapati, the king of the Kaikeyas, teaches about *ātman vaiśvānara* to six brahmins (ŚB 10.6.1.2; CU 5.11.4).[5] He is depicted as a generous patron who provides food and accommodation for brahmins and who privileges brahmins known for their knowledge of Upanishadic teachings over priests who perform sacrifices. Finally, Pravāhaṇa, the king of Pañcāla, teaches Uddālaka Āruṇi about the five fires and the two paths of the dead and claims that his knowledge is directly responsible for his royal power. Pravāhana's interactions with Śvetaketu and Uddālaka not only depict him as an ideal king, but also outline the proper etiquette by which brahmins should approach the king when seeking patronage. Taken together, these stories about kings illustrate a *kṣatriya* orientation in many teachings in the early Upaniṣads. The texts not only present kings as major characters, but also frame many of the teachings specifically within a political context that addresses the concerns of kings.

THE MYTH OF *KṢATRIYA* AUTHORSHIP

Before we look at the dialogues between brahmins and kings, let us briefly review the scholarly debate about *kṣatriya* characters and the authorship of the Upaniṣads. According to tradition, the Vedas were composed by ancient *ṛṣi*s, but have been preserved and transmitted by brahmins. However, there are a number of passages in the Upaniṣads that ascribe authorship of particular ideas to *kṣatriya*s. Richard Garbe was one of the first modern scholars to comment on these passages, concluding that some of the most consequential discourses in the Upaniṣads originated among *kṣatriya*s: 'The significance of these stories is evident . . . It shows that the authors of the elder Upanishads did not try, or did not dare, to veil the situation that was patent in their time, and claim the monistic doctrine of the Brahman-Ātman as an inheritence of their caste . . . To [the *kṣatriya*] caste belongs the credit of clearly recognising the hollowness of the sacrificial system and the absurdity of its symbolism, and, by opening a new world of ideas, of effecting the great revolution in the intellectual life of ancient India' ([1873] 2004, 77–78).

Similarly, Deussen has argued that discourses about *ātman* were developed as a direct response against ritualism and were explicitly kept secret from brahmins. Taking literally the claims of King Pravāhaṇa, he argues that the *ātman* teaching "was taken up and cultivated primarily not in Brahman but in Kshatriya circles" ([1919] 2000, 19).

Erich Frauwallner also takes seriously the narrative details that present *kṣatriya*s as important innovators of religio-philosophical ideas:

> It is striking that in a whole number of texts, it is not the Brāhmaṇas but the adherents of the Kṣatriya caste, i.e., the Kṣatriyas who impart the instruction and that it is the Brāhmaṇas who are instructed. This is evidently taken out of the actual life itself. The Brāhmaṇas, who have handed down this text would hardly think of contriving this sort of thing, if in actuality there would have been no basis for it. (1973, 34)

Frauwallner qualifies this, however, by stating that those who ascribe the chief role to the *kṣatriya*s go too far. He argues that although the *kṣatriya*s were important contributors to Upanishadic doctrines, they did not author the texts. Interestingly, Frauwallner, despite acknowledging a *kṣatriya* contribution, makes efforts to reserve the most valuable contributions for the brahmins.

This debate about authorship has had far-reaching implications. According to some scholars, teachings that the Upaniṣads ascribe to *kṣatriya*s, notably teachings about *karma* and rebirth, not only are meant to be associated with kings, but also are indications of the non-Vedic origin of these ideas. Killingley succinctly summarizes this point of view: "It is commonly asserted that belief in rebirth is not of Āryan origin, and it is often attributed to non-Āryan, or specifically Dravidian sources" (1997, 1). Thus, one of the issues often at stake in the debate about *kṣatriya* authorship is whether some of the foundational ideas of the Upaniṣads originated in Vedic or non-Vedic sources. Whether or not there may have been a non-Vedic influence on the ideas in the Upaniṣads is a question beyond the scope of this book. It is clear, however, that the ideas voiced by *kṣatriya* characters, despite what the characters claim, are not particularly new to the Vedic tradition, and that therefore, the motif of *kṣatriya* authorship is a literary fiction.

A. B. Keith was one of the first scholars to challenge the theory of *kṣatriya* authorship as proposed by Garbe and Deussen. Because of the strong connections between the Upaniṣads and earlier Vedic material, Keith refutes the suggestion that the ideas discussed by *kṣatriya* literary characters should be ascribed to actual *kṣatriya* authors: "It is absolutely certain that the Upaniṣads, as we have them, are not the work of warriors, that they are handed down by priests" ([1925] 1989, 493–94). Rather than assume *kṣatriya* authorship, Keith poses the question: why would priests want to ascribe authorship to kings? He concludes. "We must adopt a solution which explains why the whole Upaniṣad tradition is Brahmanical, and yet why the texts record actions of importance as regards the doctrines by the princes of earth" ([1925] 1989, 495).

Olivelle raises similar questions about the *kṣatriya* characters who claim to have sole possession of certain teachings, offering the speculation that identifying a teaching with a king served to align these discourses with a new age and a new urban culture: "What these stories of kings teaching new doctrines to Brahmins point to, I believe, is a divide that existed within the Brahmin tradition between the village Brahmins clinging to the old ritual religion and the city Brahmins catering to the needs of an urban population" (1992, 38).

Following both Keith and Olivelle, in this chapter I will examine why brahmin composers would want to present their own ideas as originating among the *kṣatriyas*. I will explore this issue within a more general *kṣatriya* orientation that characterizes many of the Upanishadic teachings. Indeed, *kṣatriyas* not only are prominent speakers in the texts, but also feature as ideal listeners for a number of teachings, indicated by the fact that kings are often given private instruction, and they figure as the primary audience for public debates. Moreover, a number of teachings are specifically linked to characteristically *kṣatriya* concerns such as defeating enemies and gaining political power.

Throughout, dialogues between kings and brahmins emphasize how both the presence of brahmins in the court and Upanishadic teachings themselves are indispensable to a king's political power. As we will see, the claims made by *kṣatriya* characters do not represent a true expression of a *kṣatriya* voice, but rather *kṣatriya* characters embody brahmin idealizations about the position of king. Accordingly, the most important character traits of the Upanishadic king are that he is knowledgeable in Upanishadic teachings, and generous and hospitable to brahmins.

JANAKA AND YĀJÑAVALKYA: NEGOTIATING THE BRAHMIN'S POSITION IN THE COURT

In the previous chapter we examined how the character of Yājñavalkya developed from an authoritative voice to the principal representative and founder of the Yajurvedic school. His dialogues with other brahmins, as well as with women, contributed to giving him a legendary status in Vedic literature that would serve as a prototype for the wise teacher and court priest in subsequent texts. Similarly, King Janaka of Videha achieves the status of the ideal Upanishadic king, as he is cast as both the generous patron and the knowledgeable monarch. Janaka features in several episodes in the *Śatapatha Brāhmaṇa* and the *Jaiminīya Brāhmaṇa*, and throughout these appearances he is known for hosting philosophical tournaments and for participating in debates with brahmins, both of which are characteristics shared by other kings in the Upaniṣads. Central to his depiction as king is his personable relationship with Yājñavalkya. The two of them have several dialogues with each other, and on a number of occasions they display their friendship through exchanging witty remarks. In the *Bṛhadāraṇyaka Upaniṣad*, Yājñavalkya's presence in his court establishes Janaka as a legitimate rival to the kings of Kuru-Pañcāla, indicating that Janaka's relationship with Yājñavalkya is an integral aspect of his power as king.

It is quite likely that legends about Janaka as a great king developed first, and only later was his authority attributed to his association with Yājñavalkya. This is suggested by the fact that in the earlier dialogues that include both characters, Janaka is depicted as superior in his knowledge, as well as in his debating skills. For example, in both the *Śatapatha Brāhmaṇa* and the *Jaiminīya Brāhmaṇa*, Janaka teaches Yājñavalkya, and on one occasion he overtly defeats him in a *brahmodya*. Although the *Bṛhadāraṇyaka Upaniṣad* contains a number of dialogues in which *kṣatriya*s teach brahmins, it does not contain any dialogues where Yājñavalkya does not win. It seems likely that the *Bṛhadāraṇyaka Upaniṣad*, which expands the character of Yājñavalkya in a number of ways, does not want to portray him losing an argument with anyone, even if it is Janaka. Accordingly, throughout the *Bṛhadāraṇyaka Upaniṣad*, Yājñavalkya is clearly the superior of the two, and on one occasion the king even steps down from his throne and offers the brahmin his kingdom (4.4.23).

One of the salient features of the relationship between Janaka and Yājñavalkya is that the king gives generously when the brahmin displays his knowledge. In the *Śatapatha Brāhmaṇa* (11.4.3.20) Janaka gives one thousand cows to Yājñavalkya for his knowledge of the *mitravindā* (a vegetal oblation). On another occasion, in a dialogue from the *Bṛhadāraṇyaka Upaniṣad*, he offers Yājñavalkya one thousand cows every time he refutes the argument of another brahmin. Additionally, in a discussion about the *agnihotra* (twice-daily milk offering), Janaka gives him a hundred cows (ŚB 11.3.1.2). This particular occasion is interesting because, compared to similar episodes in the

Upaniṣads, there is nothing in this teaching which makes this knowledge specifically related to the king. Yet, even though Yājñavalkya's teaching does not promise any specific rewards to Janaka as the king, he nevertheless gives Yājñavalkya one hundred cows. As we will see, a major innovation in Upanishadic teachings is that knowledge is increasingly framed for a *kṣatriya* audience.

In these examples Janaka is portrayed as much for his generosity as he is for his own knowledge. A dialogue from the *Jaiminīya Brāhmaṇa* (1.22–25) further develops Janaka's character as a generous patron. In this episode, five brahmins—including (Uddālaka) Āruṇi and Vājasaneya (Yājñavalkya)—approach Janaka because he is already known to them as an expert on the *agnihotra*: "Janaka, that king of Videha is well-informed about the *agnihotra*. He considers himself superior to us in the dispute. Come, we shall make him discuss the *agnihotra*" (1.22 tr. Bodewitz). Although the king eventually teaches the brahmins, the narrative emphasizes the gifts that Janaka bestows upon them for their presence. After they are formally announced the king prepares for them "separate seats, separate (dishes of) water, separate *ṁadhuparka* drinks (mixtures of honey and milk), separate abodes." Despite proving his superiority, Janaka nevertheless continues to be a magnanimous host, paying the brahmins abundantly for their teachings. After every brahmin speaks, Janaka praises his words and proclaims that he will pay him for his knowledge. After they all have spoken, Janaka again proves to be more knowledgeable, as he is the only one who knows the goal of the *agnihotra*. The brahmins offer him a boon for his wisdom, but rather than accepting their gift, Janaka offers them each one thousand cows and five hundred horses.

Significantly, even when he is the one doing the teaching, Janaka gives excessively, a crucial detail that is shared throughout the dialogues between brahmins and kings; whether the brahmins are teachers or students, the brahmins get paid.[6] By showing that the brahmins receive copious rewards even when they lose arguments and assume the role of the student, these dialogues emphasize that it is the presence of the eminent brahmins that is considered vital, and that in order to attract brahmins to their court kings had to pay extravagantly. As we have seen in the previous chapter, when brahmins participate in philosophical tournaments, they compete fiercely against each other for the patronage of kings. However, when brahmins discuss ideas with *kṣatriya*s there is not the same competitiveness. Brahmins get paid whether they are teachers or students and whether or not they win their philosophical debates.

Like Yājñavalkya, Janaka not only is known for his knowledge, but also is depicted as clever in his debating tactics. This dialogue from the *Jaiminīya Brāhmaṇa* tells us that before he entered a discussion with them, Janaka shaved his head and beard, cut his nails, and anointed his body, and approached them carrying a staff and wearing sandals. These details indicate that Janaka is preparing himself to be the student of the brahmins. However, when he enters into a discussion with them, he takes the initiative and asks the first question. The brahmins recognize that by means of this debating tactic, Janaka has outmaneuvered them: "You have indeed (again) out-talked us since you have taken the initiative and questioned us who are more than one" (Jaiminīya Brāhmana 1.22, tr. Bodewitz). The brahmins then, one by one, offer Janaka a teaching as a way to honor his superiority. Here, asking the first question is depicted as a crafty move whereby the king puts the visiting brahmins in the position of having to prove their knowledge. By debating tactically Janaka forces the brahmins to reveal their teachings.

Pravāhaṇa Jaivali is another king who employs this tactic in a debate with brahmins (CU 1.8.1–8). In a discussion about the *sāman* in the *Chāndogya Upaniṣad,* Pravāhaṇa establishes himself as superior to both Śilaka Śālāvatya and Caikitāyana Dālbhya. Like Janaka, he knows the importance of speaking first in a debate, as he is the first of the three to pose a question. Eventually Pravāhaṇa wins the argument, accusing both brahmins of lacking foundation in their teaching and threatening that their heads may shatter apart. The debate ends with the brahmins asking the king to be their teacher.

Returning to Janaka and Yājñavalkya, another dialogue shows how the king uses his ability to win a debate as a way to secure the services of Yājñavalkya as his court priest (ŚB 11.6.2.1). In this story, Janaka encounters Yājñavalkya, Śvetaketu Āruṇeya, and Somaśuṣma Sātyayajñi while they are driving around on chariots. Initially Janaka approaches the brahmins and asks for their expertise on how to perform the *agnihotra.* Janaka again manages to ask the first question, thus framing the course of their discussion and ensuring that they talk about something that the king knows. As we saw in the *Jaiminīya Brāhmaṇa,* the *agnihotra* is clearly a topic about which Janaka enjoys expertise, so it is not surprising that he chooses to begin the discussion with this subject. After hearing each of the priests explain his method, Janaka rejects their knowledge, mounts his chariot, and drives away.

Despite rejecting the teachings of all three brahmins, Janaka clearly shows a preference for the method described by Yājñavalkya, telling him that compared to the other priests he had inquired most closely into the *agnihotra*, and giving him one hundred cows as a reward. However, the king points out that not even Yājñavalkya has a complete knowledge of the *agnihotra*. Nevertheless, Janaka, once again, is willing to pay handsomely even when he is more knowledgeable than the brahmins.

At this point in the narrative the brahmins acknowledge among themselves that Janaka has out-talked (*ati-vad*) them, and they discuss whether they should challenge the king to a *brahmodya*. Both Śvetaketu and Sātyayajñi are eager to challenge Janaka, but Yājñavalkya has reservations: "We are *brāhmaṇas* and he is a *rājanya*: if we were to vanquish him, whom should we say we had vanquished? But if he were to vanquish us, people would say of us that a *rājanya* had vanquished *brāhmaṇas*: do not think of this!" (ŚB 11.6.2.5 tr. Eggeling). Yet having said this, Yājñavalkya mounts his chariot and catches up with Janaka.[7] Bodewitz addresses this seeming contradiction of Yājñavalkya rejecting a public debate in favor of a private instruction with Janaka, explaining that this saves Yājñavalkya the humiliation of being defeated by a king in public, as well as insures that he will not have to share the king's knowledge with his rival brahmins (1974: 89).

Yājñavalkya makes his approach by physically overtaking Janaka on his chariot. This incident highlights the competitive aspect of their discussion as their philosophical debate is likened to a chariot race.[8] When Yājñavalkya catches up with Janaka, the king then gives him further instruction about the *agnihotra*, after which Yājñavalkya admits that the king has a superior knowledge and offers the king the boon of asking him any question that he wishes. This is the only occasion in the surviving literature where Yājñavalkya is defeated in a debate; significantly, this defeat binds Yājñavalkya to surrendering his teaching services to the king. Thus, this dialogue not only displays Janaka's knowledge about the *agnihotra* but also shows how he uses this knowledge to win the services of a court priest. At the beginning of this episode Yājñavalkya is traveling around presumably as a freelance teacher, but by the end he is working for Janaka. As we will see, the link between their debate on chariots and Yājñavalkya's subsequent position in Janaka's court is expanded in the *Bṛhadāraṇyaka Upaniṣad*.

These examples suggest that in comparison with debates among brahmins, discussions between brahmins and kings tend not to be as competitive. As they do not feature threats and insults, there are no indications that anyone's life is at stake, and brahmins seem to come out ahead even when they lose the argument. Nevertheless, these episodes are important for characterizing the king as being well-versed in Upanishadic teachings, and they also suggest that by participating in debates, kings could attract brahmins to their courts and perhaps win their services by outflanking them in a philosophical discussion.

JANAKA AND YĀJÑAVALKYA IN THE *BṚHADĀRAṆYAKA UPANIṢAD*

The relationship between Janaka and Yājñavalkya further unfolds in the fourth book of the *Bṛhadāraṇyaka Upaniṣad*, which contains three dialogues between the king and the brahmin. In the first of these discussions (BU 4.1.1–7), Yājñavalkya approaches the king while he is formally seated. Janaka responds familiarly, asking if Yājñavalkya has come for cows or for a philosophical discussion. In the ensuing dialogue, which was mentioned in the previous chapter, Yājñavalkya shows his superiority over six rival brahmins by rejecting their views as they are summarized by Janaka. Once again Janaka is cast as a generous patron, as after each view that Yājñavalkya defeats, the king offers him a thousand cows and a bull as large as an elephant.

Throughout all three dialogues Yājñavalkya frames his teachings specifically for the interests of his royal audience, using many metaphors to link his discourses to the position of king. He begins by comparing the potential value of his teaching to the importance of a king equipping himself with a chariot (*ratha*) or a ship (*nāva*) before departing on a journey (BU 4.2.1), and he ends his teachings by comparing the centrality of *prāṇa* in relation to the other vital functions to the centrality of the king among his ministers (4.3.38). Finally, Yājñavalkya promises Janaka that this knowledge will help him defeat his enemies. As Yājñavalkya's livelihood relies on Janaka's patronage, it is not surprising that he packages his teachings as vital to the kings's power.

Additionally, this dialogue reinforces the particular connection between Janaka and the *brahmodya*. As we saw in the previous chapter, Janaka hosts philosophical tournaments as a means to display his political power. When he invites Yājñavalkya and the other brahmins to debate in his court, their confrontation is compared to Janaka's political struggles against both Kuru-Pañcāla and Kāśi. Although it is Janaka's political struggles that this debate plays out, the king himself is not a contestant; he proves himself not by means of his own knowledge, but through the debating skills of his court priest. This is in contrast to the depiction of Janaka in the *Śatapatha Brāhmaṇa* and the *Jaiminīya Brāhmaṇa*, where he participates in verbal disputes himself, including two episodes where he is superior even to Yājñavalkya—one where the king defeats the brahmin, the other where he teaches him. In this dialogue in the *Bṛhadāraṇyaka Upaniṣad,* Janaka is once again associated with a *brahmodya,* as he displays his understanding of Upanishadic teachings to Yājñavalkya by summarizing the views of a number of brahmins. Nevertheless, it is Yājñavalkya, not Janaka himself, who refutes the teachings of the other brahmins. Whereas in the Brāhmaṇas, Janaka's knowledge is presented as an important attribute of his character as an ideal king, in the *Bṛhadāraṇyaka Upaniṣad* he is more known for hosting *brahmodyas* than for participating in them.

The second dialogue (BU 4.2.1–4) between Janaka and Yājñavalkya appears to be a continuation of the first. This encounter begins when Janaka gets down from his seat and approaches Yājñavalkya, suggesting that Janaka, who was formally seated at the beginning of the previous conversation, is so impressed by Yājñavalkya's answers that he abdicates his position of authority to recognize Yājñavalkya's superiority. At the end of this short exchange, Janaka offers both himself and the people of Videha as the servants of Yājñavalkya, further suggesting that Janaka is, at least symbolically, stepping down as king to serve Yājñavalkya.

The final of these three dialogues (BU 4.3.1–4, 4.25) refers back to their encounter on the chariots in the *Śatapatha Brāhmaṇa.* Yājñavalkya visits Janaka thinking that he is not going to reveal his knowledge, but then the narrative recalls the chariot episode where Yājñavalkya had granted Janaka the wish to ask him questions whenever he wanted.[9] In this way, the *Bṛhadāraṇyaka Upaniṣad* mentions their previous debate to explain why Janaka can ask for a teaching even when Yājñavalkya is reluctant to disclose his knowledge: "When Janaka and Yājñavalkya discussed together about the *agnihotra,* Yājñavalkya had given him a wish (*vara*). He chose to ask any question he desired, and Yājñavalkya granted it to him. So, the king asked the first question" (BU 4.3.1).[10] This passage suggests that although Yājñavalkya is reluctant to disclose all that he knows, only by sharing his knowledge does he become free from his debt to Janaka. That Yājñavalkya is bound by his previous boon is further indicated on several occasions throughout their discussion. Janaka periodically praises Yājñavalkya for his teachings, and even continues to offer him more cows, but the king insists that Yājñavalkya will have to prove himself further in order to be released: "Sir, I give you a thousand cows. Speak further to be set free" (BU 4.3.14, 15, 16, 33).[11] At one point, Yājñavalkya acknowledges that the king is too intelligent to fool him with superficial answers: "Then Yājñavalkya was afraid, thinking: this learned king has driven me out of every corner" (BU 4.3.33).[12] Finally, Yājñavalkya concludes his teaching by offering him the "world of *brahman*." Janaka then frees him by offering Yājñavalkya both himself and his people as his slaves.

These dialogues between Janaka and Yājñavalkya show Janaka as a magnanimous king who is known for hosting the *brahmodya*. Additionally, these episodes play out the complex and mutually dependent relationship between king and court priest. As the king needs brahmins in his court to display his authority in political rivalries, the priest needs the king for his income. This dynamic between the king and his court priest is also explored in theorizations about the *brahman* and *kṣatra* powers and emerging definitions of *dharma*. The *Bṛhadāraṇyaka Upaniṣad* (1.4.11–5) explains that *brahman* created *dharma*, but that *dharma* is carried out by the king. Additionally, this account claims that a brahmin should pay homage to a *kṣatriya* during the consecration ceremony, but that the brahmin should be regarded as the womb and the source of the king's political authority. Interestingly, the relationship between Janaka and Yājñavalkya displays a similar interdependence that nevertheless privileges the role of the priest. Although the *Bṛhadāraṇyaka Upaniṣad* presents Janaka as a powerful king, ultimately Yājñavalkya, whose success against the Kuru-Pañcāla brahmins establishes the king's reputation, is portrayed as the source of his power.

Incidentally, Janaka's reputation as one who knew Upanishadic teachings and one who hosted brahmins in his court seems to have been well-known and coveted among his rivals. This is indicated in a dialogue featuring Ajātaśatru that appears in both the *Bṛhadāraṇyaka Upaniṣad* (2.1.1–20) and the *Kauṣītaki Upaniṣad* (4.1–20). In this encounter the brahmin Gārgya approaches Ajātaśatru to give him an instruction, but finding the king to be more knowledgeable, Gārgya asks to be his student.[13] When Gārgya initially offers to deliver his teaching, Ajātaśatru replies enthusiastically and promises to give Gārgya one thousand cows for his instruction.[14] Then the king proclaims: "People will rush here saying: 'A Janaka, a Janaka' " (BU 2.1.1; KṣU 4.1). These words clearly show that Ajātaśatru accepts Gārgya's offer because he recognizes that learning from an eminent brahmin and hosting him in his court would enhance his reputation and power, specifically in relation to Janaka.[15]

KINGS AS TEACHERS: AŚVAPATI TEACHES A GROUP OF BRAHMIN HOUSEHOLDERS

Aśvapati Kaikeya is another king known for both his hospitality to brahmins and his knowledge of Upanishadic teachings. Aśvapati only appears twice in Vedic literature, both times as instructing several brahmins. In the *Chāndogya Upaniṣad* (5.11–24) he is one of two kings who teaches the well-known Kuru-Pañcāla brahmin, Uddālaka Āruṇi. This dialogue begins with a group of wealthy and learned householders (*mahāśāla*) who want to know about *ātman* and *brahman*.[16] They decide to approach Uddālaka Āruṇi because he is known to study about the 'self of all people' (*ātman vaiśvānara*).[17] When they meet him, however, Uddālaka realizes that he will not be able to answer them in a complete way. Accordingly, he advises that they all approach Aśvapati, king of the Kaikeyas. When we recall what can happen to brahmins who claim to know more than they do, then perhaps it is not surprising that Uddālaka suggests they all go to another teacher.

Aśvapati receives the householders as honored guests, and when he is about to perform a sacrifice, he announces that he will give the brahmin householders wealth (*dhana*) equal to what he gives the officiating priests. Again we see the dichotomy between brahmins who specialize in Upanishadic teachings and brahmins who perform sacrifices. Aśvapati offers to pay these brahmin householders the same amount just for receiving a teaching from him as he is paying the ritual priests for actually performing a sacrifice for him. In the process, he shows his prejudice towards the householders, as he is basically paying these brahmins to listen to him. As we have seen with Janaka and Yājñavalkya, it is in the interests of the king to act as a patron to eminent brahmins. And like Janaka, Aśvapati is willing to provide gifts for the brahmins even though he is the one doing the teaching. In both cases, brahmins are paid and honored, not for their ability to teach a discourse, but rather for their authoritative presence and the opportunity they create for the king to display his own knowledge.

In the *Śatapatha Brāhmaṇa* (10.6.1.1–11) there is a different account of this story, which features Aruṇa Aupaveśi, rather than his son Uddālaka. Here, five brahmins are gathered at Aruṇa's house discussing *agni vaiśvānara*, but cannot agree. They then decide to ask Aśvapati Kaikeya. The *Śatapatha Brāhmaṇa* also emphasizes the hospitality of the king and recounts that the brahmins take up residence with him. When they go to Aśvapati, he arranges for them separate dwellings, separate honors, and separate *soma* sacrifices, each with a thousand gifts. Although the king is equally generous, in this version his gifts to the brahmin householders are not contrasted with payment to brahmin ritualists. As such, the *Śatapatha Brāhmaṇa* version, which is presented as part of the ritual, does not criticize ritual activity. The *Chāndogya Upaniṣad* account, however, expands the narrative and explicitly contrasts knowledge about *ātman* with ritual performance, as Aśvapati's teaching is about the self, rather than about the sacrificial fire. Thus, in the *Chāndogya Upaniṣad*, the *vaiśvānara* fire is recast as the *vaiśvānara* self, again emphasizing the shift away from a description of the sacrifice and presenting a teaching that focuses on the self.

Another important difference between these two presentations of this dialogue is how the characters of Uddālaka and his father are developed differently. In the *Śatapatha Brāhmaṇa* Aruṇa is not differentiated from the other brahmins in the same way that Uddālaka is in the *Chāndogya Upaniṣad*. In the *Śatapatha Brāhmaṇa* the brahmins are gathered together in Aruṇa's house, but they do not approach him specifically to learn from him, nor is he necessarily teaching them, and their decision to go to Aśvapati is not necessarily due to Aruṇa's lack of knowledge, but rather because they cannot as a group come to an agreement.[18] In the *Chāndogya Upaniṣad*, however, in contrast to his father, Uddālaka Āruṇi is singled out as lacking in essential knowledge. Although Uddālaka is once again cast as the ignorant brahmin, it is important to remember that he is effective in this role precisely because of his reputation as a respected teacher. Consequently, Aśvapati's knowledge is highlighted as he is able to do what the eminent brahmin cannot do: to teach about *ātman*.

Additionally, other attributes of Aśvapati's character are more fully developed in the *Chāndogya Upaniṣad* account, indicating that he is an exemplar for emerging conceptions about the ideal ruler. Both versions of the dialogue are in prose, yet there is a verse spoken by Aśvapati in the *Chāndogya Upaniṣad* that characterizes him as the moral protector of his kingdom: "In my kingdom there is no thief, no miser, no drunkard, no one without a sacred fire, no one who is not learned, no adulterer, much less an adulteress" (5.11.5).[19] Similarly, another dialogue in the *Chāndogya Upaniṣad* (4.1.1) describes Jānaśruti Pautrāyaṇa as the generous provider for his people, as he is known for giving cooked food and having numerous hospices built. Both of these examples coincide with a passage from the *Bṛhadāraṇyaka Upaniṣad* (1.4.14), which equates *dharma* with the king and describes the king as protecting the weak from the strong. Although these qualities are not particularly developed in the Upaniṣads, these examples point to an emerging ideal of the hospitable and generous king, attributes that would become normative characteristics for the ruler in the early Buddhist literature.[20]

UDDĀLAKA ĀRUṆI AND ŚVETAKETU: INSTRUCTIONS FOR HOW TO SEEK PATRONAGE

Another dialogue that highlights the social interaction between brahmins and kings is the story of King Pravāhaṇa and his discussions with Śvetaketu and Uddālaka Āruṇi.[21] This episode where both Śvetaketu and his father visit the king occurs three times in the early Upaniṣads. The story, as it appears in all versions, has three basic components.[22] In the first part Śvetaketu arrives at the residence of the king, who asks him a number of questions. In the *Bṛhadāraṇyaka Upaniṣad* and the *Chāndogya Upaniṣad* the king is named Pravāhaṇa Jaivali, while in the *Kauṣītaki Upaniṣad* he is known as Citra Gāṅgyāyani.[23] Unable to answer any of the king's questions, Śvetaketu leaves to return to his father. In the second part, Śvetaketu has a short dialogue with his father where he explains that he could not answer any of the king's questions. Upon hearing this, Uddālaka decides to go to the king to learn from him. The third section consists of a dialogue between Uddālaka and the king, where the king teaches him an important discourse. In both the *Bṛhadāraṇyaka Upaniṣad* and the *Chāndogya Upaniṣad* the king's teaching is about the five fires and the two paths, while in the *Kauṣītaki Upaniṣad* it is a discourse about the path after death.

At the end of this chapter we will return to the content of King Pravāhaṇa's teaching. For now, however, let us concentrate on the interactions between the characters. First, we will follow this story as presented in the *Bṛhadāraṇyaka Upaniṣad*, as this version gives us the most information about the personal dynamics. In the following section we will then compare the *Bṛhadāraṇyaka Upaniṣad* version with the accounts in the *Chāndogya Upaniṣad* and the *Kauṣītaki Upaniṣad*.

In the *Bṛhadāraṇyaka Upaniṣad* the story begins when Śvetaketu arrives at the king's residence and interrupts Pravāhaṇa while he is eating, or, as Olivelle suggests, perhaps while entertaining female attendants.[24] This initial encounter depicts Śvetaketu entering Pravāhaṇa's residence abruptly, indicating that he has not learned the proper etiquette for approaching a king. As Olivelle explains: "Śvetaketu did not know his manners and barged into the presence of [Pravāhaṇa] during an inappropriate moment" (1999, 58). Furthermore, Śvetaketu does not address Pravāhaṇa respectfully. Rather than employ the honorific *bhagavaḥ*, as he does throughout the *Chāndogya Upaniṣad*, Śvetaketu addresses the king with the word *bhoḥ*, which as Olivelle suggests, is similar to the modern colloquial word "hey."

In addition to approaching the king rudely, Śvetaketu arrogantly refuses to learn from him. The king asks the young brahmin a number of questions and then invites him to stay with him. However, when Śvetaketu cannot answer any of the questions, he refuses the king's invitation to remain at his court and hastily returns to his father. The king's questions not only cast doubt on Śvetaketu's discursive knowledge, but also bring attention to the young brahmin's lack of understanding of proper behavior.

Moreover, Śvetaketu's refusal to stay with the king is a blatant violation of a practice assumed throughout the Brāhmaṇas and Upaniṣads. As we have seen, similar narrative episodes clearly establish that there is always something at stake in a discussion and that the loser should forfeit something to the winner. When Yājñavalkya loses an argument to Janaka, for example, he offers the king a boon and then is obliged to stay with Janaka at his court. Judging from this and other situations in narrative episodes, one would expect Śvetaketu to offer firewood to the king and ask to be his student. In contrast, Śvetaketu refuses to acknowledge the king's superiority and offers neither a boon nor himself as the king's student. Instead he departs abruptly and runs back to his father.

When he returns to his father, Śvetaketu is as disrespectful to him as he was to the king, accusing him of not teaching properly. Then the young brahmin rejects his father's suggestion that they go together to learn from the king, curtly telling him to go on his own. In this scene we see a direct contrast between Śvetaketu and his father. While Śvetaketu continues to be rude and once again spurns the opportunity to receive instruction from the king, his father is patient with his son, as well as humble enough to go to learn from the king.

The remainder of the story recounts the courteous exchanges between Uddālaka and Pravāhaṇa. When Uddālaka arrives at the court, the king gives him the appropriate reception for a brahmin guest by offering a seat, providing water, and presenting him with refreshments. Notably, other dialogues in the Upaniṣads also emphasize the proper procedure for receiving guests, especially brahmins. As we have seen, Aśvapati (CU 5.11.5) receives his guests with due honor, and the *Kaṭha Upaniṣad* (1.17) specifically describes offering water as an appropriate way to appease a brahmin.[25] In fact, the *Kaṭha Upaniṣad* warns that if the proper respect is not paid to a brahmin, then the host will have to suffer the consequences, as a brahmin will take hope (*āśā*), expectations (*pratīkṣā*), friendship (*saṃgata*), joy (*sūnṛta*), efforts (*ceṣṭā*), fulfillment (*pūrtā*), children (*putra*), livestock (*paśu*), indeed everything (*sarva*), from the foolish man who does not offer him food (1.8).

After receiving him and giving him the proper refreshments, Pravāhaṇa offers Uddālaka a wish (*vara*), which is another recurring gesture towards a guest that appears throughout the dialogues. In the *Chāndogya Upaniṣad* (5.3.6) version of this dialogue, the king offers Uddālaka human riches, and in the *Kaṭha Upaniṣad* (1.9) this is part of Yama's hospitality for Naciketas, as he grants three wishes after the young brahmin had stayed in his house for three nights without food.

Returning to Pravāhaṇa and Uddālaka, the brahmin responds to the king's offer by asking to know what he had taught Śvetaketu. Pravāhaṇa is reluctant to part with his knowledge, offering wealth instead. Uddālaka, however, reminds the king that he already has an abundance of wealth—gold, cows, horses, female slaves, clothes, and garments—but that the king should not be ungenerous (*avadānyo*) with what is infinite (*ananta*) and unlimited (*aparyanta*) (BU 6.2.7).

Pravāhaṇa answers that he will instruct Uddālaka, but only if he asks in the proper manner. Accordingly, Uddālaka formally requests to become Pravāhaṇa's student: "I come to you, Sir" (BU 6.2.7).[26] Upon hearing these words, Pravāhaṇa finally agrees to teach Uddālaka, saying that he cannot refuse him when he speaks like that (BU 6.2.8). This exchange illustrates that it is Uddālaka's mode of behavior that convinces the king to teach him.

It is notable that immediately before agreeing to teach Uddālaka, the king reveals that the knowledge he is about to impart has never reached brahmins before. Thus, despite the secrecy that the king claims is involved in the transmission of this knowledge, Pravāhaṇa is impressed enough by Uddālaka's speech and actions that he cannot refuse to teach him. Uddālaka's actions illustrate both his humility and knowledge of the proper protocol, and crucially it is specifically because Uddālaka behaves properly that he earns the opportunity to learn one of the most coveted teachings in the Upaniṣads.

CONFLICTING AGENDAS FOR HOW KINGS SHOULD TEACH BRAHMINS

Thus far we have concentrated on the *Bṛhadāraṇyaka Upaniṣad* version of this story, which is the only presentation that overtly contrasts the mode of behavior between Uddālaka and his son Śvetaketu. One of the ways that the *Chāndogya Upaniṣad* differs from the *Bṛhadāraṇyaka Upaniṣad* account is that it does not describe the interaction between Pravāhaṇa and Uddālaka in as much detail, and ultimately, even though the brahmin learns from the king, he does not officially become his student. Instead, Pravāhaṇa invites Uddālaka to stay a while longer, and it is at this point in the *Chāndogya Upaniṣad* account that Pravāhaṇa announces that his teaching is known exclusively by *kṣatriyas*. Then without initiating him, the king begins to teach the brahmin.

Although these versions do not come to the same conclusion about Uddālaka's status as a student, they both show a negotiation process that establishes the grounds on which the brahmin becomes part of the king's court. In both versions the king receives Uddālaka respectfully and offers him a gift; and in both accounts Uddālaka refuses material wealth for the sake of learning the king's discourse. In this way, although the characters are presented differently, both versions of the dialogue emphasize the formal interaction between the king and brahmin as an integral aspect of the transmission of knowledge.

The *Kauṣītaki Upaniṣad* account differs from both the *Bṛhadāraṇyaka Upaniṣad* and the *Chāndogya Upaniṣad*, as it is significantly shorter and none of the characters are portrayed in as much detail. Yet the *Kauṣītaki Upaniṣad* is the only version of the story that provides an explanation for why Śvetaketu arrives at the king's residence in the first place, explaining that the king was about to perform a sacrifice and had chosen Uddālaka as his officiating priest, but that Uddālaka sent his son in his place. The entire episode where the king receives Uddālaka is absent and no negotiation takes place between Uddālaka and the king. Instead Uddālaka approaches the king with firewood already in his hands, asking to become his pupil. Another distinctive feature of this version is that the king does not present his teaching as exclusive to the *kṣatriya*s or as the explanation for the *kṣatriya* monopoly over rulership. More generally, he says that this knowledge will win him victory (*jiti*) and success (*vyaṣṭi*) (1.7).

One of the most significant differences among the three accounts pertains to whether or not Uddālaka is properly initiated as a Vedic student. In both the *Bṛhadāraṇyaka Upaniṣad* and the *Kauṣītaki Upaniṣad,* Uddālaka officially becomes the king's pupil, while in the *Chāndogya Upaniṣad* he does not. Importantly, there are other examples where the *Chāndogya Upaniṣad* version of a dialogue differs from other presentations regarding the issue of initiation. For example, in the *Śatapatha Brāhmaṇa* version of Aśvapati's teaching, he initiates the brahmins as students, yet in the *Chāndogya Upaniṣad* he does not. As Olivelle argues, these differences in the narrative reflect the conflicting agendas between the *Bṛhadāraṇyaka Upaniṣad* and the *Chāndogya Upaniṣad,* and to a lesser extent, the *Kauṣītaki Upaniṣad* (1999). It is not surprising, then, that the *Chāndogya Upaniṣad,* which places more emphasis on the teacher/student relationship, makes a point to differentiate between dialogues featuring teachers and students and those with brahmins and kings. As we have seen, even when Satyakāma and Upakosala learn Upanishadic teachings that make them "shine" like one who knows about *brahman,* because they learned these teachings from non-traditional sources they learn the same teachings again from their official teachers. Similarly, although the *Chāndogya Upaniṣad* presents

Uddālaka Āruṇi twice learning from kings, on neither occasion does he officially become their pupil. The implication is that it is all right for brahmins such as Uddālaka and Satyakāma to learn from whomever they want, but only brahmins can conduct an official teaching that includes an initiation. In contrast, the *Bṛhadāraṇyaka Upaniṣad*, which emphasizes the relationship between king and court priest, has no problem showing traditional Kuru-Pañcāla brahmins officially becoming the students of kings. This is not surprising because the *Bṛhadāraṇyaka Upaniṣad* is generally less traditional and more critical of Kuru-Pañcāla orthodoxy.

Despite these differences between the terms under which kings teach brahmins, there is no clear distinction among the early Upaniṣads in the presentation of the ideal king. In both the *Bṛhadāraṇyaka Upaniṣad* and the *Chāndogya Upaniṣad* the king is presented as knowledgeable and generous, and in both texts kings teach brahmins, whether officially or not. Furthermore, both texts claim that knowledge of Upanishadic teachings is directly responsible for political power. This is illustrated by the ability of knowledgeable kings to attract eminent brahmins to their courts, as well as explicit claims that Upanishadic knowledge will deliver to kings a favorable reputation, military success and, as we will see, even immortality.

UPANISHADIC KNOWLEDGE AS A POLITICAL DISCOURSE

So far we have explored the political dimensions of the Upaniṣads by looking at the literary portrayal of kings as both important teachers of and listeners to Upanishadic doctrines. In this section we will look at other ways that the texts link knowledge with the king and the world of politics. A number of teachings are framed as political discourses that promise success in ruling, warfare, and securing new territory.

Ajātaśatru, for example, employs several metaphors explicitly connecting his discourse to his position as king. When he responds to Gārgya's arguments, almost every one of his counterclaims emphasizes the rewards of his knowledge and many of the metaphors that he employs depict military and political struggles. For example, he says that by venerating Indra Vaikuṇṭha, one will become victorious (*aparājayiṣṇu*), invincible (*anyatatyajāyī*), and triumph over enemies (KṣU 4.7; BU 2.1.6). In the *Kauṣītaki Upaniṣad* version of this dialogue the king states: "These selves (*ātman*) depend on that self (*ātman*), as his people are of service to a chief (*śreṣṭha*)" (4.20).[27] Then Ajātaśatru asserts that knowledge of *ātman* led Indra to defeating the demons: when Indra came to know *ātman*, he smashed and conquered the demons and attained preeminence (*śraiṣṭhya*), independent rule (*svārājya*), and sovereignty (*ādhipatya*) over all beings (4.20).

In the second half of this dialogue, when Ajātaśatru begins instructing Gārgya, he teaches that when a person is asleep the cognitive powers of the *prāṇās* are in the control of the *puruṣa*.[28] During the time of sleep, breath (*prāṇa*), speech (*vāc*), sight (*cakṣus*), hearing (*śrota*), and mind (*manas*) all remain in the grasp of the *puruṣa* in the heart.[29] Ajātaśatru then explains how this affects dreams, describing a dream as the *puruṣa* moving around the body with the vital powers. Wherever the *puruṣa* may travel in his dreams, those regions become his worlds. Ajātaśatru then compares the movement of *puruṣa* around the body during dreaming to a king taking his people with him around his domain (*janapada*). This metaphor implies that just like the king, who controls his kingdom and is therefore free to roam around at will, the *puruṣa* moves freely around the body. In contrast to Gārgya's discourse, which is centered on the sacrificial arena, Ajātaśatru's teaching presents *prāṇa, puruṣa,* and the processes of life as knowledge that can secure rewards that are particularly desirable to the king.

Similarly, throughout the *Bṛhadāraṇyaka Upaniṣad* there are a number of metaphors explicitly linking knowledge with leadership and bringing harm to one's enemies. For example, one who knows the importance of food will become the patron (*bhartṛ*), chief (*śreṣṭha*), leader (*pura*), eater of food (*annāda*), and sovereign (*adhipati*). Yet anyone who is the rival of someone who knows this will not be capable of supporting his own dependents (BU 1.3.18). In another passage the *Bṛhadāraṇyaka Upaniṣad* (5.14.1–3) states that by venerating (*upās*) the *gāyatrī* (a *mantra* from the *Ṛgveda*) one can win territory extending as far as the three worlds, extending as far as the triple Veda or extending as far as there are living beings. Furthermore, knowledge can be directed against someone one hates (5.14.7). The *Kauṣītaki Upaniṣad* (2.8) has a *mantra* addressing the moon, expressing the wish that it should not become full by means of one's own lifebreath (*prāṇa*), offspring (*prajā*), and livestock (*paśu*), but that the moon should become full with the lifebreath, children, and livestock of the people one hates.[30] As the moon was considered the destination of people when they die, one who knows this *mantra* can avoid one's own death, while bringing on the destruction of one's enemies. Further on, this passage states that one's knowledge of *brahman* can lead to the death of those one hates (2.12). The *Taittirīya Upaniṣad* (3.10.4) has a passage which states that by venerating *brahman*, a person's hateful enemies (*sapatna*) and adversaries (*bhrātṛvya*) will die. The *Chāndogya Upaniṣad* proclaims that anyone who contemplates evil against one who knows the *udgītha* will be smashed to pieces like a lump of clay hurled against solid rock (1.2.8). These examples show how brahmin composers explicitly situate Upanishadic teachings within the competitive and violent context of conflicts between *kṣatriya* leaders. Throughout, there is a recurring set of metaphors that address defeating one's enemies, expanding one's territory, and maintaining one's power over others. Although the actual dialogues between brahmins and kings are not as antagonistic as the contests among brahmins, the teachings address the political and military battles between kings. In this way, brahmin composers represent Upanishadic teachings as vital for political success.

In addition to teachings that equate knowledge with specific political rewards, there are a number of passages where the king is conceptualized as qualitatively related to *ātman*. These passages do not merely suggest that the king should know about *ātman*, but that the king has a similar relationship to the social world as does *ātman* to the body or to the ontological sphere. In the *Śatapatha Brāhmaṇa*, *ātman* was already equated with political power, a tendency that continues in the *Bṛhadāraṇyaka Upaniṣad*, which equates *ātman* with the sovereign (*adhipati*), and king (*rājā*) of all beings (2.5.15). Both the king and *ātman* are like the hub of a wheel (*cakra*) to which are fastened all beings, all gods, the *prāṇās*, and the bodies (*ātman*). In a similar passage in the *Kauṣītaki Upaniṣad*, Indra teaches that *prāṇa* is comparable to the hub of a chariot wheel to which are fastened all the particles of intelligence. Subsequently, *prāṇa* is equated with *ātman*, which is described as the guardian (*pāla*) of the world, the sovereign of the world (*adhipati*), and the lord (*iśa*) of the world (3.8).[31] In these metaphors the king and *ātman* reinforce each other, as they are mutually conceptualized as that which is at the core of the human or political body; as *ātman* is the center of the ontological sphere, the king is the heart of the social world. In this respect it is important to recall that in numerous discussions in the early Upaniṣads *ātman* is described in terms of the body, what keeps it alive, and how it dies. In these examples the entire discourse about *ātman* as a living organism is presented within the metaphors of battle, sovereignty, and political power.

THE BATTLE OF THE *PRĀṆĀS* AS A POLITICAL METAPHOR

The connection between knowledge of the self and the political success of the king is further developed in the recurring myth of the competition among the *prāṇās*, which is one of the most frequently appearing mythical situations in the early Upaniṣads.[32] As Bodewitz points out, this myth first appears in the later Brāhmaṇa literature, yet in its initial occurrences there is no connection with kingship.[33] Throughout the early Upaniṣads, however, this myth is consistently presented as a political allegory where the superiority of *prāṇa* in relation to the other vital functions is likened to the supremacy of the king among his rivals and ministers. Significantly, this myth is always presented as a competition against the other vital functions where *prāṇa* has to prove superiority. All the different vital powers make claims to their authority over the others, but only after they leave the body is it evident that their power is not vital to keeping the body alive. When *prāṇa* leaves the body, however, its absence disrupts the workings of the other vital powers, leaving them to admit that the *prāṇa* is more fundamental to keeping the body alive.

Another way by which this myth operates as a political allegory is through the association between breath and food. In the sacrificial literature, food is an important political metaphor, where the prosperous king is given the epithet "eater of food" (*annāda*).[34] The *Bṛhadāraṇyaka Upaniṣad* and the *Chāndogya Upaniṣad* both directly equate breath with food, thus connecting the older discourse of the king as eater of food with the new teaching that the king is the controller of the vital functions.[35] In the *Chāndogya Upaniṣad* there is a version of this contest when the vital powers go to Prajāpati to settle their argument about which of them is the greatest. Prajāpati tells them that the one whose departure has the most adverse affect on the body is the greatest (5.1.7). Eventually *prāṇa* wins this contest and the narrative tells us that for a man who knows this there is nothing but food. In the very next section there is a description about how to make a mixture that will give a man the ability to rule.

The connection between the *prāṇa* myth and making this mixture is significant because these passages appear together both in the *Bṛhadāraṇyaka Upaniṣad* (6.1–3) and in the *Chāndogya Upaniṣad* (5.1–2), as well as in the *Śāṅkhāyana Āraṇyaka* (9). In these contexts, the *prāṇa* myth is explicitly connected with a particular ritual that promises political superiority, indicating that this myth not only is a description of a political situation, but also is considered something that a king must know in order to achieve political success. As Bodewitz argues, "The passage on the contest of the vital powers is followed by a magic rite (the Mantha ceremony) which contains obvious references to the preceding context and should be regarded as the practical application of the myth or doctrine of the superiority of the Prāṇa" (1992, 59).

In fact, the myth itself often explicitly promises political rewards. In one of the versions in the *Bṛhadāraṇyaka Upaniṣad* (1.5.21–3), those who learn the discourse become victorious in their own family, and their rivals die. Also in the *Bṛhadāraṇyaka Upaniṣad* (1.3.17) there is a similar version of the contest among the vital organs about who can sing the *udgītha*, where, once again, knowledge of the *prāṇa* myth is equated with political power: when someone knows the *prāṇa* myth, his people will gather around him and he will become their patron (*bhartṛ*), their chief (*śreṣṭha*), and their leader (*pura*); he will become an eater of food (*annāda*) and a sovereign (*adhipati*). In these examples, the battle of the *prāṇā*s is explicitly cast as a political myth, the knowledge of which promises real-world political advantages.

In a version of this myth from the *Kauṣītaki Upaniṣad* (2.13), a body emptied of the vital functions is compared to a dead and decaying dog.[36] The vital functions enter one by one, but the body continues to be lifeless. Finally, when *prāṇa* enters, the body immediately stands up, and the vital functions recognize the preeminence of *prāṇa*. At this point, all the vital functions unite together with *prāṇa* and go to heaven. The narrative then proclaims that a person who knows this myth, understands the superiority of the *prāṇa*, and unites himself with the *prāṇa* can reach heaven. As the *prāṇa* is often a metaphor for the king, this suggests that anyone who recognizes the superiority of the king and aligns oneself with him will reach heaven.

Throughout the appearances of this myth the social context that is most explicitly linked with the battle of the *prāṇā*s is the relationship between the king and the court. In one discussion Yājñavalkya teaches Janaka (BU 4.3.38) that the vital functions gather around *ātman* like the soldiers (*ugra*), magistrates (*pratyenasa*), charioteers (*sūta*), and village headman (*grāmaṇī*), who assemble around the king when he is about to depart. Similarly, the *Śatapatha Brāhmaṇa* says (3.3.2.8) that the meters act as attendants to *soma* like those who attend a king. Both of these passages are connected with the image of the living body as a healthy political body, suggesting that despite important political functions provided by the ministers, only the presence of the king is necessary to keeping the political body alive. The *Jaiminīya Upaniṣad Brāhmaṇa* (2.10–1) also has a discussion of *prāṇa*, linking it with kingship and making a connection between the vital functions and the king's ministers. The five vital powers and the corresponding cosmic powers are described as a courtly assembly (*sabhā*) in the body. In this metaphor *prāṇa* represents the king, who is assisted by an assembly consisting of the other vital powers.

The importance of this myth throughout the early Upaniṣads suggests the possibility that this scenario represents a real political situation. There is much that we do not know about the court as an institution in this period in early historic India, and given this lack of evidence it is impossible to link this myth with any specific institution or practice.[37] Nonetheless, it seems clear that this myth describes the internal dynamics between the king and his ministers, indicating that the battle among the *prāṇās* represents a power struggle within some kind of ruling administration, rather than a conflict between competing kingdoms. If this is the case, then the *prāṇa* myth is different from the other political metaphors that we examined, that tended to frame teachings within the context of political rivalries between different sovereign leaders. Rather, the imagery of the *prāṇa* myth portrays the king as central, but as continually having to prove his superiority within his own political body.

Another interesting feature of the *prāṇa* myth is that it consistently connects the relationship between the king and his ministers to the process of dying. As we have seen, the myth often contains explicit descriptions of the ministers gathering around the king as he is about to depart from the world. This link between the *prāṇa* myth and the death of the king suggests the possibility that these accounts address the problem of transferring political authority. We do not know how the position of king was decided in Upanishadic times, but these passages indicate that when the king dies there is a competition among his ministers. Was gathering around the king some kind of succession ritual? Was the position of king negotiated by means of a competition among the ministers? We do not have enough information to do anything more than ask these questions. Needless to say, however, it is clear that the *prāṇa* myth is a political allegory that reflects power struggles among the king and his ministers, and strongly suggests a connection between Upanishadic teachings and the process of transmitting political authority.

PRAVĀHAṆA AND THE TEACHING OF THE FIVE FIRES

Now that we have established the general political orientation shared by a number of teachings and myths, let us return to the particular kings portrayed in the early Upaniṣads and look at the doctrines that they teach. Other than being depicted as generally knowledgeable, is there any particular teaching that is connected to kings? In addressing this question it is important to remember that a number of the central ideas in the early Upaniṣads, such as *ātman*, *prāṇa*, and how to achieve immortality, are interrelated, and it may be distorting to present these ideas as distinct doctrines. Nevertheless, it is perhaps revealing that a number of specific themes reappear in the dialogues that feature kings.

At the beginning of the *Chāndogya Upaniṣad* version of his dialogue with Śvetaketu, Pravāhaṇa poses a question that is of central concern throughout the Upaniṣads: "Do you know where people go from here after they die?" (5.3.2). Indeed, it is Pravāhaṇa's answer to this question that he claims is the knowledge that originated among the royalty. Similarly, before one of his teachings to Janaka, Yājñavalkya asks the king: "When you are released from here, where will you go?" (BU 4.2.1). As we will see, not only are teachings about death and rebirth particular characteristics of dialogues between brahmins and kings, but they explicitly replace earlier doctrines based on ritual imagery that portrayed the king as an eater of food.

In Pravāhaṇa's teaching, the knowledge of the five fires explains human existence as a natural process that is interconnected with other forms of life. Human life is described as part of a cycle of regeneration, whereby the essence of life takes on different forms as it passes through different levels of existence. Pravāhaṇa's teaching begins by comparing five aspects of the world with a fire: the upper regions (*asau loka*), rain (*parjanya*), earth (*ayam loka*), man (*puruṣa*), and woman (*yoṣā*). The upper regions (the first fire) refers to the moon, which throughout Vedic literature is considered to be the destination of humans when they die, symbolizing death. According to Pravāhaṇa, however, the moon is not the final destination, because the deceased return to the earth in the form of rain (the second fire). When rain reaches the earth (the third fire), it nourishes the soil to produce food. Subsequently, men (the fourth fire) eat food, which is transformed in their bodies to semen. Semen is then passed into women (the fifth fire) through sexual intercourse.

After sharing this knowledge with Uddālaka, Pravāhaṇa goes on to explain that there are two kinds of people who can avoid repeated death:[38] (1) those who have the knowledge of the five fires, and (2) those in the wilderness (*araṇya*) who venerate (*upās*) faith (*śraddhā*) as truth (*satya*).[39] Interestingly, both of these groups are contrasted with those who practice sacrifice, give gifts, and perform austerities, all of whom return again following the path of the fathers. This distinction is another example of a teaching that presents those who specialize in knowledge as superior to brahmin ritualists. Presumably, Pravāhaṇa fits into the first category as he obviously has the knowledge of the five fires and, as a king, does not live in the forest.[40] Pravāhaṇa's identification of two kinds of people who have this knowledge suggests that he is claiming for himself the same kinds of soteriological rewards attributed to brahmins in the forest.

It is not surprising that the teaching associated with Pravāhaṇa addresses these particular soteriological concerns, because the goal of escaping repeated death (*punarmṛytu*) was already associated with the king in royal rituals, a number of which promised that the king would not die again.[41] In the Upaniṣads, however, this goal is achieved through knowledge, as indicated by the assumption that an understanding of Pravāhaṇa's teaching can lead to freedom from the endless cosmic cycle. The pivotal link in this chain, at least in terms of altering the cyclical process, is the time of death. As Pravāhaṇa explains, when the deceased reach the moon they become the food of gods. There, the gods feed on them, addressing the moon as King Soma and saying, "Increase, decrease" (BU 6.2.16).

Here Pravāhaṇa's teaching is informed by earlier Vedic ideas about *soma* and food. In the sacrificial literature *soma* is described as the food of the gods and is a symbol for immortality. As Brian Smith discusses (1990), the social hierarchy is often presented as a cosmic food chain where the higher classes are the eaters and the lower classes are the food. In most cases the brahmins presented themselves as at the top of the social order, but an "eater of food" was also an important epithet for a king, as many sacrifices promise that the *yajamāna* can become an eater of food.

In contrast, Pravāhaṇa's teaching rejects the eater of food theory of the ritualists in favor of a discourse that leads to escaping the food chain altogether: the only way to escape the process of regeneration is to escape becoming the food of the gods. Although, as an eater of food, one could have power on earth, one remained within the cycle of the eaters and the eaten. And, as long as one remained within the food chain, one was destined to return as food. According to Pravāhaṇa, only if a person can achieve a state beyond food, can that person avoid perpetual rebirth, and ultimately attain the world of *brahman*. The *Taittirīya Upaniṣad* also rejects the food theory, presenting a teaching of *ātman* in its place: "Different from and within one consisting of the essence-of-food (*anna-rasa*), is the *ātman*, consisting of *prāṇa*" (2.2).[42] Thus, knowledge of *ātman* offers a way out of the cosmic food cycle, as many of the teachings about *ātman* relate to this conception of regeneration and suggest that to know *ātman* is to guard against repeated death and to become immortal.

Ajātaśatru's teaching shares some of this same imagery and is also linked to a similar understanding of the process of regeneration. In his instruction to Gārgya, Ajātaśatru addresses a sleeping man by saying, "O great king, Soma, wearing white" (BU 2.1.15; KṣU 4.19). It remains unclear exactly why Ajātaśatru would approach the man in this way. However, it is interesting that in Pravāhaṇa's teaching departed souls travel to the moon, which is addressed by the gods as King Soma. This suggests that Ajātaśatru likens his own teaching about the *prāṇās* to other discourses that get one out of the cosmic food chain.

Another similarity that this dialogue shares with Pravāhaṇa's teaching is that it sets up a distinction between brahmin ritualists and those who specialize in Upanishadic teachings. In contrast to the Vedic ritualism of Gārgya, the king's teaching is about *prāṇa*, sleep, and the processes of life and death. When Gārgya approaches Ajātaśatru and offers to teach him, he makes a number of connections between *brahman* and *puruṣa* in the moon (*candra*), lightning (*vidyut*), space (*ākāśa*), wind (*vāyu*), fires (*agni*), water (*apsu*), a mirror (*ādarśa*), sound (*śabda*), the quarters (*dikṣa*), a shadow (*chāyāmaya*), and the body (*ātman*).[432] In the *Kauṣītaki Upaniṣad*, Gārgya's discourse is presented in the typical division of ritual speculation between the divine (*daivata*) and bodily (*ātman*) spheres. After every attempt to link *brahman* with the inner *puruṣa*, Ajātaśatru responds by rejecting the comparison and offering a different viewpoint. Ajātaśatru responds to each point with a sarcastic comment, saying "do not talk to me about him (*puruṣa*)" (BU 2.1.2–13).[44]

Finally, Ajātaśatru rejects Gārgya's views when he further mocks him, asking, "Is that all?" (BU 2.1.14; KṣU 4.19). This prompts Gārgya to accept defeat and ask Ajātaśatru to be his teacher. At this point, the king comments that taking on a brahmin as a student is a reversal of the norm. It is notable that in both versions of this dialogue Ajātaśatru brings attention to the exceptional circumstances of a king teaching a brahmin, despite the fact that both Upaniṣads contain other episodes with the same scenario. After making this remark, the king takes Gārgya by the hand and points out to him a man who is sleeping. By means of bringing Gārgya's attention to this sleeping man, Ajātaśatru instructs him about the process of sleeping and dreaming and how *prāṇa* behaves in the body during these processes. Ajātaśatru's teaching style and what he is teaching about are entirely different from Gārgya's discourse. Whereas Gārgya's discourse is based on knowing the connections between the sacrifice and the cosmos, Ajātaśatru uses the concrete example of a sleeping man to explain the activities of sleeping and dreaming. As we have seen, several teachings mark a shift in the general orientation of knowledge from ritual symbolism to an interest in different bodily and mental states. Accordingly, this dialogue contrasts the brahmin's ritual symbolism with the king's understanding of the processes of life and death.

Indeed, almost all the dialogues between brahmins and kings feature discussions about the processes of life and how to avoid repeated death. In the *Śatapatha Brāhmaṇa* (11.6.2.6–10) Janaka delivers a teaching to Yājñavalkya that is similar to the knowledge of the five fires. Janaka says that the two libations that are offered as the *agnihotra* rise and enter the air; from the air they enter the sky; from the sky they return to the earth; from the earth they enter man; from man they enter a woman. When a man who knows this approaches his mate, he produces a son. Janaka equates the son with the *agnihotra* and says that there is nothing higher than this. This teaching suggests that one can achieve immortality through producing a male child.

Additionally, King Citra Gāṅgyāyani has a similar teaching. As we have seen, Citra appears in place of Pravāhaṇa in the *Kauṣītaki Upaniṣad* version of the king's dialogue with Śvetaketu and Uddālaka Āruṇi. In this account there is no analogy of the five fires, yet there are similarities with the teaching of the two paths: "When people depart from this world they all go to the moon. By means of the *prāṇās*, the moon becomes full in the first half of the month. The waning of the second half of the month produces them again. Indeed, the moon is the door to the heavenly world" (1.2).[45] Here, the feasting of gods is not mentioned, but rather the moon is described as the door to heaven. As the king explains, the only way past the moon to heaven is to answer the moon's questions. Those who answer correctly are allowed to pass, but those who do not return to the earth in the form of rain (1.2). The king continues his instruction by explaining exactly what questions the moon will ask and how to answer them. Thus, in Citra's teaching the connection between the king's knowledge and his ability to achieve immortality is quite explicit.

It is clear from these examples that teachings about the processes of life and death are an important subject matter in dialogues between brahmins and kings. Taken together, Upanishadic teachings claim to offer the king powers in this life, by winning territory and defeating enemies, as well as in the world beyond, by becoming immortal. Seen within the context of the *prāṇa* myth and the recurring political and military metaphors, the *kṣatriya* characters who claim to be authors of teachings are no longer so surprising. By placing *kṣatriya*s as central figures in stories about the transmission of Upanishadic knowledge, brahmin composers could portray this knowledge as indispensable to the king's political power. As we have seen, the dialogues emphasize that regardless of who is the teacher, the brahmins get paid and are treated respectfully. In this way, brahmin composers had nothing to lose, and a lot to gain, in portraying *kṣatriya*s as the authors.

CONCLUSION

In this chapter we have looked at dialogues between brahmins and kings. Not only do a number of these episodes feature kings teaching brahmins, but King Pravāhaṇa actually asserts that his knowledge originated among the *kṣatriya*s and had never reached the brahmins before. Rather than assume that this is a literal claim, in this chapter we have considered why brahmin composers would represent their own ideas as being authored by *kṣatriya*s. As we have seen, the literary trope of the *kṣatriya* who teaches the brahmin is one of a number of narrative features in the early Upaniṣads that makes these stories directly appealing to a *kṣatriya* audience.

Throughout these dialogues the ideal king is both knowledgeable in Upanishadic teachings and generous to brahmins. The knowledgeable king in no way, however, establishes independence from brahmins, as illustrated by the fact that the very kings who are depicted as the most knowledgeable, Janaka and Aśvapati, are also represented as being the most magnanimous hosts. Furthermore, these kings, as well as others, provide both wealth and accommodation even when they are the ones giving the teaching. In these cases, the brahmins are paid for their presence in the court, suggesting that even if a king was knowledgeable he still needed the brahmin to authenticate his wisdom.

The two brahmins who feature most in dialogues with kings are Yājñavalkya and Uddālaka Āruṇi. Although Yājñavalkya is aggressive in his encounters with other brahmins, he is friendly and personable with King Janaka. In fact, he initially wins patronage from Janaka through losing his debate with the king. Similarly, Uddālaka Āruṇi is defeated in debates by kings on several occasions, with one of his most distinctive character traits being that he always admits when he does not know something. Yet far from being ridiculed for his ignorance, Uddālaka is characterized as humble and respectful, and losing discussions with kings is exactly what wins him their courtesy and patronage.

In his dialogue with Pravāhaṇa, Uddālaka's interaction with the king is presented in contradistinction to that of his son, whose rudeness not only indicates that he is not fully learned, but also is what prohibits him from hearing the king's teaching. In this example the dialogue between king and priest continues a theme that is also apparent in the dialogues between teachers and students: etiquette is a fundamental part of the teachings. In the case of Śvetaketu, he is not considered completely educated because he has not learned the social practices that accompany his discursive knowledge. This dialogue, which has clear messages for both brahmins and kings, indicates that these stories about relations between kings and priests serve as a reminder to both a priestly and kingly audience for how to treat each other. Whereas kings need brahmins to authenticate their position as kings, brahmins need kings as their employers.

In previous chapters we have discussed the different political agendas of the *Bṛhadāraṇyaka Upaniṣad* and the *Chāndogya Upaniṣad*. Whereas the *Chāndogya Upaniṣad* tends to be traditional and closely linked with the Kuru-Pañcāla heartland, the *Bṛhadāraṇyaka Upaniṣad* is more critical of Vedic orthodoxy and aligns itself with King Janaka of Videha. These opposing political agendas are also manifest in the dialogues between brahmins and kings, as the texts take different positions regarding whether kings should officially initiate brahmins as their students: while the *Bṛhadāraṇyaka Upaniṣad* shows kings formally initiating brahmins, the *Chāndogya Upaniṣad* does not. These conflicting views, however, are consistent with other differences between the texts. As we have seen, the *Chāndogya Upaniṣad* emphasizes the *upanayana* much more than the *Bṛhadāraṇyaka Upaniṣad* does and thus is reluctant to depict kings in the formal role of the teacher. The *Bṛhadāraṇyaka Upaniṣad*, however, concentrates more attention on the *brahmodya* and the relationship between the king and the court priest. With this different social orientation, as well as the text's more critical stance against the Kuru-Pañcāla establishment, the *Bṛhadāraṇyaka Upaniṣad* does not appear to have any hesitation showing brahmins officially becoming the students of kings.

Despite these differences, both texts, along with the *Kauṣītaki Upaniṣad*, consistently employ metaphors of kingship to frame fundamental Upanishadic teachings. Knowledge of discourses about *ātman* and *prāṇa* are said to lead to kingly aspirations such as supremacy (*śraiṣṭhya*), independent rule (*svārājya*), and sovereignty (*ādhipatya*); *ātman*, which is considered the center of the ontological sphere, is directly compared to the king to reinforce his position at the center of the political sphere; and the relationship between the *prāṇa* and the other vital powers is compared to the power struggles between the king and his ministers. Taken together, these examples serve to characterize Upanishadic teachings as indispensable to kings for both military and political success. In this way, political metaphors, as well as narrative frames, are used to reinforce to kings the importance of Upanishadic teachings, plus the brahmins who teach them.

As this book has demonstrated thus far, the dialogues of the Upaniṣads firmly root their teachings in the affairs of everyday life and specifically address social situations that were fundamental in defining the life of a brahmin. In this chapter we have looked at the dynamics between priests and kings and have seen how brahmins use their expertise in knowledge to secure patronage. In the following chapter we will look at dialogues between brahmins and women, examining how they relate to other aspects of a brahmin's life, such as setting up a household and having male children.

CHAPTER FOUR

Brahmins and Women

Subjectivity and Gender Construction in the Upaniṣads

INTRODUCTION

In the previous chapters we have looked at dialogues where brahmins teach students, debate with other brahmins, and discuss philosophy with kings. In these situations we have seen that the participants in the dialogues and how they interact with each other are essential aspects of the texts. As such, the Upaniṣads do not merely articulate philosophical claims, but also address how ideas are generated and circulated in the social world. In this chapter we will examine gender issues in the Upaniṣads, with particular attention to the dialogues that feature brahmins and women. It is not my aim to impose any particular theory of gender onto the Upaniṣads, but rather to investigate how issues of gender impact the teachings put forth by the texts. This chapter will demonstrate that gender is an essential aspect of philosophy in the Upaniṣads both because of the explicitly male soteriology represented by a number of the teachings and because the genders of the literary characters have an impact on what they say and how they interact with each other.

First we will examine the gender implications of the Upanishadic notions of self, especially as represented through metaphors, creations myths, and procreation rituals. Although on some occasions the Upaniṣads make appeals to a universal knowledge available to everyone, a number of teachings present an explicitly male construction of *ātman* and offer a soteriology that links a man's ability to achieve immortality to securing male children. The gender dimensions of Upanishadic ideas remain ambiguous and unresolved, but nevertheless teachings about *ātman* are targeted at a predominantly male audience and achieving selfhood is associated with a number of practices and social situations that are primarily the domain of men and that restrict the participation of women.

As we will see, the gender dimensions of Upanishadic teachings have important implications concerning the construction of brahmin male subjectivity. Satyakāma is portrayed as a householder who supports himself as a teacher by taking on students. Although it is not clear whether or not Satyakāma has any children himself, the householder lifestyle is privileged by a number of teachings that link immortality to having male children, with some teachings further claiming that this knowledge itself guarantees the production of male children. Yājñavalkya, however, challenges this ideal by including women in his philosophical discussions, as well as by teaching that immortality can be attained without having children. We will examine the differing portrayals of Satyakāma and Yājñavalkya in terms of competing ideals of the brahmin man.

Although the Upaniṣads are primarily about brahmin men, the dialogues also feature a number of female characters. In fact, because of the importance of procreation in securing immortality, the presentations of female speakers in the dialogues, as well as the practices assigned to women during procreation, are central to the philosophical claims of the texts. For the most part, the representations of women, especially as wives and procreative bodies, serve to reinforce the ideal of the male brahmin householder. Nevertheless, a number of characters point to "cracks in the veneer" of male brahmin orthodoxy.[1] These characters embody a tension regarding women throughout the Upaniṣads: whereas women are central because of their procreative role, they are defined and depicted as subordinate to men, and their participation in Upanishadic narratives tends to be marginalized and mediated. In the latter part of this chapter we will look at female characters who speak in Upanishadic dialogues, how they speak, and how they negotiate with the limitations restricting women in Upanishadic practice.

We will focus our attention on Gārgī, Jabālā, and Maitreyī. Gārgī not only speaks in the *brahmodya* at Janaka's court, but also overtly challenges Yājñavalkya's authority (BU 3.6.1, 3.8.1–12). In the process, she displays her superiority in knowledge over a number of brahmin men from Kuru-Pañcāla. Jabālā teaches her son the truth (*satya*) about his lineage that eventually leads to his recognition as a brahmin (CU 4.4.1–5). As we will see, her teaching is similar to a number of instances where the authority of a woman's words is recognized only when it is restated by a brahmin man. In Yājñavalkya's dialogue with his wife Maitreyī, we encounter a brahmin wife who discusses philosophy (BU 2.4.1–14, 4.5.1–15). Yet despite his apparent preference for Maitreyī's knowledge, Kātyāyanī, Yājñavalkya's other wife, has a knowledge that is perhaps more representative of what Upanishadic women are expected to know. One of the recurring themes among the depictions of female characters is that the text tends to reveal more about them than it seems to realize. As such, female characters are often more central to the narrative than they first appear to be.

Yet as some female characters play a central role, others are barely mentioned. Indeed, throughout the Upaniṣads the depictions of female characters are neither static nor consistent. As wives, mothers, and philosophers, female characters are not reduced to one uniform image or a single social role. Despite the diversity of the characters, however, most of the women portrayed in the Upaniṣads face similar obstacles in their discussions with men, with another recurring theme in these dialogues being the lack of authority of female speakers. Women do speak, but their speech is not assigned the same status as the words of men. Grace Jantzen makes similar observations about the participation of women in western philosophy: "The problem is not that women do not/ can not have language, but that men . . . refuse to listen" (1998, 51). In the Upaniṣads, although the presence of women is necessary, the voices of female speakers are continually restricted and muted. Taken together, the various representations of women in the Upaniṣads primarily serve to reinforce the ideal brahmin man: the married householder.

THE GENDER OF THE SELF: *ĀTMAN* AND THE MALE BODY

As discussed in the introduction, the most fundamental philosophical questions throughout the early Upaniṣads revolve around *ātman*: What is the self? How do the breaths function in keeping the body alive? What happens to the self at the time of death? As we explored earlier, many of the teachings where *ātman* figures prominently describe the world in a naturalistic way. As opposed to the ritual symbolism of the Brāhmaṇas, many Upanishadic teachings conceptualize *ātman* as an important part of a life process in the natural world. For example, when Uddālaka Āruṇi describes *ātman* in terms of bees making honey, rivers flowing into oceans, and salt dissolving into water, he does not link *ātman* directly to virility or semen, but suggests that *ātman* is a life force that transcends genders, not to mention different orders of species (CU 6.1.1–16.3). Despite the universal scope of this teaching, however, on other occasions the definition of the self and who has access to knowledge about the self is more restrictive. Indeed, the word *ātman* is masculine in gender and is often specifically connected to men. In the following two sections we will look at some of the gender implications of teachings about *ātman*, especially those that appear in creation myths and procreation rituals. On the one hand these teachings clearly privilege men and put forth a soteriology that is explicitly male, sometimes even revealing an anxiety towards women and a fear that they should not know too much. On the other hand, these teachings seem to recognize the complementarity of male and female in the process of creation and reproduction.

One of the most obvious ways that teachings about the self are connected to issues of gender is through the male teachers who articulate them. The fact that the literary characters who discuss *ātman* are predominantly male brahmins indicates that this is the group of people most associated with these teachings. Yet not only are the teachings about *ātman* conveyed by male speakers, but there is an assumed male audience illustrated by a number of androcentric metaphors that frame the discourses. For example, when Yājñavalkya is teaching Janaka, he describes knowing *ātman* as an embrace (*sampariṣvakta*) comparable to embracing a female lover, which leaves a man oblivious (BU 4.3.21). Similarly, in the *Chāndogya Upaniṣad* (5.2.9) a successful ritual performance produces a vision of a woman.[2] Although these teachings do not prohibit women from gaining access to this knowledge, they are clearly not aimed at a female audience. As we will see, Upanishadic teachings richly employ sexual metaphors, specifically relating the attainment of knowledge with male sexual pleasure.

Another aspect of the Upanishadic conception of self that privileges a male audience is the mythological connection between *ātman* and the primordial male creator gods, Puruṣa and Prajāpati. As we have seen in the introduction, the *Aitareya Upaniṣad* (1.1) has a creation myth in which *ātman* creates the universe by sacrificing, dismembering, and reconstructing his body, thus assuming the characteristics of the cosmic bodies of Puruṣa and Prajāpati. In a similar myth from the *Bṛhadāraṇyaka Upaniṣad* (1.4.1–6), the gender dimensions of *ātman* are highlighted by depicting the self as the primordial man who creates the first woman from his own body. At the beginning of creation *ātman* is alone and afraid; he thus creates a wife to have as a companion. The narrative explains that because he splits (*pat*) himself, he gives rise to husband (*pati*) and wife (*patnī*). Significantly, the female body is explicitly created from *ātman*'s body, implying that the existence of the female body is ultimately derived from the primordial male body. The first thing that *ātman* does with his wife after creating her is to copulate with her, with the result of their union being that human beings are born (1.4.3). In this myth, *ātman* is linked to a particular construction of gender relations that prioritizes male over female and defines women as created by, from, and for men.

Despite the privileging of the male role, however, procreation is represented as a process that is inherently interactive. After their initial copulation, *ātman*'s wife thinks to herself, "How can he have intercourse with me after having generated me from himself. Now, I will hide myself" (1.4.4).[3] The story then relates how she hides in the form of a cow, but then he becomes a bull and copulates with her. From this union cattle are born. She then takes the form of various other animals, and in every case *ātman* assumes the male form of each animal and copulates with her. From these unions all the animals are born.

Significantly, this account points towards later creation myths where the primordial female takes a more active role in creation.[4] At the end of this myth, *ātman* thinks to himself, "I, indeed, am creation, because I created all this" (BU 1.4.5).[5] The comments of *ātman*, however, do not seem to represent the creation process as it is described in this myth. As we have seen, each case in which the specific animals are born happens because the wife has initially taken on the identity of each animal. Thus, the first instance of every species occurs only when the wife assumes a new form for the sake of hiding. Despite the fact that *ātman* takes credit for creation, the narrative shows us that living beings did not come into existence from *ātman* alone, but by means of *patnī*'s activity. As in the Prajāpati myth, this Upanishadic account defines creation in such a way that it downplays the procreative agency of the woman, yet nevertheless illustrates the inherent complementarity among male and female in the process of creation.

Despite this active female participation, these creation myths tend to reduce the images of the female body to that of a sexual body. In a similar myth from the *Bṛhadāraṇyaka Upaniṣad*, Prajāpati creates the first woman, whose body is then compared to a *soma* sacrifice: "Her lap is the *vedi* (area between the sacrificial fires), her hair the sacrificial grass. Her skin is the *soma* press, her labia the fire in the middle" (6.4.3).[6] In the *Puruṣasūkta* (ṚV 10.90) and its subsequent mythology, Vedic literature often presents the human body as a paradigm to describe the universe and the sacrifice. However, the body of Puruṣa is a specifically male body which represents the entire universe and generates the social categories (*varṇa*), the moon and the sun, Indra and Agni. The rearticulation of this myth in the *Bṛhadāraṇyaka Upaniṣad* illustrates how the sacrificial imagery is grafted onto the male body differently from how it is grafted onto the female body. The myth begins with Prajāpati, whose body throughout Vedic literature is described and linked to both the universe and the sacrifice. However, this particular telling of the myth concludes by comparing a woman's body to a *soma* sacrifice, where only the sexual and generative organs from the woman are mentioned.[7] Whereas a man's body is a microcosm for the entire universe, the female body is reduced to a sexual and procreative body.

Admittedly, a man's body is not always likened to the entire universe. In Pravāhaṇa's instruction to Uddālaka Āruṇi, he compares the five fires to five aspects of the world: (1) the upper regions (*asau loka*), (2) rain (*parjanya*), (3) earth (*ayam loka*), (4) man (*puruṣa*), and (5) woman (*yoṣā*). In the discussion of man, his body is described in terms of the vital functions: (1) open mouth (*vyāttam*), (2) breath (*prāṇa*), (3) speech (*vāc*), (4) sight (*cakṣu*), and (5) hearing (*śrota*). The description of a woman, however, appears exclusively in terms of her sexual organs and how a man approaches her during sex: (1) lap/loins (*upastha*), (2) pubic hair (*loman*), (3) vagina (*yoni*), (4) penetration (*antaḥ karoti*), and (5) climax (*abhinandā*). These examples illustrate that while the male body is linked to sacrificial and cosmological imagery in a number of ways, the female body tends to be described particularly in relation to sexual intercourse and procreation.

As we will see, many Upanishadic teachings encourage brahmin men to engage in sexual activity in pursuit of their soteriological goals. Accordingly, it is not surprising that in some passages the male body is also described as a procreative body. Nevertheless, the male body is never reduced to its procreative role. For example, in the *Chāndogya Upaniṣad* description of the *sāman* of Vāmadeva, explicitly male sexual actions are linked to different aspects of the chant: "Inviting a woman is the *hiṅkara* (initial humming), expressing desire is the *prastāva* (prelude). Lying beside her is the *udgītha*, lying on top of her is the *pratihāra* (response). Climax is the *nidhana* (finale)" (2.13.1).[8] This passage goes on to say that one who knows the *sāman* as woven upon sexual intercourse achieves successful sexual intercourse, as well as attains a full life span, lots of children, and livestock (2.13.2). Here, the male body is also described as a sexual body, but unlike the female body that is objectified as a sexual body, the brahmin man is characterized as a sexual subject and the male body is never reduced to the sexual organs. Rather, men are encouraged to have sex for the sake of actualizing their pursuits of knowledge, and intercourse is portrayed as an activity that is part of the quest for immortality.

Not only do these examples show that the Upaniṣads tend to represent the female body differently from the male body, but by linking *ātman* with the mythology of Puruṣa and Prajāpati, these passages present a particularly male conception of the self. In these contexts, *ātman* is not a universal self in the sense that everyone has an *ātman*, but rather *ātman* is a particular construction of the self which is both explicitly male and gained through particular kinds of practices which are primarily the domain of men. Yet despite the distincly male connotations of some teachings, in other contexts *ātman* is described as operating the same way in plants and animals as in people. In these cases, the female body implicitly has an *ātman* the same way that a male body has one, thus opening up a discursive space for women such as Gārgī and Maitreyī to be knowledgeable in Upanishadic teachings. Significantly, these ambiguities concerning the gender implications of *ātman* remain unresolved.

These descriptions of a specifically male creator of the universe are closely connected to a number of teachings that emphasize the male role in procreation and birth.[9] As we have seen in the *upanayana*, the relationship between teacher and student is often described in birth metaphors, with the initiation itself considered a man's second birth, which bestows upon him a twice-born status (*dvija*). Consequently, a man's birth into society, which was defined and controlled by brahmin men, was considered more real than his natural birth. As Kumkum Roy points out with regard to the Vedic sacrifice, ritual actions often function in taking away the agency of women from the process of procreation: "The possibility of recreating such acts was open only to the male sacrificer. In effect this meant that the procreative power of women was simultaneously denied and appropriated" (1991–2, 13). At the end of the *Bṛhadāraṇyaka Upaniṣad* (6.4.10–11) there is a series of six rites, all of which address sexual intercourse and procreation. One of the themes that extends throughout this section is the male attempt to assume control over the processes of conception and birth. For example, one rite prescribes *mantras* for a man to say in order to induce and prevent pregnancy. Here, a woman's body is defined primarily as a receptacle for a man's semen, and it is the semen that is regarded as containing the power to generate life.

These rituals that deal with procreation not only promise men the ability to control conception, but also bestow the power to generate offspring with specifically desired attributes.[10] One set of instructions mentions a number of mixtures with rice and milk that should be prepared by a man's wife, for him and her to eat together (BU 6.4.15–18). There are four sets of characteristics that are then described for potential offspring and a different mixture that should be made and eaten for each one. The first desired offspring is a son with a fair (*śukla*) complexion, who will learn one Veda; the second is a son with a brown (*kapila*) and yellow (*piṅgala*) complexion, who will master two Vedas; and the third is a son with dark (*śyāma*) complexion and red eyes (*lohitākṣa*), who will learn three Vedas. Surprisingly, the fourth offspring mentioned is a daughter (*duhitā*), who is described as learned (*paṇḍitā*). Although these instructions for how to secure a female child at first seem inconsistent with the male bias of this section, in fact learned women are necessary for these rituals to work. All the procreation rituals described in this section, although they promise to give reproductive power to men, must be performed by a husband and wife together. Accordingly, female participation in the process of procreation is not restricted entirely to the role of sexual partner, but rather, as these rituals illustrate, women are also ritual partners for their husbands.

The essential role of the brahmin's wife in these procreation rituals again points to the complementary depiction of the processes of creation and procreation. Yet despite the acknowledgement that both male and female participation is needed to produce offspring, these rituals attempt to give brahmin men the ultimate control over procreative activities. This also extends to attempting to define and regulate a baby's birth and first feeding. Similar to the ceremony where a man bestows his knowledge to his son before he departs from the world, a man comes physically close to his newborn son and says in his right ear three times, "speech, speech" (*vāc*). He then feeds the baby a mixture of curd, honey, and *ghee*, while saying a *mantra* (BU 6.4.25). It is significant that this *mantra* immediately precedes the father handing over his son to the mother for the child's first breast-feeding. Roy has pointed out that this is another case where Upanishadic teachings privilege the man's role in the procreation process: "The offspring obtained, moreover, were connected with the father through rituals. For instance, the son was first fed by the father and then handed over for breast-feeding to the mother. This probably symbolically incorporated the newborn son within the patrilineage and asserted the father's role in childbirth" (1994, 257).

After the first feeding the man gives his son a name while saying, "You are the Veda" (BU 6.4.26). While there are clear instructions of how to name a male child, there are no descriptions of naming a female child. Although the text does not state that a similar naming ceremony could not take place for a daughter, its neglect is indicative of the male bias of the texts. Women are not systematically denied a place in the discourse, but rather their possibilities for selfhood are not explicitly addressed. The Upaniṣads are primarily about brahmin men and tend to address women only vis-à-vis their relation to men.

Finally, after naming the boy, the man addresses his wife, saying that a man who is born the son of a brahmin who knows this naming ritual reaches the highest point in prosperity (*śrīyā*), glory (*yaśas*), and sacred knowledge (*brahmavarcasa*) (BU 6.4.28). Here, at the end of this section, these instructions reinforce the father's role in the process of procreation and indicate that the father's knowledge ensures prosperity for his son.

THE SELF, VIRILITY, AND IMMORTALITY

As we have seen in the introduction, immortality in the Upaniṣads is often defined in terms of prolonging one's lifespan. In these contexts knowledge about how the body works is fundamental because it implies that one can manipulate the process of life in order to avert death. The *Chāndogya Upaniṣad* (3.16.7), for example, tells us that Mahidāsa Aitareya lived to be one hundred and sixteen after claiming that he would overcome death because of his knowledge. Different from, yet related to, this understanding of immortality is a soteriology that teaches that a man can pass his *ātman* to his son. In this way, a man can achieve immortality by means of having a male child, as well as by passing knowledge onto him. As we will see, this soteriology explicitly addresses the interests of brahmin men and has far-reaching implications concerning the gender status of *ātman*, as well as possible restrictions on who can achieve immortality.

The Brāhmaṇas clearly state that because a father achieves immortality through his son, only a married man can perform a sacrifice. For example, the *Aitareya Brāhmaṇa* explains that when a woman has a son, not only does she give birth to a child, but the husband himself is born again in her as the son (7.13). The *Śatapatha Brāhmaṇa* reinforces this identification of father and son: "The father is the same as the son, and the son is the same as the father" (ŚB 12.4.3.1 tr. Eggeling).

Similarly, in the Upaniṣads there are several discourses that explain how the father passes on his vital functions to his son. In the *Bṛhadāraṇyaka Upaniṣad* there is a father-son ceremony instructing that when a man is about to die he should teach his son all his Vedic learning. This passage claims that when a man who knows this dies, "he enters his son with his *prāṇās*. And if he has acted wrongly, then his son releases (*muc*) him from all that" (1.5.17).[11] Here, the father not only continues living through his son, but also through his son absolves himself from any wrongdoing. The *Kauṣītaki Upaniṣad* describes a father-son ceremony where again the father passes his *prāṇa* on to his son (2.14). According to this rite, a man should lie down and cover himself with a garment. Then the son should lie on top of him and touch his father's organs with his corresponding organs (2.14). This rite, which explains that every aspect of the father's body is passed onto his son, bestows the father's authority onto his son. This and other passages indicate the importance of passing on one's knowledge before death, emphasizing that it is not enough merely to have sons, but one must also transmit knowledge to a son.

These passages also have important implications for the relationship between knowledge of *ātman* and ritual action. As we have seen, knowledge of *ātman* is often cast as a replacement to ritual, at least to the large-scale sacrifices of the Brāhmaṇas. Yet here knowledge of *ātman* has its own accompanying procedure, as the transmission of knowledge of *ātman* from father to son is presented as a ritual. Whereas in the sacrificial texts a man had sons so that they could perform ritual actions after his death, in the Upaniṣads the father becomes alive in the son by means of a different kind of ritual, the ritual of passing on knowledge about the self.

As having a son leads to immortality, virility and sexual potency are fundamental aspects of male subjectivity. This is demonstrated by the many discourses that are either explicitly about sex or are embedded within sexual metaphors. The *Chāndogya Upaniṣad* (1.1.6), for example, describes *oṃ* as uniting in sexual union, and knowledge of the *udgītha* chant as equated with fulfilling sexual desires. For examples more specific to male sexuality, let us return to the procreation rites at the end of the *Bṛhadāraṇyaka Upaniṣad*. As Olivelle points out: "An interesting sub-text running through these rites is the fear of losing virility and merit by engaging in sexual activity" (1999, 52).

This entire section begins with the mythical account of Prajāpati creating women as a support for his semen. The imagery of this myth equates sexual intercourse with a *soma* sacrifice and promises that a man who engages in sexual intercourse with this knowledge will reap the same rewards as one who performs such a sacrifice. However, a passage that follows this myth warns that sexual activity without the proper knowledge can be potentially dangerous, as merit (*sukṛta*) could be won and lost during sex. With the proper knowledge a man can appropriate merit from a woman during their sexual activity, however if a man without this knowledge has sexual intercourse, the woman can appropriate merit for herself (6.4.3). This passage then claims that Uddālaka Āruṇi knew this when he warned that brahmin men who engage in sexual intercourse without this knowledge depart from the world impotent (*nirindriya*) and without merit (*visukṛta*) (BU 6.4.4). This reference to Uddālaka Āruṇi is quite likely an attempt to connect this teaching with the knowledge of the five fires, which appears before this passage in this same section of the *Bṛhadāraṇyaka Upaniṣad*. Thematically this would makes sense because whereas the five fires discourse explains how semen is linked to immortality, in this passage Uddālaka Āruṇi reflects that brahmins were losing their virility without this knowledge.

The importance of maintaining one's virility is further emphasized as the *Bṛhadāraṇyaka Upaniṣad* explains what to do when a man discharges semen when he is not having sexual intercourse: he should touch it and address it while saying "May my virility (*indriya*), my energy (*tejas*) and my passion (*bhaga*) return to me" (6.4.5).[12] Similarly, in his teaching of the five fires, Pravāhaṇa teaches that semen is the essence of a man's life (6.4.1). Clearly, as semen is regarded as a life force, there is a fear that losing semen will result in losing virility. The following passage tells us that if a man recites this formula and then rubs the semen between his breast and brow, he will retain his energy (*tejas*), virility (*indriya*), splendor (*yaśas*), wealth (*draviṇa*), and merit (*sukṛta*). In these examples, Upanishadic teachings are explicitly connected to a particular construction of a man, which defines masculinity in terms of sexual potency, thereby linking these instructions to virility and sexual power. Taken together, they show that male sexual activity needs to be controlled for the sake of procreation. As semen is directly linked to immortality, there is a fear of spilling one's seed outside the discursively sanctioned activity of heterosexual intercourse.

We return to the tension regarding female participation in procreation further on in this section of the *Bṛhadāraṇyaka Upaniṣad,* where there is a ritual for men to make women have sex with them. This ritual explains that a man should approach a woman who has finished menstruating and invite her to have sex with him (6.4.6–8). If she does not consent to having sex with him, he should bribe her, and if she continues to refuse, he should beat her with a stick or with his fists and overpower her. Roebuck sees this passage as an "apparent encouragement of domestic violence," yet points out that it is unclear "whether actual or symbolic violence is intended" (2003, 410). In either case, this violence is significant, especially when we remember that throughout the Upaniṣads knowledge is often framed within metaphors of antagonism and combat. Despite the fact that this passage is embedded within ritual and perhaps should be taken metaphorically, the violent and aggressive portrayal of the brahmin man is consistent with the depiction of the confrontational masculinity of verbal debates.

As the passage continues, it explains that if a woman resists the man's sexual advances and has to be overtaken by force, the man can say a *mantra* to take away her splendor (*yaśas*) (BU 6.4.7).[13] However, if she agrees to have sex with him, he can say a *mantra* to ensure that both of them can become full of splendor through sexual intercourse. Both this passage and the knowledge ascribed to Uddālaka Āruṇi emphasize the importance of Upanishadic teachings during sexual intercourse and show a brahmin male anxiety towards women. A woman, even the characteristically passive and supportive wife, is always a potential danger because she can appropriate merit (*sukṛta*) and splendor (*yaśas*) during sex.

A man's knowledge of appropriate teachings and rituals not only can make a woman have sex with him, but also can make her desire him. As he has intercourse with her he should say, "You come from every part of my body. You are born from my heart. You are the essence of my limbs. Make this woman mad about me, as if pierced by a poison arrow" (BU 6.4.9).[14] This passage, a reference to the Prajāpati myth at the beginning of the entire section, is invoked to explain that because women derive their existence from men, a man has the ability to manipulate her emotional attitude towards him.

The competitive and aggressive aspect of sexual relations is directed against not only brahmin's sexual partners, but also their sexual rivals, and guarding one's wife is considered another aspect of securing immortality. The *Jaiminīya Brāhmaṇa*, for example, claims that a wife must be protected so that another man's immortality does not grow in her: "Lest in my womb, in my world somebody else come into existence" (1.17 tr. Bodewitz).[16] In this way, a man's knowledge of discourses relating to sexual practices not only gives him power over women, but also can give him power over other men. Similarly, the *Bṛhadāraṇyaka Upaniṣad* prescribes a ritual where a man can make a mixture and perform a *mantra* if his wife has a lover whom he hates, pointing out that a man who is cursed by a brahmin with this knowledge will depart from this world without his virility and merit. These examples illustrate that a crucial aspect of brahmin subjectivity is knowledge about sex and procreation, knowledge which not only promises the reward of immortality, but also bestows power in this world over women and other men.

Another important soteriological goal in the Upaniṣads is *ānanda*, which is often translated as joy or bliss. In his study of the semantic history of this term, Olivelle argues that in the *Bṛhadāraṇyaka Upaniṣad* and the *Taittirīya Upaniṣad*, *ānanda* has overt sexual connotations: "These Upaniṣads present *ānanda* as the faculty or power of the sexual organ parallel to the sensory and motor faculties associated with other organs" (1997b, 162). Moreover, *ānanda* is often associated with knowledge of *ātman*, thus suggesting that knowledge of the self brings about orgasmic rapture.[15] As orgasmic bliss is part of the procreation process that ideally results in the birth of sons, *ānanda* is linked with immortality. Olivelle's study shows that there is an explicit connection between *ānanda* and the penis, which clearly suggests that the rapture brought about by knowledge of *ātman* is associated with a man's sexual pleasure.

Olivelle's observations about the meaning of *ānanda*, together with the repeated emphasis on male children and the rituals that are meant to control the process of procreation, point to the explicitly male soteriology assumed throughout the early Upaniṣads. This does not necessary imply that women could not be candidates for immortality, but rather the ideal candidate is undoubtedly the brahmin householder. In the following section we will see that the teachings and story of Yājñavalkya challenge this ideal, but most brahmins, such as Satyakāma, are depicted as married householders.

YĀJÑAVALKYA AND SATYAKĀMA: COMPETING IDEALS OF MALE SUBJECTIVITY

As we have discussed in previous chapters, Yājñavalkya and Satyakāma embody opposing constructions of the Upanishadic brahmin, particularly in relation to teaching and debating. In this section we will explore how their competing standards for brahminhood are developed through their interactions with female characters. Whereas Satyakāma is the embodiment of the married householder, Yājñavalkya challenges traditional views by including women in philosophical discussions and by teaching that one can attain immortality without having sons.[16]

As we discussed in the first chapter, Satyakāma's life story fits the model of the brahmin householder. Satyakāma is married, maintains a household fire, and supports himself as a teacher by taking on students. This lifestyle complies with a number of teachings, including instructions in the *Taittirīya Upaniṣad* that prescribe that brahmins should continue their family line upon their completion of Vedic studies (1.11.1). Although the presence of Satyakāma's wife is crucial to his portrayal as a householder, she remains in the shadows, as she is not mentioned by name, and Satyakāma does not acknowledge her when she speaks to him. We will return to the character of Satyakāma's wife later in the chapter. For now, however, it is important to point out that her appearance is primarily to characterize Satyakāma as the type of brahmin who gets married and maintains a household. As such, her personal identity is not specified and her words are ignored.

In contrast, Yājñavalkya has an affectionate and personable exchange with his wife. In fact, Yājñavalkya's dialogue with Maitreyī is one of two separate occasions when he speaks to women about philosophy, thus setting him apart from other Upanishadic teachers, especially the traditional Kuru-Pañcāla brahmins. In this way, Yājñavalkya's interactions with women are an integral aspect of his general character as an innovative and enigmatic figure.

In his conversation with Maitreyī, for example, he frames his teaching in a way that specifically acknowledges her relation to him as his wife: "Indeed, a husband is held dear, not for the love of a husband, but a husband is held dear for the love of the self (*ātman*). A wife is held dear, not for the love of a wife, but a wife is held dear for the love of the self (*ātman*)" (2.4.5). This affectionate prelude to his teaching is pertinent when we recall that much of the significance of Upanishadic dialogues is in outlining how brahmins should interact with their dialogical partners. In this case, as Yājñavalkya specifically relates his teaching to the particular relationship that exists between himself and his wife, this dialogue establishes a mode of address whereby brahmin men can speak to their wives about philosophy.

Additionally, Yājñavalkya's discussion with Maitreyī is remarkable in light of the fact that he is the only brahmin in the Upaniṣads to teach that having male offspring is not necessary as part of achieving immortality. As we have seen, when the procreative role of women is defined in terms of the soteriogical goals of men, women tend to be restrained and marginalized. It is perhaps because he does not equate his own immortality with this particular construction of women that Yājñavalkya can include women in his dialogues.

Furthermore, his conversation with Maitreyī can be seen as an alternative model to how a brahmin man should pass on his knowledge before he dies. This dialogue begins with Yājñavalkya about to divide his inheritance between his two wives. As we have seen, there are a number of passages that instruct how a man who is about to die should pass on knowledge to his son. Yet in this case, when Yājñavalkya is about to depart, he addresses his wife. That Yājñavalkya teaches Maitreyī under these specific conditions suggests either that Yājñavalkya can achieve his own immortality through passing his knowledge onto her, or that Yājñavalkya is instructing Maitreyī for the sake of her immortality. In either case, Yājñavalkya puts his own authority behind an alternative to the standard model of the transmission of knowledge.

Nevertheless, despite speaking to women and offering a soteriology that is more inclusive of women, Yājñavalkya appears to be condescending to both Maitreyī and Gārgī. When he speaks to Maitreyī, he indicates that she might have trouble understanding him, by telling her to "listen carefully" (*nididhyāsava*) (BU 2.4.4). Maitreyī's ability to understand Yājñavalkya's teaching is further called into question towards the end of the dialogue when Maitreyī says that she is "confused" (*muh*) by what he has said. Yājñavalkya responds rather unsympathetically: "I have not said anything confusing (*moha*)" (2.4.13).[17] Additionally, he is condescending when he debates with Gārgī. As we will discuss later in this chapter, Gārgī is the first person whom Yājñavalkya threatens in this debate, picking on her because she appears to be an easy target.

It is possible, however, that Yājñavalkya's condescending behavior towards Maitreyī and Gārgī is not necessarily directed against them as women, but is part of his aggressive and confrontational debating style. Yājñavalkya is often aggressive and ironic with his dialogical partners, and furthermore, throughout the Upaniṣads a number of teachings are framed within explicitly *kṣatriya* metaphors.[18] Although much of this rhetoric is an attempt to make Upanishadic teachings relevant to a *kṣatriya* audience, this also reflects a particular construction of the brahmin male as aggressive, competitive, and sometimes violent. As we have seen, Yājñavalkya's success is largely attributed to his ability to bully and intimidate his opponents. It is perhaps revealing that although brahmins define themselves differently from *kṣatriya*s, as experts in knowledge rather than in fighting, they nevertheless equate their success in knowledge with physical violence and military strength. Similarly, the pedagogical dialogues are more combative than supportive, as teachers often instruct students by means of confrontation, testing, and imparting false knowledge. Taken together, these different dialogical encounters illustrate that throughout the Upaniṣads, aggression, competitiveness, and suspicion are among the qualities that are needed to participate in the social world of brahmin men.

THE MYTH OF RECOVERING AN AUTHENTIC FEMALE VOICE

Now that we have looked at competing ideals of masculinity, let us turn to the depiction of female characters in the early Upaniṣads. The portrayal of women in Vedic literature is a topic of much debate. A number of scholars take a historical approach to the texts, gleaning from the portrayal of female characters evidence about the status of women in ancient India, with some scholars arguing that women enjoyed a relatively favorable position in the Vedic period. A. S. Altekar, for example, argued that the position of women was higher in ancient India than in ancient Greece and Rome ([1938] 1959, 337–38). Similarly, R. C. Dutt claimed: "No nation held their women in higher honour than the Hindus" (1972, 168–69). Uma Chakravarti argues that this trajectory of scholarship was part of the Indian nationalist project that attempted to assign a high place for women in the ancient Hindu past:

> The analysis of the position of women in ancient India has also been coloured by the fact that almost all the works have been written by scholars who would fall within the nationalist school of history. Writing at a time when Hindu social institutions were being subjected to fierce criticism by a generation that was imbibing Western education and Western values, these scholars worked hard to show that the position of women had been high in the ancient past, (1999, 74)

More recently, scholars such as Ellison Banks Findly have attempted to characterize the quite positive portrayal of female characters such as Gārgī in the Upaniṣads as representing "an era of unsurpassed advantage and opportunity for women" (1985, 38). Although Gārgī is portrayed favorably, the depiction of one literary character is not sufficient to draw any conclusions about social and gender relations in ancient India. Moreover, Gārgī's more positive characteristics tend to be presented indirectly, thus indicating that the composers and compilers of the *Bṛhadāraṇyaka Upaniṣad* are not unhesitating in their depiction of the text's most outgoing female character.

Furthermore, it is important to emphasize that the Upaniṣads are not historical accounts, and therefore it is impossible to assess the actual situation facing women in ancient India from a reading of these texts. We must keep in mind that the utterances of female characters such as Gārgī and Maitreyī are not the direct expressions of a female authorial voice. As Stephanie Jamison reminds us, we are never hearing women's voices directly in the Brahmanical literature: "From the beginning we must face the fact that we are not going to hear an authentic woman's voice—or at least not without tampering by those who have inserted it into the tradition for their own reasons" (1996, 8).

Despite the fact that we should be hesitant in making any concrete historical conclusions, there remains much to be said about gender dynamics and the representation of female characters at a textual level. In the remainder of this chapter we will look at dialogues where women participate in Upanishadic teachings, examining how female voices are represented, and how interactions between men and women are described. Although the speech and actions of women continue to be controlled by and mediated through men, we also see the construction of new kinds of female subjectivity. Rather than attempt to explain away these contradictions, it is important to recognize this tension in the Upanishadic portrayal of women, especially the female characters, as a significant aspect of the texts. As Jamison explains, "The conceptual position of women in ancient India was by nature *not* unified, not governed by a coherent set of principles and attitudes. It was contradictory, and these contradictions, found both in overt statements and in attitudes covertly reflected in narrative and ritual, are irreconcilable" (1996, 203).

Some of my observations about the female characters will be more speculative and interpretive than my comments about the male characters in previous chapters. This is due, at least in part, to the tension regarding female characters, and women in general, in the texts. Similar to the myth where *ātman*'s wife does much of the work in the process of creation, but where *ātman* takes the credit, the narrative scenes that feature female characters depict women as having much more of an impact on the outcome of the story than is ever reflected upon by the narrative itself. In other words there is often a contradiction between what female characters do and how much the text seems aware of what they do. Are these blind-spots, "accidental byproducts" as Jamison suggests? (1996, 16). Are they intentional cues for the more aware listener or reader? Or perhaps a bit of both? This, we cannot know, and I do not attempt to speculate. But what I have tried to do is bring attention to a number of often disregarded actions and non-actions of the female characters in an attempt to explore their characters more fully and to reexamine their role in the narratives.

GĀRGĪ : THE DEBATING TACTICS OF A FEMALE PHILOSOPHER

Gārgī Vācaknavī is the female character who figures most prominently in philosophical discussions in the Upaniṣads. She, along with the brahmins from Kuru-Pañcāla, challenges Yājñavalkya in the debate in King Janaka's court (BU 3.6, 3.8.1–12). Although she officially loses her debate with Yājñavalkya, in this section I will argue that there are a number of distinctive features of her challenge that distinguish her from the Kuru-Pañcāla brahmins and call into question whether her defeat is as straightforward or conclusive as it first appears: she is the first challenger to be threatened, the only one to speak twice, the only one to address the other challengers, and the only one who gets in the last word with Yājñavalkya. Moreover, she displays her knowledge both through her understanding of the discourse and her employment of a number of debating tactics. Taken together, these unique features of Gārgī's challenge suggest that, far from being silenced by Yājñavalkya, she is the strongest opponent.

The first distinguishing characteristic of her encounter is that she is the first challenger whom Yājñavalkya threatens. She begins her initial confrontation with Yājñavalkya by asking about the foundation of water: "Since all this is woven together on water, then on what is water woven together?" (BU 3.6).[19] This question initiates a verbal exchange in which Gārgī continues to ask about the foundation for every response that Yājñavalkya gives. Finally, when Yājñavalkya replies that Prajāpati is woven together upon the worlds of *brahman*, Gārgī once again demands a further answer, asking, "On what are the worlds of *brahman* woven together?" At this point Yājñavalkya warns her that if she continues to question him her head will shatter apart: "Gārgī, do not ask too many questions, or your head will shatter apart" (BU 3.6).[20]

Here, Yājñavalkya justifies his warning to Gārgī by claiming that she is asking beyond her knowledge. In chapter 2 we looked at Insler's distinction between two types of threats about head shattering. Yājñavalkya's warning to Gārgī is presented as an example of the first type because Gārgī asks beyond her own knowledge and because, according to Insler, her insufficient knowledge is implicit in the narrative:

> The vocabulary of the first type makes matters extremely clear, because the technical term employed, *atipṛchati* 'asks further

> or beyond,' implicitly requires the addition of *vidyām* 'knowledge' to complete the thought. That is to say, the questioner is asking about matters beyond the limits of [her] knowledge. (1989–90, 99)

Although it is true that the vocabulary in the narrative makes matters clear that Yājñavalkya accuses Gārgī of asking beyond her knowledge, there are a number of details that suggest that Gārgī is not speaking beyond what she knows, but that Yājñavalkya is merely employing a threat as a means to silence her. One reason to call into question Yājñavalkya's accusation is because Gārgī reenters the debate even after facing this mortal threat. Her second challenge suggests that she is confident enough in her own knowledge to feel safe from Yājñavalkya's threat.

Additionally, when Gārgī questions Yājñavalkya the second time, at first she does not address him directly, but rather appeals to all the other challengers: "Eminent Brahmins! I am going to ask him two questions. If he can answer them for me, none of you will defeat him in the *brahmodya*" (BU 3.8.1).[21] Significantly, she pays her respects to the other brahmins, by addressing them with the deferential *bhagavanta*, yet she does not refer to Yājñavalkya by name, nor does she speak to him in a respectful way, simply referring to him with the personal pronoun *imam*. None of this is surprising when we consider that these are her first words since being threatened by Yājñavalkya. Furthermore, by addressing the entire assembly, Gārgī appeals to the other brahmins to be her witnesses, perhaps in order to discourage Yājñavalkya from attempting any more debating tricks. Appealing to witnesses is a crucial tactic employed by other female characters speaking in the court of a king. For example, in the *Mahābhārata*, both Draupadī (2.60–64) and Śakuntalā (1.68–69) use the assembly to bear witness to their own truthfulness, as well as to highlight their fluency in philosophical discourse, especially when the authority of their speech is called into question.[22]

Once she has the attention of the Kuru-Pañcāla brahmins, Gārgī employs another helpful debating tactic by assuming a masculine mode of speaking.[23] Gārgī confronts Yājñavalkya: "Yājñavalkya, like a warrior-son (*ugra-putraḥ*) of Kāśi or Videha, having strung his unstrung bow and having taken in his hand two enemy-piercing arrows might challenge you, I challenge you with two questions. Answer them for me" (BU 3.8.2).[24] As we have discussed previously, by comparing herself to a warrior and positioning herself as a direct combatant to Yājñavalkya, Gārgī's challenge is aggressive and shows the competitive atmosphere and high stakes of a *brahmodya*. Even though Yājñavalkya has just accused her of ignorance and threatened that her head will shatter apart, Gārgī remains undaunted and clearly sees herself as an equal to Yājñavalkya. Gārgī's use of this trope of combat shows that when she adopts an aggressive and confrontational approach her argument is taken seriously, illustrating that she has to take on the rhetoric of a brahmin male subject to pose a serious challenge to Yājñavalkya.[25]

Similarly, Gārgī adopts Yājñavalkya's characteristic use of humor in an attempt to unsettle Yājñavalkya himself. After her aggressive challenge, Gārgī asks Yājñavalkya her first question: "That which is above the sky, that which is below the earth, what which is between sky and earth, that which people call past, present and future. On what are these woven together?" (BU 3.8.3).[26] Yājñavalkya's response is that they are all woven together upon space (*ākāśa*). Gārgī replies by praising him: "I pay my respect to you (*namaste*), Yājñavalkya. Indeed, you have answered me. Be prepared for the next question" (BU 3.8.5).[27] This response is seemingly respectful, yet when Gārgī delivers her second question it becomes clear that her praise was actually mocking Yājñavalkya: "That which is above the sky, that which is below the earth, what which is between sky and earth, that which people call past, present and future. On what are these woven together?" (BU 3.8.6). Here we see that her second question is exactly the same as her first. Olivelle has remarked on the acerbity behind Gārgī's second question: "I think that Gārgī's response is dripping with sarcasm. She is not satisfied at all with the first answer and is telling Yājñavalkya, in effect, to get serious! This, I believe, is the reason why her second question is a repetition of the first" (1996, 311n). Although Gārgī does not have the authority to threaten Yājñavalkya directly, when she responds to Yājñavalkya's answer with flattery only to ask him the same question again, she shows that she is still not satisfied with his answers. Furthermore, she openly defies his authority by mocking him in front of the assembly.

Following Gārgī's second question, Yājñavalkya responds with a teaching about the imperishable (*akṣara*), which he describes by using paradox and negation: it is neither thick nor thin, neither short nor long; it has nothing inside of it, nor outside of it; it neither eats nor is eaten. Significantly, Yājñavalkya articulates this knowledge in terms of gender, emphasizing that the imperishable is important knowledge specifically for a man to know before he dies:

> If someone in this world makes offerings, performs sacrifices and practices austerities for many thousands of years without

> knowing the imperishable, Gārgī, his work comes to an end. He who departs from this world without knowing the imperishable is miserable, Gārgī. But if someone passes from this world knowing the imperishable, Gārgī, he is a brahmin. (BU 3.8.10)[28]

Here, Yājñavalkya's teaching connects Upanishadic knowledge with a specifically male soteriology. His use of the masculine pronoun *sa*, especially when addressing a woman, suggests that only a man can become a brahmin. Accordingly, the implication of Yājñavalkya's teaching is that despite coming from a brahmin family, because of her gender, Gārgī can never truly be a brahmin.

However, we could also interpret this as Yājñavalkya indirectly bestowing the status of brahmin onto Gārgī. As we have seen, in a number of similar narrative scenes the status of brahmin is based as much upon knowledge of the discourse as it is upon birth. The *Śatapatha Brāhmaṇa* (11.6.2.10) names Janaka as a brahmin after the king proves his knowledge to Yājñavalkya, and Satyakāma is acknowledged as a brahmin despite not knowing his family lineage (CU 4.4.1–5). By implication, if Gārgī can know the imperishable then she can become a brahmin. This seems to be the interpretation supported by the text, because after equating the status of brahmin with knowledge of the imperishable, Yājñavalkya continues to teach Gārgī about the imperishable, further describing it in terms of paradox: it sees but cannot be seen, it hears but cannot be heard, it thinks but cannot be thought, it perceives but cannot be perceived. That Yājñavalkya delivers an entire discourse to Gārgī about the imperishable implies that she is capable of understanding him. Moreover, as one who can know the imperishable, Gārgī is placed in contradistinction to men who perform more traditional Vedic practices, such as making offerings, offering sacrifices, and performing austerities. In this respect, one of the functions of female characters like Gārgī, as well as *kṣatriya* characters, is to criticize more traditional brahmins.

Gārgī's superior status in relation to Yājñavalkya's other, more conservative opponents is further emphasized by the fact that she is the only one of Yājñavalkya's challengers who is not directly silenced by his words. All of his other opponents are silenced immediately after Yājñavalkya's final response to their questions. The text marks these occasions with the words "then x became silent" (*tato ha* [x] *uparārama*). In Gārgī's second challenge, however, she responds to Yājñavalkya's final words by addressing the other brahmins: "Eminent Brahmins! (*brāhmaṇā bhagavantaḥ*) You should consider it great if you escape from him by (merely) paying him respect. None of you will defeat him in a *brahmodya*" (BU 3.8.12).[29] Gārgī is the only participant in the discussion to employ the term *brahmodya* and by explicitly naming the discussion a *brahmodya*, she inscribes her own presence and voice within a discursively sanctioned activity.[30]

Moreover, with this short speech and warning to the other brahmins, Gārgī gets in the last word and consequently does not completely give in to Yājñavalkya's authority. Only after Gārgī has addressed the brahmins does the text tell us: "Then Gārgī became silent" (3.8.12). This distinction from all of Yājñavalkya other opponents suggests that she is never convinced by Yājñavalkya's answers, and that she only recognizes his superiority in relation to the other brahmins. As Findly comments, "Her silence following Yājñavalkya's rebuke is more of a courtesy than an acquiescence" (1985, 50). Additionally, with her concluding remarks she positions her own authority with Yājñavalkya's ability to defeat the other brahmins, indirectly situating herself on the winning side of the debate. Consequently, despite not winning the debate, Gārgī manages to put her own frame around their encounter and to align herself with the victor.

Furthermore, she is the one who pronounces Yājñavalkya as the superior orator. Gārgī's warning to the Kuru-Pañcāla brahmins is similar, in this respect, to Svaidāyana's warning the northern brahmins about Uddālaka Āruṇi's ability to shatter heads apart (ŚB 11.5.3.13).[31] In the case of Svaidāyana, the narrative implies that he is able to recognize Uddālaka's knowledge only because he himself has just defeated Uddālaka in a *brahmodya*. Similarly, although Gārgī does not defeat Yājñavalkya, her ability to recognize his superiority over the other brahmins suggests that she has the authority, or at least claims the authority, to pronounce the winner.

Another feature of this debate that Gārgī shares in common with both Draupadī and Śakuntalā is the intervention of an authoritative male speaker. In the *Mahābhārata*, both Draupadī and Śakuntalā have debates in which they are threatened and their reputations are questioned. Ultimately, even though they do not explicitly win their arguments, both get their way by means of an outside intervention.[32] Similarly, Gārgī is only able to challenge Yājñavalkya as fiercely as she does because of the intervention of an authoritative male speaker. As we have seen, Gārgī challenges Yājñavalkya on two separate occasions during this debate, with her second encounter made possible only due to the intervention of Uddālaka Āruṇi (BU 3.7), who joins in the *brahmodya* at precisely the moment when Yājñavalkya threatens

Gārgī, offering a counterattack in which he challenges Yājñavalkya with the same fatal consequence of his head shattering apart. It is only after Uddālaka intervenes that Gārgī resumes her challenge and it is at this point when she specifically appeals to the other brahmins to bear witness to her arguments and makes her prediction about the outcome of the debate.

Against the scholarly trajectory that presents women as silently preserving the tradition without any challenge, Findly reads Gārgī's line of questioning to Yājñavalkya as an articulation of heterodox views: "Rarely, however, have these scholars investigated the possible cracks in the veneer of India's past, cracks that may show women not only as bearers of a preserved cultural tradition but also, perhaps, as precisely the opposite: vehicles for cultural innovation and, more interestingly, for heterodox ideas and practices" (1985, 38).[33] Findly identifies Gārgī's method of regressive questioning as a new style of argumentation and suggests that this method anticipates the later Buddhist teaching of causality (*pratītyasamutpāda*). Although Findly is right to point out that Gārgī represents innovative ideas and practices, this aspect of Gārgī's character is not exemplified in her regressive questioning. Indeed, the regressive method of questioning is illustrative of an important meaning of the word *upaniṣad*, which, as we discussed in the introduction, is often used in contexts that list a chain of dependency. In these cases, an *upaniṣad* refers to the power that stands at the top of the hierarchy that governs all the other components. As Brereton points out, many teachers, especially Yājñavalkya, organize the worlds through constructing hierarchies: "Upanishadic sages set up a system of levels that show which powers include other powers or which are dependent on which others. Ultimately, by moving towards progressively deeper levels, the sage identifies the fundamental principles on which everything else is established" (1990, 124). In this case, far from showing philosophical innovation, Gārgī's method of questioning displays her familiarity with one of the most characteristic methods for organizing knowledge in the Upaniṣads.

Nevertheless, Findly is right to point out that female characters often serve to represent unorthodox or rival views. In Gārgī's case, she poses her challenge to orthodoxy not so much by what she says, but how she speaks and conducts her arguments. As we have seen, she addresses the assembly, employs sarcasm, and adopts an aggressive mode of address. By means of these debating techniques she both displays her knowledge of the practice of the *brahmodya*, and proves her superiority over the Kuru-Pañcāla brahmins.

WOMEN AND *GANDHARVAS*: THE LACK OF AUTHORITY FOR FEMALE SPEAKERS

One of the underlying issues throughout Gārgī's participation in this *brahmodya* is the lack of authority of women's speech. Despite her strong challenge, any success against Yājñavalkya is muted and indirect; her words are shown to be true and prophetic, but there is no explicit acknowledgement of her achievements. Nevertheless, at least Gārgī's participation is recognized, as she is the only woman who is explicitly represented as taking part in the debate. There are indications, however, that other female voices also are represented in the discussion, although indirectly (BU 3.3.1, 3.7.1). Similar to when Gārgī captures Yājñavalkya's attention by adopting the mode of address of a male warrior, these other women are heard only after their voices have been filtered through the identities of male subjects. As Grace Jantzen points out in a discussion about Lacan, when men control the discourse, there are severe limitations on the representation of female subjectivity: "There can be no women subjects. Women qua women, therefore, cannot speak. When women speak, when women take up subject positions, it is not as women, but as imitation males, men in drag" (1998, 43). In the Upaniṣads we see that on a number of occasions women do speak, yet the authority for female speakers is continually denied. This is the case in this *brahmodya*, where there are women whose voices are heard only when they are connected with male speakers.

When challenging Yājñavalkya in Janaka's court, both Bhujyu Lāhyāyani (BU 3.3) and Uddālaka Āruṇi (BU 3.7) preface their questions with an account from when they were wandering students and visited the brahmin teacher Patañcala Kāpya in the land of the Madras people. Bhujyu recounts that Patañcala had a daughter who was possessed by a *gandharva* (*gandharvagṛhītā*), who told him about the fate of the Pārikṣitas (an ancient dynasty). In Uddālaka's account all the details are the same, except that in this case it is Patañcala's wife who is possessed, and Uddālaka learns about the inner controller (*antaryāmin*). In both cases a female character is named, but any speech associated with them is attributed to a *gandharva*. Significantly, Bhujyu and Uddālaka do not recount merely learning from a *gandharva*, but both of them specifically mention the identities of the women who are possessed. In this way, the identities of these women are presented as necessary details in the narrative, yet the agencies of these two women as speaking subjects are completely denied. When we consider this episode in the context of the general lack of authority of female speakers in the Upaniṣads, then it is possible that both Bhujyu and Uddālaka were seeing a woman and hearing a female voice, but could not attribute the authority of the doctrine to a female speaker. Incidentally, in his analysis of the debate in Janaka's court as a ring composition, Brereton suggests that the questions of the *gandharvas* and the two challenges of Gārgī "repeat similar strategies" (1997, 12). Thus, it is possible that the structure of this scene reinforces the female source of the *gandharvas*' speeches by linking them to the two speeches of Gārgī.

Keith briefly acknowledges the possibility of attributing the speech of these *gandharvas* to the women they possessed: "Women are not excluded from contests, a maiden seized by a Gandharva . . . shows herself an adept" in Upanishadic teachings ([1925] 1989, 506). Additionally, Roebuck suggests that in these episodes the women act as oracles (2003, 487). *Gandharvas* have a special connection with women throughout Vedic literature, most notably the *gandharva* Viśvāvasu, who was known to visit brides on their wedding nights.[34] Because of this already established connection, the presence of the *gandharvas* in these episodes in the *Bṛhadāraṇyaka Upaniṣad*, rather than hiding the original speakers altogether, emphasizes their gender as female.

One of the crucial questions regarding these curious episodes is whether or not the daughter and the wife visibly assume the form of a *gandharva* or if they look the same and act as ventriloquists for the voice of the *gandharva*. In both episodes these women are described as *gandharvagṛhītā*. The Sanskrit term *gṛhīta* means to be "grasped, taken or seized," and Monier-Williams defines *gandharvagṛhīta* as "to be possessed by a Gandharva." However, in these passages we do not know exactly what it means to be a *gandharvagṛhītā*.

In the *Jaiminīya Brāhmaṇa* (2.126) there is a similar episode where a woman is possessed by a *gandharva*, however in this context the term *gandharviṇī* is used. The *Jaiminīya Brāhmaṇa* recounts that Udara, the son of Śāṇḍilya, wishes to perform an *ekatrika* sacrifice (a one-day *soma* sacrifice). He makes this decision in his mind and does not tell anyone about it. When Udara's wife is possessed the *gandharva* tells her that Udara is about to perform the sacrifice: "This Gandharva approached her and said, 'There is a rather dangerous sacrifice called the Ekatrika, and your husband wants to perform it' " (2.126 tr. O'Flaherty). After hearing this from the *gandharva*, Udara's wife warns her husband not to perform this dangerous sacrifice.

The *Jaiminīya Brāhmaṇa* simply relates that his wife became a *gandharviṇī*. Yet immediately after this, the *gandharva* approaches her and begins speaking to her. After his wife shares with Udara what the *gandharva* has said, Udara instructs her to ask the *gandharva* if he will accomplish the sacrifice. The wife then asks the *gandharva* and he again warns her of the dangers of performing the sacrifice. What is clear from this episode in the *Jaiminīya Brāhmaṇa* is that although the wife is said to be possessed or seized by the *gandharva*, her form and appearance do not change. The fact that she maintains her own identity, separate from the *gandharva*, is evident from the fact that her becoming a *gandharviṇī* is not noticeable to her husband. Also, she continues to interact with her husband and have a dialogue with the *gandharva*. The major difference between these episodes is that in the *Jaiminīya Brāhmaṇa* the husband does not even notice that the *gandharva* is inhabiting his wife's body, while in the *Bṛhadāraṇyaka Upaniṣad* both Bhujyu and Uddālaka are aware of the identities of the *gandharva*s. Nevertheless, the *Jaiminīya Brāhmaṇa* account illustrates that possession by a *gandharva* does not necessarily imply losing either form or identity.

Returning to the debate in Janaka's court, we see that these discourses, which have been ventriloquized through women, serve as consequential challenges to Yājñavalkya. This is especially the case with Uddālaka, whose dramatic entry into the debate appears between Gārgī's two challenges and who is the only interlocutor to threaten Yājñavalkya. Uddālaka links his threat with what he heard from the *gandharva* about the inner controller (*antaryāmin*), warning Yājñavalkya that his head will shatter apart if he does not know this teaching. Thus, it is Patañcala's wife's teaching, ventriloquized by the *gandharva*, then repeated by Uddālaka, that Yājñavalkya has to prove that he knows if he wants to avoid his head shattering apart.

Despite the fact that this knowledge, which is central to this *brahmodya*, is linked to female identities, Patañcala Kāpya's wife and daughter are not acknowledged as speakers. In fact, their speech is doubly removed: it is attributed to the *gandharva*s, and the *gandharva*s' speech is recounted by eminent Kuru-Pañcāla brahmins. Here, the words of women are accepted within Vedic discourse, yet women themselves are given no authority.

THE AMBIGUITIES OF SATYAKĀMA'S MOTHER AND WIFE

Jabālā is another female character whose words are authoritative, yet whose speech is mediated by male speakers. Jabālā, the mother of Satyakāma, is one of the most fascinating, yet underappreciated characters in the Upaniṣads. Commentators and scholars focus on the truthfulness of her son Satyakāma, who becomes recognized as a brahmin by honestly admitting that he is uncertain about his lineage (CU 4.4.1–5). Indeed, in chapter 1 we looked at this tale from the point of view of Satyakāma as a model *brahmacārin*, exploring how his story addresses the importance of a pedagogical lineage in contrast to a family lineage. This story begins when Satyakāma asks his mother about his lineage because he wants to be a Vedic student. And later, when he approaches the teacher Hāridrumata, he repeats what his mother had told him: he states that he does not know his lineage because his mother moved around a lot when she was younger and consequently does not know the identity of his father. He then relates that his mother told him to introduce himself as Satyakāma Jābāla.[35] After offering this explanation, Satyakāma is praised by Hāridrumata for his honesty: "Only a brahmin is able to explain like that. Bring firewood, my boy. I will initiate you. You have not abandoned the truth (*satya*)" (CU 4.4.5).[36] As discussed in chapter 1, it remains ambiguous whether Satyakāma was already a brahmin or if he earns the status of a brahmin. In both readings, however, the emphasis is on Satyakāma and his truthfulness.

A different picture emerges when we focus on how this dialogue portrays his mother Jabālā. Although it is described, it is not emphasized in the narrative how Satyakāma learns the truth that he is later praised for telling. When Satyakāma asks his mother about his lineage, it is she who is admirably truthful: "My son, I do not know what your lineage (*gotra*) is. I became pregnant in my youth when I was a servant and moved around a lot. Because of this I do not know your lineage. But my name is Jabālā and your name is Satyakāma. You should merely say you are Satyakāma Jābāla" (CU 4.4.1).[37] When we consider Jabālā's explanation in light of Upanishadic attempts to define women as wives and sexual partners for brahmin men, it is quite extraordinary that she is so honest about her nonconforming sexual activity. In this respect, we could consider Jabālā the real truth lover (*satyakāma/ā*), because she is admitting details about herself that are not in accordance with the Upanishadic ideal of a woman as a faithful and supportive wife.

Furthermore, it is significant that Jabālā's explanation is repeated word for word by Satyakāma when he explains his lineage to Hāridrumata. Indeed, it is her speech, not his, that is the means by which Satyakāma is recognized as a brahmin. Of course, it is unlikely that Jabālā would report such information to a male brahmin teacher, but it is notable that when her words are repeated by her son they are praised for their truthfulness: when Hāridrumata responds to

Satyakāma's verbatim account of his mother's story, he exclaims that no one who is not a brahmin would be able to speak like this. Surely Jabālā would not have been praised as a brahmin if she had spoken directly to Hāridrumata. Perhaps it is the case that brahmins are not the only ones who can speak like Satyakāma, but that brahmins are the only ones who would be praised, while others would be censured.

However, it is also possible to read Jabālā's character as deliberately untruthful. Despite the fact that Satyakāma quotes his mother directly, he does not do what his mother tells him to do. After Jabālā explains why she does not know her son's lineage, she instructs him to introduce himself as Satyakāma Jābāla, perhaps implying that she wants her son to conceal her murky past. As Roebuck suggests: "Jabālā wants the boy to give the impression that he is the son of a man called Jabāla, by forming a patronymic rather than a metronymic from her name" (2003, 419n). However, it is not so clear that Jabālā intends to be deceitful. According to Olivelle, Jābāla is meant to be a matronym meaning "son of Jabālā" (1996, 341n). This reading would imply that Jabālā is simply giving her son a surname because she anticipates that he will be asked for one, not as a means to mask information about her past. Thus we are left with two possible ways to interpret Jabālā's instructions to her son. Either she is deceiving: "You should present your name as a patronym to make it seem like you know the true identity of your father"; or she is merely helpful: "Because we do not know the name of your father, why don't you just use my name instead." Both interpretations have decisive implications concerning female speakers. If we see her as dishonest then it follows that Satyakāma's truthfulness is linked to betraying the advice of his mother, as his identity as a brahmin is recognized at the moment when he exposes his own mother as a scheming liar. Yet if we see Jabālā as truthful, then she is not explicitly presented negatively, but is not given sufficient credit for providing her son with the truth with which he becomes Hāridrumata's student.

It is not only Satyakāma's mother whose motives and actions remain unclear, as his wife is presented in a similarly ambiguous way. Satyakāma's wife, who is not given a name, appears in a brief narrative scene that immediately follows the story featuring his mother. When Satyakāma is about to go on a journey and leave his student Upakosala behind, his wife warns him: "The student (*brahmacārin*) has practiced his austerities (*tapas*) and properly tended the fires. Teach him before the fires tell him first" (CU 4.10.2).[38] Instead of listening to his wife, Satyakāma leaves his home. Upon his return, he finds that his student, as his wife had anticipated, has been taught by the fires. In this story, Satyakāma's wife both predicts that his student will learn in his absence and displays a certain understanding of the process of Vedic learning.

Furthermore, the speech of Satyakāma's wife and that of the fires is almost exactly the same. Before the fires begin teaching Upakosala, they remark, "The student (*brahmacārin*) has performed his austerities (*tapas*) and properly tended us" (CU 4.10.4).[39] The similarity in speech establishes a connection between Satyakāma's wife and the teaching of the fires. Keeping in mind how the teachings of female speakers can be ventriloquized through male characters, it is significant that through speech Satyakāma's wife is connected to the fires, who become Upakosala's teachers. This connection points to the possibility that she is Upakosala's real teacher. Additionally, it is her advice to Upakosala to eat some food that initially leads to his instruction from the fires. When Satyakāma departs on his journey, his wife notices that Upakosala is not eating and encourages him to eat something, perhaps suggesting that she is familiar with Uddālaka's teaching (CU 6.7.1–6) that one cannot learn without proper nourishment. Admittedly, it is speculative to suggest that Satyakāma's wife is the real teacher of this discourse, but the similarity between her speech and the words of the fires indicates that there is a link between what she says and what Upakosala learns from the fires.

Another reading suggests that the connection between Satyakāma's wife and the fires might have sexual connotations. Simon Brodbeck (Pers. comm. Jan. 2005) points out that "being taught by the fires" could be a euphemism for a sexual relationship between Satyakāma's wife and his student. A sexual relationship between a teacher's wife and student is a common theme in later texts such as the *Mahābhārata*, and as we have seen in the Upaniṣads, a fire can be a metaphor for a woman's sexual organs: "A fire, that's what a woman is" (BU 6.2.13; CU 5.8.1). Additionally, it is pertinent that Satyakāma's wife offers Upakosala food, because throughout the Brahmanical literature there are clear connections between food and sex. Furthermore, the way in which Upakosala refuses his teacher's wife—referring to the desires (*kāma*) within him—suggests that more is being offered to him than food: "The desires (*kāma*) in this man are many and various. I am overwhelmed with sickness. I will not eat" (4.10.3).[40]

Despite the numerous subtle references and innuendos, we cannot say definitively that Satyakāma's wife is Upakosala's teacher or sexual partner, if not both. Similarly, the characterization of Jabālā remains ambiguous. Yet regardless of the uncertainties of their stories, Satyakāma's mother and wife are alike in that they are underdeveloped characters who initially appear to be marginal, but have much more active roles in the story of Satyakāma than usually recognized, even if the exact nature of their roles remains unclear. Although any negative actions they perform are more implicit than explicit, suspicion is cast on both of them: one perhaps for trying to conceal her past from her son's future teacher, the other perhaps for seducing her husband's student.

MAITREYĪ AND KĀTYĀYANĪ: KNOWLEDGE OF *ĀTMAN* VERSUS *STRĪPRAJÑĀ*

Although Gārgī and Jabālā are characteristic for their independence, and Satyakāma's wife is perhaps not as devoted to him as he would assume, the most standard representation of women in the Upaniṣads is in the role of the dutiful wife. In this way, the early Upaniṣads share with the Brāhmaṇas a similar view of the importance of marriage. According to the sacrificial texts, the ideal wife was the partner to her husband in ritual practices. As Jamison explains:

> One of the main technical requirements for being a Sacrificer is that he must be a householder (gṛhastha); he must be *married*. Not only that but the presence and participation of his wife is required to all solemn rituals. Sacrificer's Wife (patnī in Sanskrit) is a *structural role* in ritual with particular duties and activities that cannot ordinarily be performed by anyone else. (1996, 30)

Not only was the sacrificer's wife essential in terms of her mere presence, but her actions, although restricted, were both symbolically important and unique, in the sense that they could not be performed by anyone else. Jamison points out that the *patnī* "acts independently of her husband: she is not merely his double or shadow in ritual performance" (1996, 38).

Similarly, a number of stories in the Upaniṣads present the brahmin's wife as both necessary and marginal. Like Gārgī and Jabālā, brahmin wives often speak about the same things as eminent brahmin teachers, yet their speech is not granted the same legitimacy. Despite these limitations, we see that when the social location of Upanishadic teachings is the brahmin household, there is a certain amount of knowledge that is required for women to learn in order for knowledge to be able to produce the results that it promises. Brahmin wives are expected, therefore, to know certain teachings and participate in rituals for the sake of their husband's material gain and soteriological goals.

The story of Yājñavalkya and his two wives offers two competing ideals of the brahmin wife. Whereas Maitreyī is praised for her interest in Upanishadic teachings, the knowledge of Yājñavalkya's other wife, the voiceless Kātyāyanī, is equally reinforced. Besides Gārgī, Maitreyī is the only other female character who is explicitly depicted discussing philosophy in the Upaniṣads. She appears twice, in almost identical dialogues in the *Bṛhadāraṇyaka Upaniṣad* (2.4.1–14, 4.5.1–15).[41] In both dialogues, Yājñavalkya wants to make a settlement between Maitreyī and Kātyāyanī before he departs. Although these versions are quite similar, there are some important differences, eliciting different interpretations of Maitreyī's character.

In the first version, Yājñavalkya approaches Maitreyī saying, "I am about to depart from this state. Look, I will make a settlement between you and Kātyāyanī" (BU 2.4.1).[42] When we look at this episode in the context of other dialogues, it is relevant that Yājñavalkya initiates the conversation, but does not end up learning from Maitreyī. Throughout the Upaniṣads, we have seen three kinds of dialogues that feature two participants. In the first type, a student, usually carrying firewood, approaches his teacher and asks for instruction. The second case is the private *brahmodya*, in which two brahmins debate and the winner becomes the teacher of the loser. The third kind involves a brahmin and a *kṣatriya*, where the brahmin usually speaks first to the king, only to end up as his student. In all of these cases, the person who approaches the other becomes the student, either initially or eventually. Not only does Maitreyī's dialogue differ from others in this way, but also there are no formal indicators, such as firewood, to make this conversation an official teaching. This suggests that even when brahmins do teach women, it is not presented as a formal instruction and women cannot claim the authority of a proper education.

Rather than the typical circumstances for an Upanishadic teaching, the occasion for Yājñavalkya's instruction is his imminent departure (*ud yā*). Yājñavalkya's departure has usually been interpreted as his taking up a life of asceticism, yet in the first version of the dialogue the reasons for Yājñavalkya's departure remain unclear.[43] As Olivelle notes, although "it is traditionally assumed that he was leaving home to assume an ascetic way of life . . . in this version . . . the setting is probably the imminent death of Yājñavalkya, which would necessitate the partitioning of his estate" (1996, 306n). In light of the lack of any details suggesting renunciation, it is worth considering that discussions about *ātman* are often associated with understanding the process of death, and that much of this discussion with Maitreyī is related to immortality. Additionally, Yājñavalkya begins teaching Maitreyī after she suggests that Yājñavalkya's wealth is not important to her because it could not make her immortal, further suggesting that Yājñavalkya's imminent departure is related to death.

As we discussed earlier in this chapter, this dialogue is reminiscent of the several passages that describe the transmission of knowledge from father to son before the father's death (BU 1.5.17; KṣU 2.14). This dialogue is also about passing on knowledge, but presumably because he does not have any sons, Yājñavalkya passes his knowledge onto his wife instead. Taken in this way, this discussion between husband and wife perhaps represents an alternative to the father-son ceremony. This certainly seems possible when we take into consideration the fact that on other occasions it is Yājñavalkya who teaches that a man does not need to have sons to achieve immortality. Here he indicates that he can achieve his soteriological goals by means of passing on knowledge to his wife.[44]

The second version gives us much more information regarding the characters of both Maitreyī and Kātyāyanī: "Maitreyī was a *brahmavādinī*, while Kātyāyanī had only the knowledge of women (*strīprajñā*)" (BU 4.5.1).[45] Here Maitreyī is described favorably, while Kātyāyanī functions as a counterpoint to emphasize Maitreyī's interest in philosophical discussion. Moreover, Maitreyī does not seem interested in Yājñavalkya's inheritance, as she questions the value of wealth because it will not make her immortal. This comment further endears her to her husband, as indicated by Yājñavalkya's response: "You have always been dear to me. Now you have become more dear" (BU 4.5.5).[46] These words clearly show that Maitreyī earns preference in Yājñavalkya's eyes explicitly because of her interest in discussing philosophy.

Although she is praised for this interest, both accounts suggest that she does not completely comprehend Yājñavalkya's teaching. In the first version, she specifically states that he confuses (*muh*) her by saying there is no consciousness after death (2.4.13).[47] In the second version she expresses her confusion in more general terms, suggesting that she is confused by Yājñavalkya's discourse as a whole: "You have made me completely bewildered. I do not understand this at all" (4.5.14).[48] Thus, in the first version of the dialogue, Maitreyī is not confused by philosophy in general, but rather is merely challenging Yājñavalkya on a specific point. In fact, the precision of her question suggests that she has been following quite well what Yājñavalkya has been saying. As Rasmus Reinvang suggests, "Maitreyī is worried and confused as the fact that there, supposedly, is no consciousness after death would seem to make a state of immortality impossible . . . Maitreyī anticipates the unraveling of how one may attain immortality, but is being told that there is [no] knowledge of anything after death" (2000, 181–82). This reading of the dialogue implies that Maitreyī's confusion is not necessarily brought about by her own inability to understand, but rather by Yājñavalkya's muddled explanation. In fact, Reinvang considers whether Yājñavalkya is "deliberately obscuring" how his teaching relates to immortality. Taken this way, perhaps it is not so much that Maitreyī is confused, as she is pointing out to her husband that he is not making sense. In this way, it is possible to see Maitreyī's claim to be confused as a polite way of challenging her husband. As we have seen, Gārgī sarcastically praises Yājñavalkya as a way of indirectly pointing out that he has not answered her questions. Perhaps Maitreyī is being similarly indirect, stating her own confusion as a way of prompting her husband to deliver a more coherent teaching.

Another difference between the two accounts is that the first dialogue ends inconclusively, while the second version ends by saying that Yājñavalkya taught Maitreyī everything about immortality. Again, these details serve to portray Maitreyī differently. Whereas in the first version what Maitreyī learns remains unresolved, in the second version, despite the fact that her confusion is made more explicit, the conclusion indicates that Maitreyī has learned everything about immortality.

Maitreyī's character takes on other dimensions when we compare her to Kātyāyanī, Yājñavalkya's other wife. Kātyāyanī is named, yet she does not speak herself. In the first version there is no description of her character, but in the second version she is characterized as a woman who is only interested in women's knowledge (*strīprajñā*) (BU 4.5.1). As Maitreyī's interest in learning philosophy is praised, Kātyāyanī and her women's knowledge are presented as less important.

As a *brahmavādinī*, Maitreyī learns about *ātman*, but what is the *strīprajñā* that is associated with Kātyāyanī? Śaṅkara glosses *strīprajñā* as "minding household needs" (Findly 1985, 46). Roebuck, however, suggests that *strīprajñā* is specific to the knowledge of a brahmin wife, claiming that *strīprajñā* does not refer to "what all women know" but rather to "what every priest's wife knows: what food and robes her husband will need for each ritual, etc." (2003, 242n).[49] Other dialogues suggest that this knowledge would also include managing the household and filling in for the priestly duties of her husband in his absence.

Another example of *strīprajñā* might be the knowledge of Āṭikī, whose "women's knowledge" is an important survival skill that ultimately is responsible for Uṣasti securing the job as chief priest at a sacrifice (CU 1.10.1–6). As we have seen in chapter 2, Uṣasti is portrayed as a brahmin who is struggling for food and money and has to beg to support both himself and Āṭikī. The narrative recounts that after eating the leftovers he received from a rich man, Uṣasti took what remained to his wife. She, however, had already collected alms, so she took the food Uṣasti gave her and saved it. This scene shows that Āṭikī is not dependent on her husband for food and in fact feeds both of them due to her own resourcefulness.

The story continues, relating that the next day Uṣasti said, "If we could obtain food, we could obtain some money" (CU 1.10.6). This remark is similar to Uddālaka's teaching to Śvetaketu that one cannot remember the Vedic chants properly without food (6.7.1–6). In this case, it implies that Uṣasti can only earn money as an officiating priest if he eats. At this point in the story, Āṭikī speaks for the first time: 'Here, my dear, is the grain (*kulmāṣa*)" (CU 1.10.7). The narrative relates that he then ate the grain and was able to successfully perform the sacrifice, and consequently earn a lot of money. Although the story does not explicitly credit Āṭikī for her part in earning the money, it is clear from the details of the story that it is due to her ingenuity that Uṣasti is able to perform the sacrifice correctly. Similar to other female characters, Āṭikī's character is generally underdeveloped, yet her actions are crucial to the outcome of the story.

Another pertinent detail of this characterization of Āṭikī is that she is presented as the one who controls the food for her husband and herself. In addition to Āṭikī, in all the descriptions of procreation practices where a mixture was to be made and then eaten, the text explicitly states that the brahmin's wife should prepare the food. Additionally, as we have seen, Satyakāma's wife is linked with food, as she is the one who encourages Upakosala to eat. These examples indicate that a vital aspect of *strīprajñā* was cooking and distributing food in the household. Furthermore, they return us to the complexities surrounding female agency in the Upaniṣads. Whereas Āṭikī is depicted as an individual with considerable autonomy, who exercises influence over her husband, her agency is derived from her position as wife. Jamison makes a similar point in regard to how female characters are represented in the *Mahābhārata*: through marriage a woman "gains access to whatever active roles exist for women" (1996, 354). In the Upaniṣads, women who are married tend to assume the active roles of ritual participants and dispensers of food.

Returning to Kātyāyanī, although she does not display philosophical knowledge, she perhaps stands to gain more through *strīprajñā* than most people in the marketplace of Upanishadic teachings. As we have seen, her husband Yājñavalkya accumulates more wealth than any other character in the Upaniṣads, and as he cynically states before the debate at Janaka's court, wealth is the real objective of Upanishadic knowledge. Accordingly, if the cows, not to mention the gold, are the ultimate prizes for philosophical knowledge, then Kātyāyanī is the real winner in her settlement with Yājñavalkya, especially when we consider the gender bias of the texts that generally calls into question the ability of women to achieve immortality. As we have seen, towards the end of her discussion, Maitreyī admits that she is confused by what Yājñavalkya tells her, and the first version ends with a question that Yājñavalkya poses, but which remains unanswered (BU 2.4.13–14). As Yājñavalkya's teachings leave Maitreyī a confused *brahmavādinī*, Kātyāyanī's preference for *strīprajñā* might be exactly what makes her a very rich woman; as Maitreyī rejects Yājñavalkya's offer of material wealth for a confusing teaching, perhaps the voiceless Kātyāyanī is quite wise in her silence.

CONCLUSION

We began this chapter by looking at creation myths and procreation rituals. Significantly, in a number of accounts of creation, *ātman* is equated with the specifically male bodies of Puruṣa and Prajāpati. Yet despite privileging the male body and the male role in creation, these myths also recognize the complementary roles of male and female in creation. In this way, these sections are representative of the ambiguous and unresolved portrayal of gender in the Upaniṣads.

Next, we looked at how procreation rites contribute to defining an Upanishadic ideal of masculinity. As soteriological goals such as knowing *ātman* and achieving immortality are inextricably linked to producing male children in order to ensure male progeny, the ideal brahmin man must not only be married, but be virile and have control over his wife. Accordingly, much of the discourse that addresses the interaction between brahmins and women attempts to define and control the process of procreation.

Additionally, the brahmin male world is depicted as aggressive and competitive, and one of the ways that brahmins prove their superiority over each other is through their ability to control their wives' sexual behavior. In this respect, Yājñavalkya's interactions with Gārgī and Maitreyī offer an interesting challenge to brahmin orthodoxy. As

Yājñavalkya teaches that immortality is not connected to producing male children, thus suggesting that there is less at stake in controlling sexual relations, he is able to share his knowledge with women without threatening his own soteriological goals.

Indeed, despite the numerous hesitations, qualifications, and modifications surrounding the role of women in the discourse, there are a number of active female participants in Upanishadic narratives. One of the recurring themes in the dialogues between brahmins and women is how female speakers negotiate with the limitations that restrict their participation. Gārgī circumvents these restrictions by debating tactically and thereby putting herself on the winning side of the argument; Jabālā, rather than attempt to become a brahmin herself, uses her knowledge to prepare her son for his education; Kātyāyanī accumulates vast amounts of wealth by remaining silent. Another theme that connects these female characters, as well as others, is that they often have a central role in the drama of the narrative scenes in which they appear, even when they initially seem to be marginal figures.

Additionally, many of the narratives indicate that there are some Upanishadic teachings that women, at least the wives of brahmins, are expected to know. In these cases, a wife's contributions to her husband's soteriological ambitions are not merely reduced to her procreative capacity, but are established in her role in running the household, taking part in procreative rituals, and even contributing to the transmission of knowledge. The fact that there are a number of discourses and practices that a wife needs to know, points to the possibility that women, at least the wives of brahmins, were an anticipated audience of Upanishadic teachings.

The principal audience, however, was brahmin men, and it is important to keep in mind that the female characters are mostly depicted in ways that reinforce the ideals of brahmin men. Although these interactions with women are crucial, they are only one aspect of the lives of brahmins and their quest to achieve selfhood. As we have seen, throughout the Upaniṣads the dialogues indicate that achieving selfhood is as much about what one does and how one lives one's life, as it is about what one knows: that much of understanding *ātman* is tied into becoming a brahmin. Accordingly, brahmins not only must learn from the proper teacher (chapter 1), compete with other brahmins (chapter 2), and win patronage from kings (chapter 3), but also must have wives and produce children (chapter 4).

Conclusion

Both commentators within the Indian tradition and modern scholars have treated the Upaniṣads primarily as a collection of abstract philosophical doctrines, analyzing the transcendental claims without taking into consideration how philosophy is rooted within a social and historical context. It has been the intention of this book to look at the social dimensions of Upanishadic philosophy. Through highlighting and examining the dialogues, I have demonstrated that the narrative episodes are not merely superfluous information or literary ornamentation, but fundamental aspects of the philosophical claims of the texts.

I have focused on the social context that is provided by the texts themselves. As we have seen throughout this book, the social world of the Upaniṣads is not the realm of myth or fantasy, but rather represents the real, at least in an idealized representation, social world of ancient Indian brahmins. This is not to claim that the concrete scenes depicted in the stories and dialogues are historically true: I have not claimed that the *brahmodya* in King Janaka's court actually happened, or that Pravāhaṇa really taught the doctrine of the five fires to Uddālaka Āruṇi. Rather, this book maintains that these scenes represent the kinds of episodes that were part of the social world of brahmins. As a way of exploring the social dimensions of the Upaniṣads, I have discussed the dialogues in terms of four groups: (1) instructions passed from teachers to students, (2) debates between rival brahmins, (3) discussions between brahmins and kings, and (4) conversations between brahmins and women.

Throughout all four kinds of dialogues, *ātman* is the idea that is discussed most, although it is defined and explained in a number of ways by different literary characters. Despite the differences, however, knowledge of *ātman* consistently represents the new Upanishadic knowledge that is defined in contradistinction to the traditional Vedic knowledge about the sacrifice. The dialogues not only serve to highlight teachings about *ātman*, but also connect this knowledge to specific people and particular situations, indicating that knowledge of the self is particularly important to brahmins and to a number of specific situations in a brahmin's life. Thus, by means of looking at the dialogues, we have seen that the Upanishadic notion of the self is not merely a philosophical insight, but a way of living one's life.

We began by examining dialogues between teachers and students. These dialogues show an interest in the moment of instruction and record how knowledge is transmitted. By means of describing the interactions of specific characters, the dialogues outline modes of address and modes of behavior that accompany the transmission of knowledge. Different teachers employ different means of instruction, but in all cases they follow the script of the *upanayana*, and they all impart discourses about the self.

One of the central activities for brahmins is participating in the *brahmodya*. As we have seen, there are two main types of *brahmodya* that feature in the Upaniṣads: the private debates that establish a relative hierarchy among brahmins, and the public tournaments, which are depicted as competitive, and where the reputations of brahmins, and sometimes political power, is at stake. The *brahmodya* is especially emphasized in the *Bṛhadāraṇyaka Upaniṣad*, where Yājñavalkya uses the public debate as a forum for establishing authority for both himself and his patron, King Janaka of Videha. Yājñavalkya proves his superiority not only by displaying his knowledge of the discourse, but also by how he advances his arguments and marshals debating tactics. In addition to establishing himself as superior to a number of Kuru-Pañcāla brahmins, Yājñavalkya also emerges quite wealthy. As performing sacrifices is no longer the primary occupation of brahmins, Yājñavalkya is an example of how brahmins make a living in a changing world.

In addition to his success in winning philosophical debates, Yājñavalkya is also known for his friendly relationship with King Janaka. Indeed, the conversations between Yājñavalkya and Janaka are among several dialogues between brahmins and kings throughout the Upaniṣads. These dialogues often depict the king teaching the brahmin and in some cases even claim that particular doctrines originated among kings. As we have seen, however, many of these same doctrines are recorded in earlier Brahmanical literature and thus these claims cannot be taken as historically accurate. Nevertheless, this literary strategy taken by brahmin composers indicates that forging relationships with kings was an important aspect of establishing oneself as a successful brahmin. By linking philosophical doctrines to political power and describing the ideal king as one who hosts philosophical debates and gives generously to brahmins, the dialogues present both brahmins and their teachings as indispensable to a king's political and military success. As such, the dialogues between brahmins and kings outline the proper modes of address and behavior for brahmins to seek patronage from kings and for kings to secure the presence of brahmins in their court.

Besides kings, the other essential dialogical partners for brahmins are women. Many of the teachings in the Upaniṣads are concerned with securing immortality and connect immortality with having male children. Accordingly, a crucial aspect of Upanishadic teachings is about how to control sexual relations and the process of birth. Furthermore, these discourses establish idealized gender roles for men and women. Brahmin men are depicted as confrontational and aggressive, both in their interactions with other brahmin men and in their relations with their wives. Women are defined primarily as procreative bodies and supportive wives, helping their husbands maintain the household fires and helping to prepare mixtures in procreation rites. Nevertheless, Gārgī and Maitreyī have a more active participation in Upanishadic philosophy, as Gārgī in particular not only shows her knowledge of the discourse, but also demonstrates her understanding of the practice of philosophy by debating both tactically and aggressively.

Through focusing on the social situations provided by the dialogues, I have also explored a number of related issues regarding the historical context of ancient India. The most fundamental matter is a shift in attitude concerning the sacrifice. As discussed in the introduction, it seems unlikely that economic or political pressures contributed to an actual decline in the practice of sacrifice. However, the early Upaniṣads strongly criticize the sacrifice and focus on other activities as the practices which most give knowledge authority. This movement away from sacrifice at a textual level indicates that the composers and editors of the Upaniṣads were attempting to define their roles as brahmins in different ways to audiences who no longer found the sacrifice favorable. In fact, not only do brahmins define themselves as teachers and court priests rather than as ritualists, but also the ideal king is one who learns philosophy and hosts philosophical debates rather than one who is the patron of the sacrifice. In this way, the early Upaniṣads not only replace sacrifice with a number of different practices for brahmins, but promote discursive knowledge as the new political currency for brahmins that promises political and military success to kings.

Inextricably related to changing attitudes about the sacrifice are new means of establishing the status of brahmins. As we have seen, the Upaniṣads, on several occasions, criticize those who are merely brahmins based on their family lineage, and offer new ways to consider individuals as brahmins. The new ideal was not someone born as a brahmin, but one who becomes a brahmin by learning about the self. However, these changes do not suggest that the status of brahmin was open to everyone, but rather these new means for defining brahmins was mostly an attempt to establish a hierarchy within the brahmin community. In most of the dialogues that make a point of distinguishing those who are brahmins by birth from those who are brahmins because of their knowledge, the individual in question is already a brahmin. For example, Śvetaketu is encouraged to go receive a proper education, and Naciketas rejects the ritualism of his father. Both students are already brahmins by birth before they are initiated into the Upanishadic teachings of the self. In these cases the point is not that knowledge about the self is enough to make one a brahmin, but rather for those who are already brahmins, it is better to learn and teach about the self than to perform rituals. Defining a brahmin is fundamental because, as we have seen, one of the central aspects of knowledge about the self is not merely the content of the discourse, but also who is teaching the discourse. The dialogues illustrate that knowledge of the self is not an insight that can be achieved through solitary introspection, but rather has to be received from the proper teacher by means of the accepted method of transmission; one can only understand the meaning of the self through someone else who knows.

The changing attitude about sacrifice and the new ways of defining brahmins are prominent themes in both the *Bṛhadāraṇyaka Upaniṣad* and the *Chāndogya Upaniṣad*; however, the two texts differ in how they respond to these social changes. The *Chāndogya Upaniṣad* is more traditional, offering up the ideal brahmin as both teacher and householder. Like the *Bṛhadāraṇyaka Upaniṣad*, the *Chāndogya Upaniṣad* presents knowledge of the self as more beneficial than performing sacrifices, yet the *Chāndogya Upaniṣad* is more conservative in who can have access to this new knowledge by insisting that the teacher is more valuable than the knowledge itself and refusing to depict brahmins being initiated by kings.

The *Bṛhadāraṇyaka Upaniṣad*, however, pushes the critique of ritualism much further. Yājñavalkya, for example, establishes his knowledge, not by means of learning from the proper teacher, but through directly defeating more orthodox brahmins. Additionally, the *Bṛhadāraṇyaka Upaniṣad* does not refrain from showing brahmins being initiated by kings. The most radical change in the *Bṛhadāraṇyaka Upaniṣad*, however, is its critique of the brahmin household. Both through the teachings of Yājñavalkya and his interaction with female characters, the *Bṛhadāraṇyaka Upaniṣad* challenges the assumption that only married brahmin men with sons can achieve selfhood and immortality. Significantly, this anticipates the Buddhist critique of Brahmanism, which also attempts to forge relationships with kings based on philosophy but which takes the critique of the householder even further.

Despite the competing agendas of the *Bṛhadāraṇyaka Upaniṣad* and *Chāndogya Upaniṣad*, both Upaniṣads employ the dialogue form to present their teachings. In both texts, the dialogue form is used to critique the Vedic sacrificial paradigm, to set up new ideals for brahmins, and to connect these new ideals to specific doctrines and practices. Indeed, as much as any particular doctrine, the use of the dialogue is one of the most consequential legacies of the Upaniṣads in relation to subsequent Indian literature. Most generally, the dialogue form itself characterizes philosophy as a social practice. Although the Upaniṣads are sometimes represented as the abstract insights of renunciates, the texts depict philosophy as an interactive process: philosophy is something that is achieved through discussion and debate, confrontation and negotiation. Despite emphasizing knowledge about individual selves, this knowledge can only be achieved through dialogue with others.

Furthermore, the dialogue form focuses attention on a number of specific individuals, many of whom were already authoritative figures in Vedic literature. Characters such as Śāṇḍilya, Uddālaka Āruṇi, and Yājñavalkya were already known as famous priests and textual composers, but the Upanishadic dialogues further develop their personalities, creating legends of ideal teachers and court priests. The stories not only use the names of these individuals to authorize specific teachings, but also use the narratives to portray these individuals as leading a specific kind of life. In this way, the Upanishadic portrayals of its literary characters are similar to hagiographies, as they anchor religio-philosophical claims to specific ways of leading one's life. Whereas Satyakāma lives the life of a teacher and married householder, Yājñavalkya represents a challenge to this ideal as the priest who debates in the court and leaves his household without any male heirs. Both Satyakāma and Yājñavalkya embody their teachings, their different stories offering two distinct models of how to be a brahmin.

These features of the dialogues not only help us understand doctrines about the self, but they also can be instrumental in exploring how the Upaniṣads have influenced subsequent Indian texts. Many scholars note that the Upaniṣads have influenced early Buddhism. Yet similar to how Upanishadic philosophy is characterized in general, the influence of the Upaniṣads on early Buddhism is described as taking place in the hermetically sealed realm of ideas. The early Buddhist texts, however, like the Upaniṣads, use both narrative and dialogue to present the message of the Buddha's teachings. Furthermore, there are a number of specific literary tropes and narrative situations that are quite similar. Both Yājñavalkya and the Buddha leave a life of riches that is associated with the court and the household for a life of renunciation. Also, the Buddha, like Yājñavalkya, debates against several opponents in the presence of the king. Whereas all of Yājñavalkya's opponents represent different Vedic schools, the Buddha's opponents represent rival religio-philosophical movements. These similarities suggest that one of the major influences of the Upaniṣads on the early Buddhist texts is the mode of presentation. Both textual traditions present philosophical ideas in the form of a dialogue, as well as attach teachings to specific individuals in particular moments in space and time.

Similarly, the Upaniṣads have had a crucial influence on subsequent Brahmanical literature. Knowledge continues to be portrayed as both elusive and dangerous, and the reluctant teacher and eager student remain as standard tropes. In particular, the dialogue form continues to be the most common mode of presentation for religio-philosophical ideas in the Brahmanical tradition. Not only is the *Bhagavad Gītā* presented as a conversation between Kṛṣṇa and Arjuna, but even texts such as the *Mahābhārata* and the Purāṇas are framed within a dialogue. In this way, in addition to representing the birth of philosophy in ancient India, the Upaniṣads mark the beginning of the dialogical presentation of philosophical ideas. By means of this particular literary device, philosophical ideas are presented in the form of discussions and debates, formal instruction and secret teachings; and in the context of public tournaments and courtly assemblies, financial exchanges and intimate relations. By means of the dialogue form, philosophy is connected with a number of specific social practices, and is characterized as entrenched within the affairs of everyday life.

Notes

INTRODUCTION

1. *ṛgvedaṃ bhagavo' dhyemi yajurvedaṃ sāmavedamātharvaṇaṃ caturthamitihāsapurāṇaṃ pañcamaṃ vedānāṃ vedaṃ pitryaṃ rāśiṃ daivaṃ nidhiṃ vākovākyamekāyanam devavidyāṃ brahmavidyāṃ bhūtavidyāṃ kṣatravidyāṃ nakṣatravidyāṃ sarpadevajanavidyāmetadbhagavo' dhyemi // so'ham bhagavo mantravidevāsmi nātmavit* / CU 7.1.2–3. The translations of passages from the Upaniṣads are my own. See Roebuck's notes for the meaning of a number of the terms in this passage (2003, 423–24).

2. Deussen, Hume, and Radhakrishnan have all focused primarily on the identification with *brahman* as the most fundamental teaching of *ātman*. Olivelle, as well as scholars such as Bodewitz and Brereton, have paid more attention to the diversity of teachings about *ātman*, as well as other important ideas.

3. Throughout this book, the word 'dialogue' will be used to refer to conversations in the Upanishadic literature between two or more people, much like this word is used to refer to the dialogues of Plato. The use of this word is not intended to invoke the works of philosophers such as Gadamer and literary theorists such as Bakhtin, who employ this word in technical and idiosyncratic ways.

4. Olivelle dates the *Bṛhadāraṇyaka Upaniṣad* and *Chāndogya Upaniṣad* between the seventh and sixth centuries BCE and the *Kauṣītaki Upaniṣad*, the *Taittirīya Upaniṣad*, and the *Aitareya Upaniṣad* between the sixth and fifth centuries BCE (1996, xxxvi). These dates take into consideration recent scholarship that has placed the Buddha's death between 375 and 355 BCE.

5. Edgerton, for example, is one of several scholars to a make this distinction between the Upaniṣads and previous Vedic texts: "The Upaniṣads are the earliest Hindu treatises, other than single hymns or brief passages, which deal with philosophic subjects" (1965, 28).

6. Although it is important to note that the Upaniṣads and Indian thought in general have a number of features that are distinct from European philosophy, I see no reason to limit the term 'philosophy' to the Western tradition. Lipner (1998) and Mohanty (1993, 313–30; 1992, 21–25) are two scholars who have argued exhaustively and convincingly, in my opinion, that the term 'philosophy' is perfectly legitimate for the Indian context.

7. Scholarly consensus has dated these texts between 300–100 BCE and has regarded them as post-Buddhist compositions (Olivelle 1996, xxxvii).

8. The *Aitareya Upaniṣad* appears as *Aitareya Āraṇyaka* 2.4–6. Also there are two other sections in the *Aitareya Āraṇyaka* that are known as Upaniṣads: the *Mahaitareya* (or *Bahvṛcabrāhmaṇa*) *Upaniṣad* (AĀ 2) and the *Saṃhitā Upaniṣad* (AĀ 3). See Keith ([1909] 1995, 39–41) for further discussion.

9. The *Taittirīya Upaniṣad* appears as sections 7, 8, and 9 of the *Taittirīya Āraṇyaka*.

10. There are four extant Āraṇyakas: the *Aitareya Āraṇyaka*, the *Taittirīya Āraṇyaka*, the *Śāṅkhāyana Āraṇyaka*, and the *Bṛhadāraṇyaka Upaniṣad*.

11. For example, see the *Śatapatha Brāhmaṇa* (6.1.1.8). Smith (1989, 57) calls Puruṣa the 'alter ego' of Prajāpati. See also Gonda (1986).

12. For further discussion see Smith (1989, 58).

13. Brereton explains that creation myths like this one are not meant to recount the actual process of creation, but rather to establish "the connections that now exist within the world" (1990, 120).

14. *tad yathā tṛṇajalāyukā tṛṇasyāntaṃ gatvā anyam ākramam ākramya ātmānam upasaṁharati / evam evāyam ātmā idaṃ śarīraṃ nihatya avidāṃ gamayitvā anyam ākramam ākramya ātmānam upasaṃharati* // BU 4.4.3.

15. The exact meanings of the terms designating the bodily winds continue to be contested among scholars. Olivelle translates them as breathing out (*prāṇa*), breathing in (*apāna*), breathing that moves up (*udāna*), the breath that traverses (*vyāna*), and the breath that equalizes (*samāna*). Bodewitz explains succinctly that sometimes the *prāṇā*s are the breaths and sometimes they are the senses, the power behind the senses or even the organs of sense. For a detailed account of the semantic range of *prāṇa* from the *Ṛgveda* to the Upaniṣads, see Ewing (1901). For other discussions of *prāṇa* see Zysk (1993), Connolly (1997), Bodewitz (1992), and Roebuck (2003, xxx–xxxi).

16. Sometimes it is a competition between *prāṇa* and the life-breaths, while at other times it is a contest between *prāṇa* and the vital functions. On one occasion, the *prāṇā*s are linked to deities (*devas*) (KṣU 2.13).

17. The *Chāndogya Upaniṣad* (3.12.4) also describes the *prāṇā*s as resting within the heart.

18. . . . / *taṃ na kaścana pāpmā spṛśati* / CU 8.6.3.

19. Olivelle describes the world of the fathers as a conception "closely connected with social memory and the inheritance of property" (1997a, 434).

20. See Olivelle (1997a) for a further discussion of the many interrelated meanings of *amṛta* in Vedic literature.

21. *puruṣe ha vā ayam ādito garbho bhavati yad etad retaḥ / tad etat sarvebhyo 'ṅgebhyas tejaḥ saṃbhūtam ātmany evātmānaṃ bibharti / tadyadā striyāṃ siñcatyathainajjanayati / tad asya prathamaṃ janma // tad striyā ātmabhūyaṃ gacchati yathā svam aṅgaṃ tathā / tasmād enāṃ na hinasti / sāsyaitam ātmānam atra gataṃ bhāvayati* // AU 2.1–2.

22. Witzel refers to this legend as an origin myth for the Videha kings. In this respect it is significant that Agni Vaiśvānara is the same Agni which is invoked in the very first hymn of the *Ṛgveda*.

23. Witzel explains that "this is *not* a legend of the Indo-Aryan settlement of the east . . . but it is a tale of Sanskritization, of the arrival of Vedic (Kuru-Pañcāla) orthopraxy in the east" (1997, 311).

24. For example, King Pravāhaṇa's teaching of the five fires, which he claims in both the *Bṛhadāraṇyaka Upaniṣad* (6.2.8) and the *Chāndogya Upaniṣad* (5.3.7) had never reached the ears of brahmins before, appears in the *Jaiminīya Brāhmaṇa* (1.4.5), but without a frame dialogue (Bodewitz 1973, 216).

25. As Theodore Proferes explains, the Upaniṣads represent an editorial moment as much as a philosophical one (pers. comm., April 2003).

26. The *Kūṭadanta Sutta* (DN 5), for example, describes the excess violence of sacrifice in vivid detail. Also the Aśokan inscriptions indicate that the king effectively outlawed the practice of sacrifice during the Mauryan Empire (Thapar 1984, 97; Fitzgerald 2001, 2004, 114–23).

27. In his enjoyable and provocative book, Grinshpon (2003) has also looked at the relationship between form and content in the Upaniṣads, with quite different results than those found in this book. He employs what he calls a "Good Enough" reading, arguing that many of stories in the Upaniṣads depict a personal crisis, the experience of which leads the character to knowledge.

28. I am using the term *ārya* strictly in its Sanskrit sense as denoting a cultured person who knows Sanskrit and behaves according to the sensibilities of orthodox Brahmanism. In this sense, *ārya* is a term denoting a particular cultural and social identity and does not in any way imply a racial identity.

29. Some of the dialogues in the late Brāhmaṇas and early Upaniṣads do contain enigmatic questions similar to the Rigvedic style riddle. For example, in the *Jaiminīya Brāhmaṇa* (1.19–20) Yājñavalkya poses a riddle to Janaka about the mind (*manas*).

30. *mahātmanaś caturo deva ekaḥ kaḥ sa jagāra bhuvanasya gopāḥ / taṃ kāpeya nābhipaśyanti martyā abhipratārin bahudhā vasantam* // CU 4.3.6.

31. *ātmā devānāṃ janitā prajānāṃ hiraṇya daṃṣṭro babhaso 'nasūriḥ / mahāntam asya mahimānam āhuranadyamāno yad anannam atti* // CU 4.3.7.

CHAPTER ONE. TEACHERS AND STUDENTS

1. Many of these literary tropes such as the reluctant teacher and the enthusiastic student, which are employed subsequently throughout Indian texts, are first seen in the late Brāhmaṇas and early Upaniṣads.

2. The genealogical lists are found in BU 2.6.1–3, 4.6.1–3, and 6.5.1–4. Śāṇḍilya's teaching about *ātman* and *brahman* is in CU 3.14.1–4.

3. . . . / *eṣa ma ātmāntar hṛdaye / etad brahma / etam itaḥ pretyābhisambhavitāsmi* . . . / CU 3.14.4.

4. Chattopadhyaya remarks, "Uddālaka was about the only prominent thinker in the Upaniṣads in whose discourse the word Brahman never occurs at all" (1986–87, 41).

5. *Uktha* is the technical term for the verses of the *Ṛgveda* that are recited during a sacrifice. Thus, in this passage, *ātman* is identified with the three types of Vedic formulas: the *uktha* refers to the verses of the *Ṛgveda*, the

sāman refers to the chants of the *Sāmaveda*, and the *brahman* refers to the *yajus* formulas of the *Yajurveda*. See Olivelle (1996, 301n).

6. There are also a number of different meanings of *brahman* in subsequent literature related to the Upaniṣads, such as the *Bhagavad Gītā* and texts within the Vedānta tradition. See Lipner (1986).

7. Additionally, *brahman* is closely connected to sound, often considered to be a verbal expression of the ultimate reality. As Olivelle points out, "It is important to remember that the concept always retains its verbal character as the 'sound expression' or truth or reality" (1996, lvi). For a further discussion of *brahman*, see Gonda (1950).

8. Furthermore, Hume maintains that the composers of the Upaniṣads "were always aware of the underlying unity of all being" ([1921] 1975, 1).

9. Connolly also argues that too much emphasis has been put on *ātman* and *brahman*. He is especially critical of the Advaita Vedānta philosophers, who, he maintains, "willfully misrepresented the teachings of the Upaniṣads" (1997, 36–37). Connolly makes a good case that some of the conceptions of *ātman* and *brahman* "were originally employed to characterize *prāṇa*" (1997, 21).

10. As Witzel suggests, the Vedic use of the demonstrative pronoun indicates that "these texts were taught and recited on the offering ground" (1997, 259).

11. Also Mahidāsa is quoted in the early Upaniṣads (CU 3.16.7; JUB 4.2).

12. Other teachers whose names are employed to authorize a teaching, but who do not feature in a dialogue include Vāmadeva (AU 2.5), Prācīnayogya (TU 1.6.2), Triśaṅku (TU 1.10), Kauṣītaki (CU 1.5.2), Nāka Maudgalya, and Kumārahārita (BU 6.4.4).

13. Both Kenneth Zysk (1991) and D. P. Chattopadhyaya (1986–87) argue that these discussions about *ātman* and the body are some of the earliest articulations of medical knowledge in ancient India.

14. *ta iha vyāghro vā siṃho vā vṛko vā varāho vā kīṭo vā pataṅgo vā daṃśo vā maśako vā yad yad bhavanti tad ābhavanti* // CU 6.9.3, 6.10.2.

15. Roebuck raises objections to Brereton's argument, pointing out that "there are numerous places in the Upaniṣads where the authors have departed from the strict rules of grammatical gender to make a teaching point" (2003, 423n).

16. Other discourses in the Upaniṣads are also presented as naturalistic. As Killingley observes, the *Bṛhāraṇyaka Upaniṣad* version of the teaching about the five fires and two paths "can be read as describing a biological process in which life descends in the form of rain and is eventually born as a living being" (1997, 17).

17. This connection is implied in other dialogues as well. See, for example, CU 1.10.6 and 4.10.3.

18. There are similar descriptions of the *upanayana* in the *Pāraskara Gṛhyasūtra* (2.2), the *Aśvalāyana Gṛhyasūtra* (1.20), and the *Śāṅkhāyana Gṛhyasūtra* (2.1), as well as the *Mānava Dharmaśāstra* (2.36–249). However, as the material in the Brāhmaṇas is more closely associated with the Upaniṣads, we will confine our description of the *upanayana* to how it appears in the *Śatapatha Brāhmaṇa*.

19. The Sāvitrī is a verse from the *Ṛgveda* (3.62.10) dedicated to Savitṛ, the sun. In later texts such as the *Mānava Dharmaśāstra*, reciting the Sāvitrī is considered to be one of the most essential aspects of an initiation ritual. The verse is divided into three parts, each of which is considered to contain the essence of one of the three Vedas. See Olivelle (2004, 238, 240n) and Roebuck (2003, 389n).

20. Although Kaelber is keen to present the *upanayana* as having an archaic origin, there is no evidence that this description in the *Śatapatha Brāhmaṇa* harkens back to an earlier practice. In fact, Eliade does not "demonstrate" that the *upanayana* is of archaic origin, but merely speculates that the *upanayana* is a "homologue to primitive puberty initiations" (1958, 53).

21. There are exceptions: the *Chāndogya Upaniṣad* mentions a *brahmacārin* who settles permanently at his teacher's house (2.23.1). Olivelle, following Böhtlingk and Senart, takes this passage as a late interpolation (1996, 334–35n). Additionally, Indra is a *brahmacārin* for 101 years (CU 8.11.3). See Olivelle (1993) for a discussion on how the life of a *brahmacārin* became incorporated as the first of the four stages of life represented by the *āśrama* system (the other stages are: married householder, retired householder and renouncer).

22. In the introduction, I briefly mention that Upanishadic dialogues represent real life situations and situate philosophy within everyday social practices. How do we then account for the appearance of Prajāpati, Indra, and Virocana? As I have mentioned, these mythical characters connect the Upaniṣads with the authority of traditional Vedic figures. These examples show how the composers of the Upaniṣads use legendary figures from Vedic folklore to add legitimacy to new doctrines. For the most part, however, Upanishadic characters are based on humans rather than on gods. Even in this scene, except for the exaggerated life span of Indra, the words and actions of all the main characters are consistent with depictions of humans in other dialogues.

23. This myth also appears in other places in the Upaniṣads. In the *Chāndogya Upaniṣad* (1.2.1), the *devas* and *asuras* compete with each other over the *udgītha* (the chanting of the *Sāmaveda*).

24. Prajāpati also appears as a teacher in the *Bṛhāraṇyaka Upaniṣad* (5.2.1), where he instructs *devas*, *asuras*, and humans.

25. The Lokāyatas, also known as the Cārvākas, were a materialist school of philosophy who accepted only sense perception as a valid means for acquiring knowledge. Although perhaps originally one of the branches of Vedic learning, in post-Upanishadic times the Lokāyatas were often represented by Hindu philosophical doxologies, along with the Buddhists and the Jains, as one of the main rival positions to the orthodox *darśanas* (See Mohanty 2000; King 1999, 16–23). Chattopadhyaya claims that in the *Chāndogya Upaniṣad* (1.12), Baka Dālbhya expresses views associated with the Lokāyatas (1959, 76–79). For other references to the Cārvāka school see R. Bhattacharya (2002).

26. This practice of treating the body of the deceased is similar to how the Buddha's body is treated in the *Mahāparinibbāna Sutta*: "Then the Mallas ordered their men to bring perfumes and wreaths, and all the musicians, and with five hundred sets of garments they went to the sāl-grove where the

Lord's body was lying. And there they honoured, paid respects, worshipped and adored the Lord's body with dance and song and music, with garlands and scents, making awnings and circular tents in order to spend their day there" (DN 16.6.13 tr. Walshe).

27. Roebuck translates *ativādin* as one who "speaks boldly" (see 2003, 425 n.27). Olivelle, who translates *ativādin* as a man who "out-talks" (1996, 353n), agrees that this term can be used both positively and negatively. Radhakrishnan translates *ativādin* as "excellent speaker" ([1953] 1992, 483n) and Hume renders this term as "superior speaker" ([1921] 1975 *passim*).

28. O'Flaherty suggests that this story may have been inspired by *Ṛgveda* 10.135 (1981, 56).

29. The fact that this episode in the *Kaṭha Upaniṣad* appears almost exactly as it does in the *Taittirīya Brāhmaṇa* has led most scholars to think that this *adhyāya* is one of the older portions of the Upaniṣads. Also it is commonly assumed that this dialogue was originally part of the *Kāṭhaka Brāhmaṇa*. Passages 1, 2, and 4 of the *Kaṭha Upaniṣad* are exactly the same as passages in the *Taittirīya Brāhmaṇa*. In the *Taittirīya Brāhmaṇa* his wishes are (1) to return to his father, (2) to learn the durability (non-decaying) of sacrifice and rituals acts (*'na + kṣit'*: a play on words of Naciketas. He not only is named after a fire altar, but also is one who does not decay), and (3) to learn how to ward off death.

30. Another meaning of *naciketas* is "I do not know." Although Whitney demonstrates the linguistic foundation for this rendering, he himself is skeptical of this interpretation: "This, though not entirely without parallels, would be an irregular and an odd thing in Sanskrit derivation" (Whitney 1890, 91). However, there is no reason to assume that only one meaning was intended. Considering that Naciketas plays the role of the student in this dialogue, his name as one who does not know is quite appropriate.

31. This metaphor continues throughout the Upaniṣads as well. For example, the *Taittirīya Upaniṣad* states that the *puruṣa* in a man and the *puruṣa* in the sun are the same (2.8). See also *Chāndogya Upaniṣad* (1.7.5).

32. Another section in the *Chāndogya Upaniṣad* states that only a man with knowledge could carry out a sacrifice (2.24.1).

33. O'Flaherty comments briefly on this story, suggesting that this episode expresses the theme of the son who emerges as better than his father, which she argues is an important motif throughout Vedic literature (1985, 43–44).

34. The aspects of the sacrifice mentioned are the offering (*iṣṭa*), the protracted sacrifice (*sattrāyaṇa*), the vow of silence (*mauna*), the period of fasting (*anaśakāyana*), and also the way of the forest (*araṇyāyaṇa*).

35. Here, we see the symbolism connecting initiation with procreation. The *brahmacārin* is considered the embryo of his teacher, his initiation representing his second birth.

36. As we will see, Satyakāma leaves his student in his house for a prolonged period of time as well.

37. As part of his first wish, Naciketas also wants his father's anger to subside and wants his own death to be symbolic rather than actual. In his first

wish we see that Naciketas desires to reestablish his connection with the world, thus illustrating the importance of family lineage. Although the dialogue with Satyakāma, as we will see, suggests that the lineage of teachers is more important than the lineage of families, the Upaniṣads nevertheless place importance on the relationship between father and son.

38. *ā mā yantu brahmacāriṇaḥ svāhā / vi mā yantu brahmacāriṇaḥ svāhā / pra mā yantu brahmacāriṇaḥ svāhā / damāyantu brahmacāriṇaḥ svāhā / śamāyantu brahmacāriṇaḥ svāhā //* TU 1.4.2. The meaning of this passage is unclear (see Olivelle 1998, 573n). What does seem clear, however, is that this passage represents a teacher's plea for students.

39. *yaśo jane 'sāni svāhā / śreyān vasyaso 'sāni svāhā /* TU 1.4.3.

40. A man should not steal gold, drink liquor, kill a brahmin, or sleep with a brahmin's wife (CU 5.10.9).

41. . . . *ācāryaḥ pūrvarūpam // antevāsy uttararūpam / vidyā sandhiḥ / pravacanaṃ saṃdhānam /* TU 1.3.2–3.

42. See Grinshpon for a detailed survey of the interpretations offered in the scholarly literature (2003, 45–56). Although I think Grinshpon overinterprets this story in suggesting that Jabālā is a *śūdra* (member of the lowest class), he makes some interesting speculations about the possible conflict between mother and son.

43. It is quite possible that the text is supposed to be ambiguous. Although this story opens up the possibility that Satyakāma does not originally come from a brahmin family, his mother's family name already appears in earlier texts. On two occasions in the *Śatapatha Brāhmaṇa,* we see the character Mahāsāla Jabālā. The texts give no indication, however, what the relation is between Mahāsāla and Satyakāma. On one of the occasions where Mahāsāla appears in the *Śatapatha Brāhmaṇa,* he is one of the five wealthy householders that approach Aśvapati for a teaching about *ātman* (10.6.1). Curiously, in the version of this dialogue that appears in the *Chāndogya Upaniṣad,* all the names of the householders are the same except that Mahāsāla is replaced by Prācīnaśāla Aupamanyava. It seems possible that as the editors of the *Chāndogya Upaniṣad* want to emphasize the uncertainty of Satyakāma's family lineage, they omit the one other Vedic character who shares his family name. Indeed, if there is a relation between Mahāsāla and Satyakāma, then Satyakāma was perhaps already a brahmin. The *Bṛhāraṇyaka Upaniṣad* (4.6.1) mentions a similar name, Jābālāyana, in one of its genealogies.

44. There are several other examples of students who take care of their teachers' cows. The *Śatapatha Brāhmaṇa* (3.6.2.15) tells us that a student should guard his teacher, his teacher's house, and his cows. Also Yājñavalkya instructs his student to take care of the cows that he claims before his debate with the Kuru-Pañcāla brahmins (BU 3.1.2).

45. Here I am following Roebuck in taking *magdu* as cormorant (2003, 419n).

46. Another example of this exchange of work for teaching occurs in the *Aitareya Āraṇyaka* (3.1.6). In this episode Tārukṣya guards his teacher's cows for one year just for the sake of learning a secret teaching (*upaniṣad*).

47. This point is also part of Uddālaka's instruction to Śvetaketu (CU 6.14.2).

48. Here, I am following Roebuck's rendering of *sādhiṣṭhaṃ prāpati* as 'attains the best.' See Roebuck (2003, 420n).

49. . . . *ha na kiṃ cana vīyāyeti vīyāyeti* . . . // CU 4.9.3.

50. Satyakāma's teaching is closely related to the discourse of the five fires, which we will discuss in more detail in chapter 3.

CHAPTER TWO. DEBATES BETWEEN BRAHMINS

1. See Renou and Silburn (1949), Brereton (1999), Thompson (1997, 1998), Houben (1998), and Johnson (1980).

2. Witzel points out that the *brahmodya* was usually part of large-scale *soma* rituals and the *aśvamedha* (1987a, 385).

3. Both *brahmodya*s begin with the same question: who is it that walks alone. In both cases the answer is the sun. The eighth question in the first *brahmodya* is the sixth question in the second (q: who is the tawny one; a: the night and day). The fifth question of the first *brahmodya* is also the fifth question of the second (q: what is the first conception; a: the sky). Additionally, some of the same exchanges that appear in these two examples also appear in *Vājasaneyi Saṃhitā* 23.45–46. See Thompson for a further discussion of these types of riddles (1997, 14–15).

4. For a discussion about this dialogue and its relation to the *agnihotra* (twice-daily milk offering) and *prāṇāgnihotra* (offering of food to the breaths) see Bodewitz (1973, 220–29). Another version of this episode appears in the *Gopatha Brāhmaṇa* (1.3.14).

5. The *vedi* is the sunken area between the fires in the consecration ground of a Vedic ritual. The area, strewn with grass, was where the gods were invited to sit as guests, while priests sang hymns and made offerings in their honor.

6. Elsewhere I suggest that there is a third situation: when one character uses the threat of head shattering to force his or her opponent into answering a direct question. This characterizes Yājñavalkya's warning to Śākalya in Janaka's court, as well as the Buddha's challenge to Ambaṭṭha in the *Ambaṭṭha Sutta* (Black, forthcoming).

7. Bodewitz describes chariots as the luxury cars for the Vedic elite (1974, 90).

8. Witzel points out that a gold coin is given in a similar dialogue in *Gopatha Brāhmaṇa* (1987a, 367).

9. The *Bṛhadāraṇyaka Upaniṣad* further portrays Yājñavalkya as an inventive figure by the language used in the sections attributed to him. As Fišer argues, the style of the Yājñavalkya sections is more innovative, and a number of new words are coined: "Yājñavalkya's individuality is documented by his language" (1984, 60–61).

10. Yājñavalkya discusses the *agnihotra* with Śvetaketu, Sātyayajñi, and Janaka (ŚB 11.6.2.1); he is quoted as an expert on the *agnihotra* (12.4.1.10; 2.3.1.21).

11. In the *Śatapatha Brāhmaṇa* he is known only as Yājñavalkya, whereas both names are used in the *Jaiminīya Brāhmaṇa* and the *Bṛhadāraṇyaka Upaniṣad.*

12. As Fišer explains, "In most cases the stock phrase 'as to this/ point/ however, Yājñavalkya said' (*tad u hovāca yājñavalkyaḥ*) introduces a new idea that implies, at the same time, an objection to what was said immediately before" (1984, 59 n.10). There is a similar episode where Yājñavalkya's views are presented in contrast to Śaulvāyana's (ŚB 11.4.2.17). In this case Yājñavalkya's views are again presented last and predicated by the same phrase (*tad u hovāca yājñavalkyaḥ*).

13. In the Brāhmaṇas, attributing views to a *ṛṣi* is often a way of quoting the *Ṛgveda.*

14. Śāṇḍilya is quoted and no one else is mentioned (7.5.2.43); he teaches the Katīyas (9.4.4.17); Śāṇḍilya quotes Tura Kāvaśya (9.5.2.15); he disputes with his student (although this exchange is contentious, this dialogue is presented as a teacher/student dialogue) (10.1.4.11); Śāṇḍilya teaches about *ātman* (10.6.3.2).

15. The compilation of the *Śatapatha Brāhmaṇa* suggests a personal rivalry between Śāṇḍilya and Yājñavalkya. While Yājñavalkya is mentioned more than anyone else in the *Śatapatha Brāhmaṇa,* his appearances are almost entirely limited to the sections of the text ascribed to him. In sections six through nine, attributed to Śāṇḍilya, Yājñavalkya is not mentioned at all.

16. Grinshpon interprets this tournament as describing Yājñavalkya's "self-transformation from a person who does not know into a sage who does" (1998, 381). Although an interesting reading, this *brahmodya,* as we will see, seems to be much more about how Yājñavalkya uses his knowledge, rather than about what he learns during the process of the debate. In fact, this is a key difference that distinguishes the *brahmodya* from the *upanayana,* which does describe the process of learning.

17. Brereton argues that the debate in Janaka's court is a ring composition that is similar in structure to the framework of the Vedic sacrifice (1997, 3). Although my own analysis of this debate is more concerned with the unfolding of the narrative and the interaction between the characters, I generally accept Brereton's argument. I believe that these two approaches do not contradict each other, and that, in fact, the text operates on both levels. Furthermore, both approaches are similar in the sense that they attempt to read the Upaniṣads as "coherent composition[s]" (1997, 3n.7) rather than merely the gathering together of diffuse fragments.

18. Witzel suggests that "there may have been a sudden movement of the Aitareyins towards the east" (1987a, 404). That the *Ṛgveda* had an established presence in Videha is suggested by the fact that the only priest other than Yājñavalkya who is specifically associated with Janaka is the *hotṛ* priest Aśvala.

19. Bhadrasena Ājātaśatrava does not appear anywhere else in Vedic literature. Eggeling speculates that he was the son of King Ajātaśatru ([1882–97] 1994, Part 3:141).

20. The *Jaiminīya Brāhmaṇa* (1.58–9) version of this discussion does not mention Uddālaka Āruṇi. See Bodewitz (1973, 183) for further discussion.

21. In this case Uddālaka's name only appears as Āruṇi, yet he is addressed as Guatama. Yājñavalkya is referred to as Vājasaneya.

22. Buḍila Āśvatarāśvi also appears in the *Śatapatha Brāhmaṇa* (10.6.1.7) and as a student of Janaka in the *Bṛhadāraṇyaka Upaniṣad* (5.14.8).

23. The Jain sources claim that Chandragupta Maurya, the first Mauryan emperor, was a patron of the Jains and that he converted to Jainism towards the end of his life by giving up the throne and joining a monastery. His son Bindusāra, is associated with the Ājīvikas, but is thought to have been a patron of brahmins as well as of Parivrājakas (religious wanderers). Aśoka, who is known to have favored the Buddhists, also supported the Ājīvikas and Jains. See Thapar (2002, 164–65; 1994, 11–25). See also Basham for the doctrinal differences between the Buddhists, Jains, and Ājīvikas (1951).

24. Fišer points out that of the three occasions where Yājñavalkya is quoted in the fourth book of the *Śatapatha Brāhmaṇa*, twice his views are cast into doubt (1984, 69).

25. . . . / *sa eṣa neti nety ātmā / agṛhyo na hi gṛhyate / aśīryo na hi śīryate / asaṅgo na hi sajyate / asito na vyathate / na riṣyati* / BU 4.2.4.

26. That Yājñavalkya wins his arguments by means other than his philosophical knowledge is similar to Socrates, who does not always win arguments according to their logical consistency. Many of Socrates' arguments are "fallacious or unsound" (Beversluis 2000). Or as Vlastos points out, Socrates "wins every argument, but never manages to win over an opponent" (1971, 2).

27. Olivelle points out that these terms have a double meaning in this passage: "Within the ritual, *graha* refers to the cup used to draw out *soma* and *atigraha* refers to the offering of extra cupfuls of *soma*. Within the context of the body, *graha* is a sense organ and *atigraha* is the sense object grasped by it. The passage attempts to show how the grasper itself is grasped by what it grasps, i.e., the sense object" (Olivelle 1996, 309n).

28. Additionally, this teaching is different from those given by other Upanishadic teachers. Both Ajātaśatru and Prajāpati offer teachings that suggest that the breaths do depart from the body at the time of death.

29. . . . / *yatrāsya puruṣasya mṛtasyāgniṃ vāg apyeti vātaṃ prāṇaś cakṣur ādityaṃ manaś candraṃ diśaḥ śrotram pṛthivīṃ śarīram ākāśam ātmā . . . kvāyaṃ tadā puruṣo bhavati* / BU 3.2.13.

30. . . . / *āharạ somya hastam ārtabhāga / āvām evaitasya vediṣyāvo na nāv etat sajana* . . . / BU 3.2.13.

31. In the *upanayana* in the *Śatapatha Brāhmaṇa* (11.5.4.12), the teacher takes the student by the right hand. Also Ajātaśatru takes Dṛpta-Bālāki by the hand when he receives him as a student (BU 2.1.15).

32. Eggeling translates *aṃsala* as "tender" ([1882–97] 1994 Part 2: 11). Fišer offers "juicy" or "fleshy" (1984, 69).

33. I would like to thank my friend and colleague Steven Lindquist for pointing out Yājñavalkya's pragmatic attitude regarding ritual (pers. comm., Nov. 2002).

34. This *brahmodya* is based on a similar episode in the *Śatapatha Brāhmaṇa* that also takes place in Janaka's court and features both Yājñavalkya and Śākalya. However, in the *Śatapatha Brāhmaṇa,* Śākalya is the only challenger. Similar to Svaidāyana he debates with Yājñavalkya on the behalf of a number of other brahmins (11.6.3.1–11). A similar account is in the *Jaiminīya Brāhmaṇa* (2.76–77).

35. It is interesting that in the *Śatapatha Brāhmaṇa* (11.6.3.2) version there is no mention of Yājñavalkya's student Sāmaśravas, whose name suggests that he is connected to the *Sāmaveda.* Indeed, this is the only occasion where Yājñavalkya is depicted as having a student and his very brief appearance illustrates that Yājñavalkya is much more known for his participations in debates than he is as a teacher. That Yājñavalkya asks Sāmaśravas to drive away the cows is not surprising, as we saw in the previous chapter that taking care of a teacher's cows was an important duty for students.

36. . . . / *namo vayaṃ brahmiṣṭhāya kurmo gokāmā eva vayaṃ sma . . .* / BU 3.1.2.

37. Witzel argues that there are three conditions for the splitting of the head during a philosophical debate: (1) insufficient knowledge and lack of admission of this, (2) perpetration of forbidden actions, and (3) asking a forbidden question (1987a, 375). Insler points out that this is one of just two occasions where this threat is used in response to improper ritual procedure (the other is in ŚB 3.6.1.23). Rather than head shattering, the usual threats for not performing the ritual correctly are the ruin or death of the sacrificer and his family (1989–90, 100).

38. There are exceptions to this. Insler, however, agrees that although these instances are not all *brahmodyas,* the topics are "phrased in this narrative with the prevalent terminology of theological disputes" (1989–90, 101).

39. Both Hume and Radhakrishnan translate this phrase as the "head will fall off"; Roebuck's rendering is "your head will split apart"; Olivelle's translation is "your head will shatter apart."

40. For a more detailed study of this episode in the *Ambaṭṭha Sutta,* as well as other parallels with the Upaniṣads, see Black (forthcoming).

41. *sattadhā muddhā phalissati.*

42. *sacâyaṃ Ambaṭṭho māṇavo Bhagavatā yāva tatiyakaṃ sahadhammikaṃ pañhaṃ puṭṭho na vyākarissati etth' ev' assa sattadhā muddhaṃ phālessāmi.*

43. "And at the sight, Ambaṭṭha was terrified and unnerved, his hairs stood on end, and he sought protection, shelter and safety from the Lord" (DN 3.1.21 tr. Walshe).

44. Insler explains: "the vocabulary of the JB tales is quite distinct from that of the other Brahmanic stories concerning theological discussions. Where the latter employ the uniform collocation *mūrdha vipatati* and the like, the JB narratives appear with the verbs *praharati* and *prajaghāna* (*mūrdhānam*)" (1989–90, 105). Although it is clear that the *Jaiminīya Brāhmaṇa* story is a different

kind of story than the narrative accounts of the *brahmodya*, it is not necessarily the case that this is also true of the Ambaṭṭha tale. In fact, the Ambaṭṭha tale has a number of features that indicate similarities with Upanishadic stories (Black, forthcoming).

45. Part of Insler's argument is also based on the similarities between the head shattering incidents and an episode in the *Ṛgveda* (4.9) where a young poet loses his concentration while trying to compose a poem in front of his father.

46. Brereton argues that the shared details from the *Śatapatha Brāhmaṇa* version of the story frames the entire *Bṛhadāraṇyaka Upaniṣad* episode (1997). This seems quite likely, especially when we take into consideration the importance of embedding and framing within ancient Indian literature (Minkowski 1989; Witzel 1987b). My point here, however, is that the change in the narrative between the *Śatapatha Brāhmaṇa* and the *Bṛhadāraṇyaka Upaniṣad* accounts of Śākalya's death highlights the threat of head shattering and presents Yājñavalkya as responsible, at least on some level, for Śākalya's death.

47. In Bhujyu Lāhyāyani's account, Patañcala Kāpya's daughter is possessed by a *gandharva* and the identity of the *gandharva* is Sudhanvan Āṅgirasa. We will discuss the issue of *gandharva* possession in more detail in chapter 4.

48. . . . / *tac cet tvaṃ yājñavalkya sūtram avidvāṃs taṃ cāntaryāmiṇam brahmagavīr udajase mūrdhā te vipatiṣyati* / BU 3.7.1.

49. . . . / *tad eva bahu manyedhvaṃ yad asmān namaskāreṇa mucyedhvam* / BU 3.8.12.

50. Witzel points out that Śākalya's name is a double entendre. One of the meanings of his name is "the clever one." This is appropriate as Yājñavalkya's victory in the debate is more meaningful when Śākalya is cast as a strong opponent. However, his name can also mean "burnt up," "cremated," or "decomposed," all of which foreshadow his eventual fate in this *brahmodya* (Witzel 1987a, 405).

51. *śākalya . . . tvāṃ svid ime brāmaṇā aṅgārāvakṣayaṇam akratā u* . . . // BU 3.9.18.

52. . . . / *taṃ tvaupaniṣadaṃ puruṣaṃ pṛcchāmi* / *taṃ cen me na vivakṣyasi mūrdhā te vipatiṣyati* . . . / BU 3.9.26.

53. Rather curiously, after recounting his death, the text adds that his bones were later stolen by thieves, who mistook them for something else. Witzel discusses this cryptic detail (1987a, 380).

54. As discussed in the previous chapter, there are a number of criticisms of sacrifice in the early Upaniṣads. Most of the Upanishadic teachings generally, and especially the dialogues, take the position that discursive knowledge is more important than ritual activity.

55. Heesterman (1985), Tull (1989), and Biardeau (1994) all emphasize the continuity of the tradition, especially the notion that the sacrifice was internalized. Thapar (1984) argues that the sacrifice declined because of economic factors.

56. Although Yājñavalkya is associated with his desire for wealth in the *Bṛhadāraṇyaka Upaniṣad*, in the *Śatapatha Brāhmaṇa* he is contrasted with Aupoditeya, who explicitly asks for cows. Here it is Aupoditeya who is depicted as seeking the material rewards of the sacrifice, and Yājñavalkya is cast as the more traditional brahmin who strives for the correct performance of the ritual. Yājñavalkya says, "For at this indeed the brahmin should strive, that he be a *brahma-varcasin* (illumined by the *brahma*, or sacred wit)" (ŚB 1.9.3.16 tr. Eggeling). By the time of the Upaniṣads, however, Yājñavalkya is the brahmin most associated with material wealth.

57. . . . / *kim artham acārīḥ paśūn icchannaṇvantān* . . . / BU 4.1.1.

58. Initially, the steward cannot find Raikva, but Jānaśruti instructs him to search again "in a place where one would search for a non-brahmin" (CU 4.1.8). Here we see an example of someone who is not a brahmin by birth, but who is treated with the respect of a brahmin because of his reputation for being knowledgeable.

59. This is the only instance in the Upaniṣads where land is given in exchange for an Upanishadic teaching. In fact, Jānaśruti's gift to Raikva resembles the *brahmadeyya* as described in the early Buddhist literature. These were tracts of land given as "royal gifts" from the king to eminent brahmins. Gokhale describes these dwellings as villages "predominantly inhabited by Brahmanas . . . designed in a proprietary way for the residence and maintenance of learned brahmins" (1994, 28–29). Additionally, the marriage represented in this dialogue resembles the practice of bride price. As Witzel points out, this type of marriage is extremely rare in the Brahmanical textual tradition (1996, 164). For more discussion on bride price in ancient Indian texts, see Jamison (1996, 213–15).

60. In response to Aśvala at the *brahmodya* in Janaka's court, Yājñavalkya shows he knows all the other priestly duties.

61. Madeleine Biardeau also emphasizes the continuity of the tradition, especially the notion that the sacrifice was internalized: "[After the Brāhmaṇas] sacrifice is not abandoned, but instead of offering it to the gods, in real fire, it is offered to one's *ātman*, in the fire of breath. All the outward observances are thus, partially at least, internalized" (1994).

62. Some might suggest that Pravāhaṇa's teaching of the two paths of the dead (BU 6.2.15; CU 5.10) also indicates a renunciate culture, as the king distinguishes between those who live in the forest (*araṇya*) and those who perform sacrifices and give gifts. It seems clear that these passages are contrasting the kind of brahmins that we see in Upaniṣads with the paradigmatic Vedic ritualists, who are ridiculed on many occasions. However, it is far from clear that the people living in the forest, as mentioned in this passage, are necessarily renunciates. Additionally, Pravāhaṇa states that there are two kinds of people who can avoid repeated death: those who live in the forest and those who know about the five fires. Thus, even if those who live in the forest are meant to be renunciates, the king's teaching inidicates that one need not be a renunciate to know and benefit from this teaching.

63. . . . / *etam eva viditvā munir bhavati* / *etam eva pravrājino lokam icchanaḥ pravrajanti* / BU 4.4.22.

64. . . . / *te ha sma putraiṣaṇāyāś ca vittaiśaṇāyāś ca lokaiṣaṇāyāś ca vyutthāya atha bhikṣācaryaṃ caranti* / BU 4.4.22.

65. *same śucau śarkarāvahnivālukāvivarjite śabdajalāśrayādibhiḥ* / *mano 'nukūle na tu cakṣupīḍane guhānivātāśrayaṇe prayojayet* // SU 2.10.

66. In the *Chāndogya Upaniṣad* Satyakāma is quoted after an account of the battle of *prāṇās*, whereas in the *Bṛhadāraṇyaka Upaniṣad* he is quoted after the *mantha* rite.

CHAPTER THREE. KINGS AND BRAHMINS

1. . . . / *yatheyaṃ na prāk tvattaḥ purā vidyā brāhmaṇān gacchati* / *tasmādu sarveṣu lokeṣu kṣatrasyaiva praśāsanam abhūd* . . . / CU 5.3.7.

2. Bodewitz also has a more recent article (1996a) in which he explores the development of the *pañcāgnividyā*, again demonstrating that this teaching originally appeared in texts without the frame narrative. Additionally, Killingley analyzes the connections between the *pañcāgnividyā* in the *Bṛhadāraṇyaka Upaniṣad* and the *Chāndogya Upaniṣad* with similar passages in the *Śatapatha Brāhmaṇa* and the *Jaiminīya Brāhmaṇa* (1997).

3. A similar teaching appears in the *Aitareya Āraṇyaka* (2.1.3), and the five fires appear as a secret teaching of the *agnihotra* in the *Śatapatha Brāhmaṇa* (11.6.2.6–10).

4. Olivelle comments, "It is naive, therefore, to accept the literary evidence of the Upaniṣads regarding their *Kṣatriyas* authorship at face value and as historical fact . . . The most we can say is that some segments of the Brahmanical community must have perceived it as advantageous to present doctrines they favored as coming from the royal elite" (1996, xxxv).

5. *Ātman vaiśvānara* means the "self of all people." For further discussion see the section about Aśvapati in this chapter.

6. This is especially true of Janaka, as we will see in the following examples. Also, Aśvapati gives the brahmins who have come to study from him as much as he pays priests to perform a sacrifice (CU 5.11.5). Similarly, Ajātaśatru offers Gārgya one thousand cows but then ends up teaching the brahmin himself (BU 2.1).

7. It is interesting that in this episode brahmins such as Yājñavalkya, Śvetaketu, and Sātyayajñi are all depicted riding chariots. As we have seen, Uddālaka Āruṇi also appears in a chariot when he is riding around the northern country of Madras (JUB 3.2.4.8; ŚB 2.4.1.6). Bodewitz has challenged Heesterman's suggestion that the connection between chariot driving and theological discussion might relate back to older ritual practices. Instead, he argues that there is no ritual connection and that chariots represent the luxury car of the Vedic elite (1974, 90). When we recall that brahmins commanded high rewards for their teachings, then it is not surprising that they traveled around on chariots. This tendency of brahmins to conspicuously display their

wealth becomes the subject of ridicule in the early Buddhist texts. For example, in the *Ambaṭṭha Sutta* the Buddha accuses the brahmin Ambaṭṭha and his teacher of indulging in luxurious pleasures such as riding in chariots drawn by mares with braided tails (DN 3.2.10).

8. Bodewitz argues that this episode does not imply a chariot race (1974, 89). This is likely to be true in the sense that there is no reason to take this episode as a description of an actual or a ritual race. Nevertheless, metaphorically, the fact that both king and brahmin are featured on chariots undoubtedly adds competitive symbolism to their verbal dispute.

9. Here Yājñavalkya resembles other reluctant teachers such as Prajāpati and Yama.

10. . . . / *atha ha yaj janakaś ca vaideho yājñavalkyaś cāgnihotre samudāte* / *tasmai ha yājñavalkyo varaṃ dadau* / *sa ha kāma praśnam eva vavre* / *taṃ hāsmai dadau* / *taṃ ha samrāḍ eva pūrvaṃ papraccha* // BU 4.3.1.

11. . . . / *so'ham bhagavate sahasraṃ dadāmi* / *ata ūrdhvaṃ vimokṣāya brūhi* . . . // BU 4.3.14; 15; 16; 33. Many translators have assumed that Yājñavalkya is teaching Janaka how to attain final liberation (*mokṣa*). Radhakrishnan, for example translates this line: "Sir, please instruct me further for the sake of my liberation" ([1953] 1992, 259–60). Taking into account the reference to the *Śatapatha Brāhmaṇa*, my understanding of this dialogue is as a confrontation between priest and king, where Yājñavalkya is attempting to release himself from the wish he had granted to Janaka. Olivelle (1996, 316n) maintains that the terms *mokṣa* and *vimokṣa*, both of which mean 'release' in a general sense, are not used in the early Upaniṣads specifically in connection with final liberation.

12. . . . / *atra ha yājñavalkyo bibhayāṃ cakāra medhāvī rājā sarvebhyo māntebhya udarautsīd* . . . // BU 4.3.33.

13. As compared with the *Bṛhadāraṇyaka Upaniṣad* account, the *Kauṣītaki Upaniṣad* version provides more information about Gārgya, describing him as a man who is learned (*anūcāna*) and well-traveled.

14. It is significant that the number of cows is the same amount that Janaka offers to Yājñavalkya. However, unlike the cows offered to Yājñavalkya, the cows offered to Gārgya are not adorned with gold.

15. Ajātaśatru's attempt to achieve a status on par with Janaka not only shows the political importance of Upanishadic teachings, but further brings to attention the particular rivalry between Kāśi and Videha, a rivalry that is also articulated by Gārgī Vācaknavī when she is debating against Yājñavalkya in Janaka's court. As we have seen, when she questions Yājñavalkya on the second occasion, she compares her challenge to that of a warrior from Kāśi or Videha (BU 3.8.2). Although the *Bṛhadāraṇyaka Upaniṣad* generally describes Yājñavalkya's opponents as brahmins from Kuru-Pañcāla, Gārgī's challenge suggests that she herself might be from Kāśi. As Gārgī presents her own challenge as representing a fight between Videha and Kāśi, she indicates that, as Yājñavalkya is associated with Videha, she is a warrior from Kāśi. That Gārgī perhaps has a connection to Kāśi is interesting because her name suggests that she is related to the Gārgya, who is teaching Ajātaśatru, the king of

Kāśi. Witzel proposes that Gārgī's name makes her a member of the Gārga family, indicating that she would "represent the (originally) more Western schools like the one to which Uddālaka belonged" (1987a, 403). Although her family may have originally come from the west, these two examples bring up the possibility that this name is associated with Kāśi.

16. In the *Chāndogya Upaniṣad* their names are Prācīnaśāla Aupamanyava, Satyayajña Paulusi, Indrayumna Bhāllaveya, Jana Śārkarākṣya, and Buḍila Āśvatarāśvi. In the *Śatapatha Brāhmaṇa*, Mahāsāla Jābāla appears instead of Prācīnaśāla Aupamanyava. It is pertinent that the *Chāndogya Upaniṣad* specifically designates these brahmins as householders (*mahāśāla*), a point that we will explore further in the next chapter.

17. Both Olivelle and Roebuck render *ātman vaiśvānara* as the "self of all men." Roebuck suggests that this term is not meant to refer to a specific doctrine of the self, but rather to a general understanding of the self: "Later, the term is specialised to refer to just one form of the *ātman* (e.g., ManU [*Māṇḍūkya Upaniṣad*] 3) but here it seems to be used of the self in the widest sense" (Roebuck 2003, 421–22n). As we will see, the primary reason for specifying what kind of self Aśvapati teaches about, is that it is in contradistinction to a similar dialogue in the *Śatapatha Brāhmaṇa* where he teaches about the *agni vaiśvānara*.

18. This is following Eggeling's rendering that *samiyāya* should be taken impersonally to mean that there was no argument among them. Sāyaṇa, however, interprets this passage to mean that Aruṇa was unable to instruct them. See Eggeling ([1882–97] 1994, 4:393).

19. . . . / *na me steno janapade na kadaryo na madyapaḥ* / *nānāhitāgnir nāvidvān na svairī svairiṇī kutaḥ* // CU 5.11.5.

20. See Chakravarti (1996, 150–76), Gokhale (1994, 110–20), and Tambiah (1976).

21. See Black (forthcoming) for a comparison of the structure of this story with that of the *Ambaṭṭha Sutta* in the *Dīgha Nikāya*.

22. The three narrative sections are pointed out by Söhnen (1981, 179).

23. Actually, in the *Bṛhadāraṇyaka Upaniṣad* his name appears the other way around, as Jaivali Pravāhaṇa.

24. Olivelle argues that the grammatical form of *pari-car* as *paricārayamāṇam* refers to serving food, yet also has sexual connotations (1999, 58).

25. The particular reception described in the *Chāndogya Upaniṣad* is part of the traditional way of receiving guests as outlined in the Gṛhyasūtras: the *Āśvalāyana Gṛhyasūtra* 1.24.7 and the *Pāraskara Gṛhyasūtra* 1.3.1. See Olivelle for further discussion (1999, 60–61).

26. . . . / *upaimyahaṃ bhavantam* . . . / BU 6.2.7.

27. . . . / *tam etam ātmānam eta ātmāno 'nvavasyante yathā śreṣṭinaṃ svāḥ* / *tad yathā śreṣṭhī svair bhuṅkte* . . . / KṣU 4.20.

28. In the *Bṛhadāraṇyaka Upaniṣad* version of this dialogue the word *ātman* does not occur. Rather, *puruṣa* is described as the site where the *prāṇā*s gather together, a description often associated with *ātman*.

29. There is a similar passage in *Śatapatha Brāhmaṇa* (10.5.2.11), where the loss of consciousness during sleep is presented in explicitly sexual terms. The persons of the right and left eyes are specifically gendered as male and female, and during sleep these two persons unite together within the cavity of the heart. The bliss (*ānanda*) that they experience through their union is linked with the loss of consciousness that one experiences during sleep. See Olivelle (1997b).

30. Throughout Vedic literature, the moon is depicted as where people go when they die. As we will see in Pravāhaṇa's teaching, those who go to the moon and make it become full are not released from the karmic cycle, but return to the earth again as rain. Thus, knowing the *mantra* not only brings death to one's enemies, but further ensures that they do not escape the karmic cycle to become immortal.

31. Similarly, in the *Taittirīya Upaniṣad* (1.6.2), the *puruṣa* within the heart is compared to a king. When *puruṣa* obtains sovereignty (*svārājya*) over the other organs of sense, it becomes lord (*pati*).

32. This myth appears at *Chāndogya Upaniṣad* 5.1.6–5.2.2; *Bṛhadāraṇyaka Upaniṣad* 1.5.21, 6.1.1–14; *Kauṣītaki Upaniṣad* 2.13, 3.3; *Praśna Upaniṣad* 2.1–4; and *Śāṅkhāyana Āraṇyaka* 9.

33. Bodewitz (1992, 54) further claims that the kingship of *prāṇa* was originally a theme of the *Sāmaveda* that was then developed in the *Bṛhadāraṇyaka Upaniṣad*.

34. For a further discussion see Smith (1990). Also, we will discuss this metaphor in the section about Pravāhaṇa and the teaching of the five fires.

35. According to the *Bṛhadāraṇyaka Upaniṣad*, when a man knows that breath is food, nothing he eats is considered improper food (6.1.14). Similarly, in the *Chāndogya Upaniṣad* (5.2.3) Satyakāma teaches that breath is food. See also *Taittirīya Upaniṣad* 1.5.

36. Here the *prāṇā*s are called *devas*.

37. Several scholars have attempted to define the institution of the court in Upanishadic times (Rau 1957; R. S. Sharma 1999b; Drekmeier 1962). However, connecting the Upaniṣads with a specific conceptualization of the court is difficult because the terminology employed by the texts to describe the residence of the king is inconsistent. For example, all three versions of the story of Uddālaka, Śvetaketu, and Pravāhaṇa/Citra use different terms to refer to the residence of the king. The *Bṛhadāraṇyaka Upaniṣad* uses the word *pariṣad*, the *Chāndogya Upaniṣad* uses *samiti*, and the *Kauṣītaki Upaniṣad* uses *sadas*. Furthermore, the *Chāndogya Upaniṣad* (8.14.1) refers to Prajāpati's court as the *sabhā*. Although we do not have enough information to understand the specific nature and workings of the court during Upanishadic times, it is clear that the myth of the *prāṇā*s shows a courtly orientation.

38. Killingley points out that this part of Pravāhaṇa's teaching, which he calls the "Two Paths pericope" has a different set of antecedents in Vedic literature than his teaching of the five fires. The allegory of two paths was first used in the *Ṛgveda* (10.88.15), and there are a number of passages parallel to

Pravāhaṇa's presentation of two paths in the Brāhmaṇas and Upaniṣads (1997, 13–16). According to Killingley, one of the most important innovations of Pravāhaṇa's teaching is that, as it appears in the *Bṛhadāraṇyaka Upaniṣad* and the *Chāndogya Upaniṣad*, it is the first teaching that combines the five fires with the two paths of the dead, both of which are themes found in older Vedic material (1997, 17).

39. Killingley rightly points out that this part of Pravāhaṇa's teaching appears slightly differently in its two versions (1997, 7–8). In the *Chāndogya Upaniṣad*, the two groups of people who avoid repeated death are those who have knowledge of the five fires and those who venerate faith as austerity (*tapas*).

40. We might assume that Uddālaka fits into the first category as well, as the dialogues suggest that he is frequently the guest of kings.

41. See the *Aitareya Brāhmaṇa* (8.25) and the *Śatapatha Brāhmaṇa* (11.5.6.9, 10.4.3.9). Bodewitz (1996b, 36) argues that repeated death is more of an argument against anti-ritualists than a belief. In other words, not only is the ritual effective against death, but it would be effective against multiple deaths. See also Olivelle (1997a).

42. *tasmād vā etasmād annarasamayāt / anyo 'ntara ātmā prāṇamayaḥ / tenaiṣa pūrnaḥ* / TU 2.2.

43. Gārgya's name is also Dṛpta-Bālāki, which can mean "the proud Bālāki." Olivelle comments that it is unclear whether *dṛpta* is part of his name or merely an epithet (1996, 302 n.).

44. . . . / *mā maitasmin saṃvadiṣṭhāḥ* / BU 2.1.2–13. Olivelle equates this phrase with modern vernacular quips like "Give me a break!" (1999, 66). These remarks resemble the verbal exchanges of a *brahmodya*.

45. *ye vai ke cāsmāl lokāt prayanti candramasam eva te sarve gacchanti / teṣāṃ prāṇaiḥ pūrvapakṣa āpyāyate / tān aparapakṣeṇa prajanayati / etad vai svargasya lokasya dvāraṃ yac candramāḥ* / KṣU 1.2.

CHAPTER FOUR. BRAHMINS AND WOMEN

1. This phrase is borrowed from Findly (1985), whose work on Gārgī we will discuss later in this chapter.

2. The vision of a woman that indicates a successful ritual performance is also mentioned in the *Śāṅkhāyana Āraṇyaka* (9). Bodewitz suggests that the vision of a woman is sometimes connected with kingship (1992, 59).

3. . . . *kathaṃ nu mātmana eva janyitvā saṃbhavati / hanta tiro 'sānti* / BU 1.4.4.

4. This is similar to the Puranic creation myth of Puruṣa and Prakṛti where Prakṛti is the active and dynamic force in creation. In this passage, as well as the Puranic myth, it is the woman who puts creation in motion.

5. . . . *ahaṃ vāva sṛṣṭir asmyahaṃ hīdaṃ sarvam asṛkṣi* . . . / BU 1.4.5.

6. *tasyā vedir upastho lomāni barhiś carmādhiṣavaṇe samiddho madhyatastau muṣkau* / BU 6.4.3. The word *vedi* is feminine and is often homologized with masculine words in the Brahmanical ritual literature. The feminine dimen-

sion of the *vedi* is further highlighted by the fact that its hourglass shape is often compared to a woman with large breasts and full hips, and a slender waist.

7. Another example appears in the *Jaiminīya Brāhmaṇa* (1.45–6) where *agni vaiśvānara* is compared to both the male and female body. The male is defined in terms of the five sense capacities, while the female is defined in terms of the sexual organs.

8. *upamantrayate sa hiṃkāraḥ / jñapayate sa prastāvaḥ / striyā saha śete sa udgīthaḥ / prati strīṃ saha śete sa pratihāraḥ / kālaṃ gacchati tan nidhanam / pāraṃ gacchati tan nidhanam / etad vāmadevyaṃ mithune protam* // CU 2.13.1.

9. Indeed, defining and controlling the process of birth within a male-dominated discourse is characteristic of a number of religious and mythological traditions. There are many religious myths that attribute the act of giving birth to men. For example, in Greek mythology Athena is born from the head of Zeus. In the Torah, Eve is created from Adam's body. For a discussion about the male appropriation of birth in the Western philosophical tradition see Jantzen (1998, 141–43).

10. Similarly, in the *Chāndogya Upaniṣad* (1.5.2), Kauṣītaki teaches that one can manipulate how many children one has according to how one venerates (*upa ās*) *ātman*.

11. . . . / *sa yadyanena kiṃ cid akṣṇayā kṛtaṃ bhavati tasmād enaṃ sarvasmāt putro muñcati* . . . / BU 1.5.17.

12. . . . / *punar mām aitvindriyaṃ punas tejaḥ punar bhagaḥ* / BU 6.4.5.

13. Similarly, the *Chāndogya Upaniṣad* states that one who knows the *vāmadevya sāman* as woven upon sexual intercourse reaches a full life-span, lives well, has many children and cows, and achieves great fame. He should not hold back from any woman (2.13.2).

14. . . . / *aṅgād aṅgāt saṃbhavasi hṛdayād adhijāyase / sa tvam aṅga kaṣāyo 'si digdha viddhām iva mādayemāmamūṃ mayi* . . . // BU 6.4.9.

15. See, for example, the *Śatapatha Brāhmaṇa* (10.3.5.12–14) and the *Taittirīya Upaniṣad* (2.2–5). For more examples, particularly those that equate *ānanda* with *ātman/brahman*, see Olivelle's seminal article (1997b).

16. The texts do not tell us explicitly that Yājñavalkya does not have sons, but this is suggested not only by what he teaches, but also by the fact that he settles his inheritance between his two wives.

17. . . . / *na vā are 'ham mohaṃ bravīmi* / BU 2.3.13.

18. Brian Smith makes similar observations: "Although the Veda was certainly composed by the priestly and intellectual class (i.e., the Brahmins), the ideology propounded in it is shot through with the martial values ordinarily associated with warriors (i.e., kshatriyas)" (1990, 178).

19. . . . / *yad idaṃ sarvam apsv otaṃ ca protaṃ ca kasmin nu khalv āpa otāś ca protāś ca* . . . / BU 3.6. *Ota* and *prota* are technical terms that refer to the back and forth movement of the shuttle in the process of weaving. As Roebuck points out, the traditional interpretation takes water to be the warp and weft threads, with the air as the loom (2003, 402n). This metaphor is also used in

the *Ṛgveda*. Findly (1985, 29) suggests that Gārgī's familiarity with this metaphor illustrates that she is generally familiar with Vedic discourse.

20. . . . / *gārgī mātiprākṣīḥ / mā te mūrdhā vyapaptat* / BU 3.6.

21. . . . / *brāhmaṇā bhagavanto hanta aham imaṃ dvau praśnau prakṣyāmi / tau cen me vakṣyati na vai jātu yuṣmākam imaṃ kaścid brahmodyaṃ jeta* . . . / BU 3.8.1.

22. Although the *Mahābhārata* comes much later than the early Upaniṣads, there are a number of similarities regarding the representation of female characters.

23. Gārgī merely talks like a man, but as we will see, a number of female characters actually assume a male identity. This tactic can also be seen in the *Ṛgveda* (10.39.6) where Ghoṣā speaks to the gods as a son rather than as a daughter.

24. . . . / *ahaṃ vai tvā yājñvalkya yathā kāśyo vā vaideho vā ugraputraḥ ujjyaṃ dhanur adhijyaṃ kṛtvā dvau bāṇavantau sapatna ativyādhinau haste kṛtvā upottiṣṭhed evam evāhaṃ tvā dvābhyām praśnābhyām upodasthām / tau me brūhi* . . . / BU 3.8.2.

25. The metaphors that Gārgī employs are not merely explicitly male, but more precisely they are associated with a particular kind of male: a *kṣatriya*. As we have seen, a number of brahmins invoke imagery associated with *kṣatriya*s as a way to make their interactions more combative and competitive. Additionally, as we have seen in chapter 3, metaphors associated with *kṣatriyas* are often used to frame innovative teachings. From this perspective, it is possible that Gārgī depicts herself as a *kṣatriya* in order to associate herself with the kinds of doctrines taught by Pravāhaṇa and Ajātaśatru.

26. . . . / *yad ūrdhvam yājñvalkya divo yad avāk pṛthivyā yad antarā dyāvāpṛthivī ime yad bhūtam ca bhavac ca bhaviṣyaccetyācakṣate kasmiṃs tad otaṃ ca protaṃ ca* // BU 3.8.3.

27. . . . / *namaste 'stu yājñavalkya yo ma etaṃ vyavoco' parasmai dhārayasva* . . . / BU 3.8.5.

28. *yo vā etad akṣaraṃ gārgyaviditvāsmiṃl loke juhoti yajate tapas tapyate bahūni varṣasahasrāṇy antavad evāsya tad bhavati / yo vā etad akṣaraṃ gārgyaviditvāsmāl lokāt praiti sa kṛpaṇaḥ / atha ya etad akṣaraṃ gārgī viditvāsmāl lokāt paraiti sa brāhmaṇaḥ* // BU 3.8.10.

29. . . . / *brāhmaṇā bhagavantas tad eva bahu manyedhvaṃ yad asmān namaskāreṇa mucyedhvam / na vai jātu yuṣmākam imaṃ kaścid brahmodyaṃ jeta* / . . . / BU 3.8.12.

30. Thompson argues that there is a close connection between the *brahmodya* and the *satyakriyā*: A *brahmodya* (utterance of *brahman*) "is a means of *self-display*, on the one hand, of one's mastery of the esoteric lexicon and, on the other hand, of one's personal authority or power. It therefore provides an area also for the performance of a *satyakriyā*" (1997, 20).

31. This dialogue was discussed in chapter 2.

32. The heavenly voice in Śakuntalā's story is implicitly male, suggested by Duḥṣanta's use of the masculine noun *devadhūta*.

33. Here Findly is referring specifically to Sengupta and Altekar, who, according to her, perpetuate the traditional view of women as "silent and invisible bearers of culture" (1985, 37).

34. The final section of the *Bṛhadāraṇyaka Upaniṣad* indicates that it is familiar with this tradition: "Get up Viśvāvasu. Go find some other young woman. Leave this wife here with her husband" (BU 6.4.19). This passage is similar to a passage in the *Ṛgveda* (10.85.21).

35. Jabālā explains that when Satyakāma was conceived, she was young (*yauvana*) and was traveling around as a maid-servant (*carantī paricāriṇī*). Jabālā implies, at least, that she had several relationships, and it is clear that Satyakāma was born out of wedlock.

36. . . . / *naitad abrāhmaṇo vivaktum arhati / samidhaṃ somya āhara / upa tvā neṣye na satyād agā* . . . / CU 4.4.5.

37. . . . / *nāham etad veda tāta yad gotras tvam asi / bahv ahaṃ carantī paricāriṇī yauvane tvām alabhe / sāham etan na veda yadgotras tvam asi / jabālā tu nāmāham asmi / satyakāmo nāma tvam asi / sa satyakāma eva jābālo bruvīthā* . . . // CU 4.4.1.

38. . . . / *tapto brahmacārī kuśalam agnīn paricacārīt / mā tvāgnayaḥ paripravocan / prabrūhy asmā* . . . / CU 4.10.2.

39. . . . / *tapto brahmacārī kuśalaṃ naḥ paryacārīt* / CU 4.10.4.

40. . . . / *bahava ime 'smin puruṣe kāmā nānātyayāḥ / vyādhibhiḥ pratipūrṇo 'smi / nāśiṣyāmi* . . . // CU 4.10.3.

41. For the purpose of this discussion we will refer to *Bṛhadāraṇyaka Upaniṣad* 2.4.1–14 as the first version and *Bṛhadāraṇyaka Upaniṣad* 4.5.1–15 as the second version. Reinvang offers the explanation that most probably each of the two recensions of the *Bṛhadāraṇyaka Upaniṣad* at one point adopted the Upanishadic section of the other recension so that both recensions came to include two versions of the dialogue between Yājñavalkya and Maitreyī (2000, 146–47). Hock, however, suggests that these two versions frame what he calls the "Yājñavalkya core," "producing a highly visible ring composition" (2002, 283). Although his argument is not conclusive, it seems to me that this is the more likely explanation as to why this same dialogue would appear twice within the same Upaniṣad, especially when we take into consideration the importance of framing and embedding in other texts such as the *Ṛgveda*, Brāhmaṇas, and *Mahābhārata*. See Brereton (1997), Minkowski (1989), and Witzel (1987b).

42. . . . / *ud yaśyan vā are 'ham asmāt sthānād asmi / hanta te 'nayā kātyāyanyāntaṃ karavāṇi* . . . // BU 2.4.1. That Yājñavalkya intends to divide his estate between his two wives, indicates that women could own wealth and property. This is in contrast to earlier Vedic texts that not only deny women inheritance rights, but claim that the wife did not have her own possessions, and indeed did not even own herself. Findly argues that this passage "casts Yājñavalkya as an early champion of economic rights" (1985, 46). Witzel cites numerous texts that explicitly deny a woman entitlement to inheritance (1996, 165).

43. Radhakrishnan, for example, comments, "Yājñavalkya wishes to renounce the stage of the householder, *gṛhastha* and enter that of the anchorite, *vānaprastha*" ([1953] 1992, 195).

44. That a wife can be the student of her husband is also suggested by the *Mānava Dharmaśāstra* (*The Law Code of Manu*), which equates marriage with the *upanayana* for women (MDS 2.67).

45. Most scholars agree that these additional details in the second version are an interpolation. See Reinvang (2000).

46. . . . *priyā vai khalu no bhavatī satī priyam avṛdhat* / BU 4.5.5.

47. Reinvang attributes these narrative differences of the second version to the addition of a number of interpolations in Yājñavalkya's teaching: "Maitreyī's objection has been reformulated from the original remark that she does not understand there is no *saṃjña* [awareness] after death, to a more general statement saying that she does not understand 'this' (*idam*)." He argues that consequently, Yājñavalkya's teaching in the second version does not fit together: "the substantial edition of the latter part of the text ends up presenting the reader with a less coherent exposition of the nature of immortality" (2000, 191–92). Hock, however, suggests that the different details in the second version can be explained by the fact that they provide "a stronger closing" to this entire section of the *Bṛhadāraṇyaka Upaniṣad*, which he suggests is a ring composition (2002, 281).

48. . . . / *atraiva mā bhagavān mohāntam āpīpipat* / *na vā aham imaṃ vijānāmi* . . . / BU 4.5.14.

49. Fišer points out that managing the household of Yājñavalkya must have been a considerable task when we take into account the wealth that he amasses: "She was probably thought of as having been in charge of Yājñavalkya's household which must have been at least for those times, an establishment of considerable size—provided that we are to accept the hints of large royal donations bestowed on Yājñavalkya" (1984, 84).

Glossary

adhvaryu: The name of one of the four priests associated with the large-scale Vedic sacrifice (*yajña*). The *adhvaryu*, a specialist in the *Yajurveda*, is the officiant priest who is responsible for carrying out most of the ritual actions.

agni: The Sanskrit word for fire, which was an essential component of all Vedic sacrifices. *Agni* is also the god of fire and is associated with the sacrificial priests.

agnicayana: The name of a particular sacrifice (*yajña*) that consists of building a fire altar. The performance of the *agnicayana* is strongly linked to the mythology of Puruṣa and Prajāpati. For a detailed study of the *agnicayana* see Staal (1983).

agnihotra: The twice-daily milk offering. For a detailed study see Bodewitz (1976).

amṛta: Literally meaning 'not-dieable,' *amṛta* is the Sanskrit word for immortal. At the time of the Upaniṣads, *amṛta* was understood in a number of different ways, including being preserved in the social memory, becoming one with the essential being of the universe, and surviving death in the heavenly world. For a detailed study of this word and its various meanings see Olivelle (1997a).

apsarā: A class of female divinities; the female counterpart to *gandharva*.

ārya: A cultured person who knows Sanskrit and behaves according to the sensibilities of orthodox Brahmanism. In this sense, *ārya* is a term denoting a particular cultural and social identity and does not imply a racial identity.

ātman: In the earliest Vedic material, *ātman* was a reflexive pronoun meaning 'self.' The word continued to be used as a pronoun, but by the time of the late Brāhmaṇas and early Upaniṣads, *ātman* also became a philosophical term that could be associated with a wide range of meanings including body and soul, and could sometimes refer to the ontological principle underlying all reality.

ātman vaiśvānara: The self of all people. This is an Upanishadic reformulation of Agni Vaiśvānara, who is invoked in the very first hymn of the *Ṛgveda*.

brahmacārin: A student of the Vedas.

brahman: Originally meaning 'sacred speech,' *brahman* also can refer to the power or essence of the priestly class. In the Upaniṣads this meaning is often extended to designate the underlying reality of all things.

brahmin: The Anglicized form of the Sanskrit word *brāhmaṇa*, the name of the priestly class, the first of the four classes (*varṇa*).

brahmodya: Debate or verbal contest.

ekatrika: The name of a particular type of one-day *soma* sacrifice.

gandharva: A class of male divinities; the male counterpart of *apsarā*.

hotṛ: The name of one of the four priests associated with the large-scale Vedic sacrifice (*yajña*). The *hotṛ*, a specialist in the *Ṛgveda*, is the invoking priest who is responsible for praising the gods and inviting them to the sacrifice.

kṣatra: The power or essence of the *kṣatriya* class.

kṣatriya: The name of the second of the four classes (*varṇa*). Originally referring to warriors, the term *kṣatriya* came to designate members of the aristocracy. In the Upaniṣads kings are members of the *kṣatriya* class.

mantra: A sacred verse, formula, or series of sounds. Often used to refer to verses from the Vedas.

mokṣa: In the early Upaniṣads *mokṣa* tends to mean 'release' in the everyday sense of the word. Subsequently, *mokṣa* developed the connotation of final emancipation, which was considered the soteriological goal for a number of Hindu traditions.

pañcāgnividyā: Literally meaning 'knowledge of the five fires,' the *pañcāgnividyā* refers to the first part of the discourse that King Pravāhaṇa Jaivali delivers to Uddaka Āruṇi in the *Bṛhadāraṇyaka Upaniṣad* (6.2.9–14) and the *Chāndogya Upaniṣad* (5.3.4–9).

prāṇa: The most general meaning is 'breath,' but it can have different connotations in different contexts. In its plural form, the *prāṇā*s refer to either the bodily winds or to the five vital functions.

ṛṣi: Literally meaning 'seer,' *ṛṣi* refers to the divinely inspired poets who composed the Vedas.

sāman: The melodic chants of the *Sāmaveda*.

saṃsāra: The cycle of life, death, and rebirth. This term is not used in the early Upaniṣads, but became a central idea in later Brahmanism and Buddhism.

Sāvitrī (also called Gāyatrī): The Sāvitrī is a verse from the *Ṛgveda* (3.62.10) dedicated to Savitṛ, the sun. In later texts such as the *Mānava Dharmaśastra*, reciting the Sāvitrī is considered to be one of the most essential aspects of an initiation ritual. The verse is divided into three parts, each of which is considered to contain the essence of one of the three Vedas. See Roebuck (2003, 389) for a translation and discussion of this verse.

soma: The food of the gods and a symbol of immortality. Made from a sacred plant, the preparation and consumption of *soma* is a central feature of many Vedic sacrifices.

śūdra: The name of the fourth social class (*varṇa*). In the Upaniṣads *śūdra* is considered the lowest class.

udgātṛ: The name of one of the four priests associated with the large-scale Vedic sacrifice (*yajña*). The *udgātṛ*, a specialist in the *Sāmaveda*, is the chanting priest who is responsible for singing the melodies during the sacrifice.

upanayana: The initiation ceremony of a brahmin student (*brahmacārin*).

varṇa: Literally meaning 'color,' *varṇa* refers to the social classes, of which there are traditionally four: brahmin (priests), *kṣatriya* (warriors, kings), *vaiśya* (farmers, merchants), and *śūdra* (laborers). The *varṇa* system is famously articulated in the *Puruṣasūkta* hymn of the *Ṛgveda* (10.90), where the four classes are derived from different parts of the body of the cosmic man. *Varṇa* can also refer to the hierarchical system that organizes all the components of the universe under one basic structure (see Smith 1994).

vedi: The sunken area strewn with grass between the fires in the consecration ground of a Vedic ritual, where the gods were invited to sit as guests. The word *vedi* is feminine and is often homologized with masculine words in the Brahmanical ritual literature. The feminine dimension of the *vedi* is further highlighted by the fact that its hourglass shape is often compared to a woman with large breasts and hips, and a slender waist.

yajamāna: Literally meaning 'sacrificer,' the *yajamāna* is the sponsor of the sacrifice. He must be a member of one of the first three social classes (*varṇa*) and he must be married.

yajña: The Vedic sacrifice.

yakṣa (*yakkha* in Pāli): A class of divinity often associated with nature and wealth. *Yakṣas* appear in both the Brahmanical and Buddhist traditions.

Bibliography

SOURCE TEXTS: SANSKRIT AND ENGLISH

Bodewitz, H. W., trans. 1973. *Jaiminīya Brāhmaṇa I, 1–65: Translation and Commentary with a Study Agnihotra and Prāṇāgnihotra.* Leiden: E. J. Brill.

Buitenen, J. A. B. van, trans. 1962. *The Maitrāyaṇīya Upaniṣad: A Critical Essay with Text, Translation and Commentary.* The Hague: Mouton.

———, trans. 1973–78. *The Mahābhārata Books 1–5.* Chicago: Chicago Univ. Press.

———, trans. 1981. *The Bhagavad Gītā in the Mahābhārata: A Bilingual Edition.* Chicago: Chicago Univ. Press.

Deussen, Paul. [1897] 1980. *Sixty Upaniṣads of the Veda.* Trans. V. M. Bedekar and G. B. Palsue. Delhi: Motilal Banarsidass.

Eggeling, Julius, trans. [1882–97] 1994. *Śatapatha Brāhmaṇa.* Parts 1–5. The Sacred Books of the East. Delhi: Motilal Banarsidass.

Fitzgerald, James L., trans. 2004. *The Mahābhārata Books 11 and 12.* Chicago: Chicago Univ. Press.

Griffith, Ralph T. H., trans. [1889] 1973. *The Hymns of the Ṛgveda.* Delhi: Motilal Banarsidass.

Hume, Robert, trans. [1921] 1975. *The Thirteen Principal Upanishads.* London: Oxford Univ. Press.

Keith, A. B., trans. [1909] 1995. *Aitareya Āraṇyaka.* London: Oxford Univ. Press.

———, trans. [1920] 1981. *Aitareya and Kauṣītaki Brāhmaṇas of the Rigveda.* Delhi: Motilal Banarsidass.

Müller, F. Max, trans. [1879–84] 2000. *The Upaniṣads, Parts I and 2.* Delhi: Motilal Banarasidass.

Oertel, H., trans. 1897. The Jaiminīya or Talavakāra Upaniṣad Brāhmaṇa. *Journal of the American Oriental Society* 16:79–260.

O'Flaherty, Wendy Doniger, trans. 1981. *The Rig Veda.* London: Penguin Books.

Olivelle, Patrick, trans. 1996. *The Upaniṣads.* Oxford: Oxford Univ. Press.

———, trans. 1998. *The Early Upaniṣads: Annotated Text and Translation.* New York: Oxford Univ. Press.

———, trans. 2004. *The Law Code of Manu.* Oxford: Oxford Univ. Press.

Radhakrishnan, Sarvepalli, trans. [1953] 1992. *The Principal Upaniṣads.* New Jersey: Humanities Press.

Roebuck, Valerie, trans. 2003. *The Upaniṣads*. London: Penguin Books.

Walshe, Maurice, trans. 1995. *The Long Discourses of the Buddha: A Translation of the Dīgha Nikāya*. Boston: Wisdom Publications.

Weber, Albrecht, ed. 1964. *The Śathapatha Brāhmaṇa in the Mādhyadina-śākhā*. Varanasi: Chowkhamba Sanskrit Series.

SCHOLARLY LITERATURE

Ali, Daud. 2000. From Nāyikā to Bhakta: A Genealogy of Female Subjectivity in Early Medieval India. In *Invented Identities: The Interplay of Gender, Religion and Politics in India*, ed. Julia Leslie and Mary McGee, 157–80. Oxford: Oxford Univ. Press.

Altekar, A. S. [1938] 1959. *The Position of Women in Hindu Civilization*. Delhi: Motilal Banarsidass.

Alter, Robert. 1981. *The Art of Biblical Narrative*. New York: Basic Books.

Asad, Talal. 1993. *Genealogies of Religion: Discipline and Reasons of Power in Christianity and Islam*. Baltimore: John's Hopkins Univ. Press.

Bakhtin, M. M. 1981. *The Dialogical Imagination*. Austin: Univ. of Texas Press.

Basham, A. L. 1951. *History and Doctrine of the Ājīvikas: A Vanished Indian Religion*. Delhi: Motilal Banarsidass.

Beversluis, John. 2000. *Cross-Examining Socrates: A Defense of the Interlocutors in Plato's Early Dialogues*. Cambridge: Cambridge Univ. Press.

Bhattacharya, Ramakrishna. 2002. Cārvāka Fragments: A New Collection. *Journal of Indian Philosophy* 30:597–640.

Bhattacharya, Sibesh. 1983. Political Authority and *Brāhmaṇa-Kṣatriya* Relationship in Early India: An Aspect of the Power Elite Configuration. *The Indian Historical Review* 10 (1–2): 1–20.

Biardeau, Madeleine. 1994. *Hinduism: The Anthropology of a Civilization*. Delhi: Oxford Univ. Press.

Black, Brian. In press. Eavesdropping on the Epic: Female Listeners in the Mahābhārata. In *Gender and Narrative in the Mahābhārata*, ed. Simon Brodbeck and Brian Black. London: Routledge.

———. Forthcoming. Ambaṭṭha and Śvetaketu: Literary Connections between the Upaniṣads and Early Buddhist Narratives. In *Essays in Honor of Patrick Olivelle*, ed. Steven E. Lindquist. Firenze: Firenze Univ. Press.

Blondell, Ruby. 2002. *The Play of Character in Plato's Dialogues*. Cambridge: Cambridge Univ. Press.

Bodewitz, H. W. 1974. Vedic Dhāvayati "To Drive." *Indo-Iranian Journal* 16:81–95.

———. 1976. *The Daily Evening and Morning Offering (Agnihotra) According to the Brāhmaṇas*. Leiden: E. J. Brill.

———. 1992. King Prāṇa. In *Ritual, State and History in South Asia: Essays in Honour of J. C. Heesterman*, ed. A. W. van Den Hoek, D. H. A. Kolff, and M. S. Oort, 50–64. Leiden: E. J. Brill.

———. 1996a. The *Pañcāgnividyā* and the *Pitṛyāna/Devayāna*. In *Studies on Indology: Professor Mukunda Madhava Sharma Felicitation Volume*, ed.

A. K. Goswain and D. Chutia. Sri Garib Das Oriental Series 201. Delhi: Sri Satguru Publications.

———. 1996b. Redeath and its Relation to Rebirth and Release. *Studien zur Indologie und Iranistik* 20:27–46.

Brereton, Joel. 1986. "Tat Tvam Asi" in Context. *Zeitschrift der Deutchen Morgenländischen Gesellschaft* 136:98.

———. 1990. The Upanishads. In *Approaches to the Asian Classics,* ed. Wm. T. de Bary and I. Bloom, 115–35. New York: Columbia Univ.

———. 1996. Yājñavalkya's Curse. *Studien zur Indologie und Iranistik* 20:47–57.

———. 1997. Why is a Sleeping Dog like the Vedic Sacrifice?: The Structure of an Upaniṣad *Brahmodya.* In *Inside the Texts, Beyond the Texts,* ed. Michael Witzel, 1–14. Columbia, MO: South Asian Books.

———. 1999. Edifying Puzzlement: *Ṛgveda* X.129 and the Uses of Enigma. *Journal of the American Oriental Society* 119:248–60.

Brockington, John. 1998. *The Sanskrit Epics.* Leiden: E. J. Brill.

Bronkhorst, Johannes. 1996. Śvetaketu and the *Upanayana. Asialische Studien* 50:592–601.

Buitenen, J. A. B. van. 1968. *The Pravargya: An Ancient Indian Iconic Ritual Described and Annotated.* Poona: Deccan College Postgraduate and Research Institute.

Chakravarti, Uma. 1996. *The Social Dimensions of Early Buddhism.* Delhi: Munishiram Manoharlal.

———. 1999. Beyond the Altekarian Paradigm. In *Women in Early Indian Societies,* ed. Kumkum Roy. Delhi: Manohar.

———. 2000. Vedic Sacrificer and the Officiating Priest. *The Indian Historical Review* 27 (1–2): 1–20.

Chattopadhyaya, Debiprasad. 1959. *Lokāyata: A Study in Ancient Indian Materialism.* Delhi: People's Publishing House.

———. 1977. *Science and Society in Ancient India.* Calcutta: Research India Publications.

———. 1986–87. Uddālaka Āruṇi: The Pioneer of Science. *The Indian Historical Review* 13 (1–2): 37–57.

Clarke, J. J. 1999. *Oriental Enlightenment.* London: Routledge.

Connolly, Peter. 1997. The Vitalistic Antecedents of the Ātman-Brahman Concept. In *Indian Insights: Buddhism, Brahmanism and Bhakti: Papers from the Annual Spalding Symposium on Indian Religions,* ed. Peter Connolly and Sue Hamilton. London: Luzac Oriental.

Dasgupta, Surenranath. [1922] 1988. *A History of Indian Philosophy.* Vol. 1. Delhi: Motilal Banarsidass.

Deussen, Paul. [1919] 2000. *The Philosophy of the Upanishads.* Delhi: Oriental Publishers.

Doniger, Wendy. 1999. *Splitting the Difference: Gender and Myth in Ancient Greece and India.* Chicago: Univ. of Chicago Press.

Drekmeier, Charles. 1962. *Kingship and Community in Early India.* Stanford: Stanford Univ. Press.

Dumont, Louis. 1966. *Homo Hierarchicus: The Caste System and its Implications.* London: Weidenfeld and Nicolson.

Dutt, R. C. 1972. *A History of Civilization in India.* Delhi: Vishal Publishers.

Eagleton, Terry. 1983. *Literary Theory: An Introduction.* Oxford: Basil Blackwell.

Edgerton, Franklin. 1965. *The Beginnings of Indian Philosophy.* London: George Allen and Unwin.

Eliade, Mircea. 1958. *Rites and Symbols of Initiation: the Mysteries of Birth and Rebirth.* New York: Harper Torch Books.

———. 1969. *Yoga, Immortality and Freedom.* New York: Princeton Univ. Press.

Ewing, A. H. 1901. The Hindu Conception of the Functions of Breath. *The Journal of American Oriental Society* 22:251–308.

Falk, Harry. 1986. Vedisch *upaniṣád. Zeitschrift der Deutschen Morgenländischen Gesellschaft* 136:80–97.

Findly, Ellison Banks. 1985. Gārgī at the King's Court: Women and Philosophical Innovation in Ancient India. In *Women, Religion and Social Change,* ed. Yvonne Yazbeck Haddad and Ellison Banks Findly. Albany: State Univ. of New York Press.

Fišer, Ivo. 1984. Yājñavalkya in the Śruti Tradition of the Veda. In *Acta Orientalia* Vol. 45, 56–87.

Fitzgerald, James L. 2001. Making Yudhiṣṭhira the King: The Dialectics and the Politics of Violence in the *Mahābhārata. Rocznic Orientalistyczny* 54:63–92.

Flood, Gavin. 1999. *Beyond Phenomenology: Rethinking the Study of Religion.* London: Cassell.

Frauwallner, Erich. 1973. *History of Indian Philosophy.* Delhi: Motilal Banarsidass.

Fujii, Masato. 1997. On the Formation of the Jaiminīya-Upaniṣad-Brāhmaṇa. In *Inside the Texts, Beyond the Texts,* ed. Michael Witzel, 89–102. Columbia, MO: South Asian Books.

Garbe, Richard. [1897] 2004. *The Philosophy of Ancient India.* Montana: Kessinger Publishing.

Gokhale, Balkrishna Govind. 1977. The Merchant in Ancient India. *Journal of the American Oriental Society* 97 (1–2): 125–30.

———. 1994. *New Light on Early Buddhism.* London: Sangam Books.

Gonda, J. 1950. *Notes on Brahman.* Utrecht: J. L. Beyers.

———. 1965. *Bandhu* in the Brāhmaṇas. *Adyar Library Bulletin* 29:1–29.

———. 1986. *Prajāpati's Rise to Higher Rank.* Leiden: E. J. Brill.

Grinshpon, Yohanan. 1998. The Upaniṣadic Story and the Hidden *Vidyā*: Personality and Possession in the Bṛhadāraṇyakopaniṣad. *Journal of Indian Philosophy* 26:373–85.

———. 2003. *Crises and Knowledge: The Upanishadic Experience and Storytelling.* Delhi: Oxford Univ. Press.

Grube, G. M. A. 1980. *Plato's Thought.* Indiana: Hackett Publishing Company.

Halbfass, Wilhelm. 1988. *India and Europe: An Essay in Understanding.* Albany: State Univ. of New York Press.

———. 1995. *Philology and Confrontation: Paul Hacker on Traditional and Modern Vedanta.* Albany: State Univ. of New York Press.

Heesterman, J.C. 1985. *The Inner Conflict of Tradition.* Chicago: Univ. of Chicago.

———. 1993. *The Broken World of Sacrifice.* Chicago: Univ. of Chicago.

Helfer, James S. 1968. The Initiatory Structure of the *Kaṭhopaniṣad. History of Religions* 7:348–67.

Hock, Hans Heinrich. 2002. The Yājñavalkya Cycle in the *Bṛhad Āraṇyaka Upaniṣad. Journal of the American Oriental Society* 122 (2): 278–86.

Houben, Jan E. M. 1998. The Ritual Pragmatics of a Vedic Hymn: The 'riddle hymn (Ṛgveda 1.164) and the Pravargya-ritual. *Journal of the American Oriental Society* 120 (4): 499–537.

Inden, Ronald. 1990. *Imagining India.* London: Hurst.

———. 1992. Changes in the Vedic Priesthood. *Ritual, State and History in South Asia: Essays in Honour of J. C. Heesterman,* ed. A. W. Van den Hoek, D. H. A. Kolff, and M. S. Oort, 556–77. Leiden: E. J. Brill.

Insler, Stanley. 1989–90. The Shattered Head Split in the Epic Tale of Shakuntalā. *Bulletin d'Etudes Indiennes* 7–8:97–139.

Jamison, Stephanie. 1991. *The Ravenous Hyenas and the Wounded Sun: Myth and Ritual in Ancient India.* Ithaca: Cornell Univ. Press.

———. 1996. *Sacrificed Wife, Sacrificer's Wife: Women, Ritual, and Hospitality in Ancient India.* Oxford: Oxford Univ. Press.

Jantzen, Grace M. 1995. *Power, Gender and Christian Mysticism.* Cambridge: Cambridge Univ. Press.

———. 1998. *Becoming Divine: Towards a Feminist Philosophy of Religion.* Manchester: Manchester Univ. Press.

Johnson, Willard. 1980. *Poetry and Speculation in the Ṛg Veda.* Berkeley: Univ. of California Press.

Kaelber, Walter. 1989. *Tapta Mārga: Asceticism and Initiation in Vedic India.* Albany: State Univ. of New York Press.

Keith, A. B. [1925] 1989. *The Religion and Philosophy of the Veda and the Upanishads.* Delhi: Motilal Banarsidass.

Killingley, Dermot. 1997. The Paths of the Dead and the Five Fires. In *Indian Insights: Buddhism, Brahmanism and Bhakti: Papers from the Annual Spalding Symposium on Indian Religions,* ed. Peter Connolly and Sue Hamilton. London: Luzac Oriental.

King, Richard. 1999a. *Indian Philosophy: An Introduction to Hindu and Buddhist Thought.* Edinburgh: Edinburgh Univ. Press.

———. 1999b. *Orientalism and Religion: Postcolonial Theory, India and 'The Mystic East.'* London: Routledge.

Kosambi, D. D. 1994. *The Culture and Civilization of Ancient India in Historical Outline.* Delhi: Vikas Publishing House.

Kuiper, F. B. J. 1960. The Ancient Aryan Verbal Contest. *Indo-Iranian Journal* 4:217–81.

Kulke, H. 1992. The Rājasūya: A Paradigm of Early Indian State Formation? In *Ritual, State and History in South Asia: Essays in Honour of J. C. Heesterman,* ed. A. W. Van den Hoek, D. H. A. Kolff, and M. S. Oort, 188–98. Leiden: E. J. Brill.

Larson, Gerald. 1969. *Classical Sāṃkhya.* Delhi: Motilal Banarsidass.

Leslie, Julia. 2003. *Authority and Meaning in Indian Relgions: Hinduism and the Case of Vālmīki.* Aldershot: Ashgate.

Lindstrom, Lamont. 1990. *Knowledge and Power in a South Pacific Society.* Washington: Smithsonian Institution Press.

Lipner, Julius. 1978. An Analysis of Kaṭha 6.4 and 5, with some observations on Upanishadic Method. *Journal of Indian Philosophy* 5:243–53.

———. 1986. Applying the Litmus Test: A Comparative Study in Vedāntic Exegesis. In *A Net Cast Wide: Investigations into Indian Thought in Memory of David Freidman,* ed. Julius Lipner and Dermot Killingley. Newcastle upon Thyne: Grevatt and Grevatt.

———. 1998. Philosophy and World Religions. In *Philosophy of Religion: A Guide to the Subject,* ed. Brian Davies. London: Cassell.

Lloyd, Genevieve. 1993. *The Man of Reason: 'Male' and 'Female' in Western Philosophy.* London: Routledge.

Malamoud, Charles. 1996. *Cooking the World: Ritual & Thought in Ancient India.* Delhi: Oxford Univ. Press.

McKim, R. 1988. Shame and Truth in Plato's Gorgias. In *Platonic Writings/ Platonic Readings,* ed. C. Griswold. New York: Routledge.

Minkowski, Christopher. 1989. Janamejaya's *Sattra* and Ritual Structure. *Journal of the American Oriental Society* 109:401–20.

Mohanty, J. N. 1992. *Reason and Tradition in Indian Thought: An Essay on the Nature of Indian Philosophical Thinking.* Oxford: Clarendon Press.

———. 1993. Are Indian and Western Philosophy Radically Different? In *J. N. Mohanty: Essays on Indian Philosophy,* ed. Purushottama Bilmoria. Oxford: Oxford Univ. Press.

———. 2000. *Classical Indian Philosophy.* Lanham: Rowman and Littlefield.

Monier-Williams, Monier. [1899]. 1993. *A Sanskrit-English Dictionary, Etymologically and Philologically Arranged with Special Reference to Cognate Indo-European Languages,* rev. ed. Delhi: Motilal Banarsidass.

Müller, F. Max. [1883]. 2000. *India: What Can It Teach Us.* Delhi: Penguin Books India.

Nehemas, Alexander. 1998. *The Art of Living: Socratic Reflections from Plato to Foucault.* Berkeley: Univ. of California Press.

O'Flaherty, Wendy Doniger. 1985. *Tales of Sex and Violence: Folklore, Sacrifice, and Danger in the Jaiminīya Brāhmaṇa.* Chicago: Univ. of Chicago Press.

Oldenberg, Hermann. [1908] 1991. *The Doctrine of the Upaniṣads and the Early Buddhism,* trans. Shridhar Shrotri. Delhi: Motilal Banarsidass.

Olivelle, Patrick. 1992. *Saṃnyāsa Upaniṣads.* New York: Oxford Univ. Press.

———. 1993. *The Āśrama System.* New York: Oxford Univ. Press.

———. 1997a. Amṛtā: Women and Indian Technologies of Immortality. *Journal of Indian Philosophy* 25:427–49.

———. 1997b. Orgasmic Rapture and Divine Ecstasy: The Semantic History of Ānanda. *Journal of Indian Philosophy* 25:153–80.

———. 1999. Young Śvetaketu: A Literary Study of an Upaniṣadic Story. *Journal of the American Oriental Society* 119 (1): 46–70.

Parks, Ward. 1990. *Verbal Dueling in Heroic Narrative: The Homeric and Old English Traditions*. Princeton: Princeton Univ. Press.

Patton, Laurie L. 2005. *Bringing the Gods to Mind: Mantra and Ritual in Early Indian Sacrifice*. Berkeley: Univ. of California Press.

Ranade, Ramchandra Dattatraya. 1926. *A Constructive Survey of Upanishadic Philosophy*. Poona: Oriental Books Agency.

Rau, W. 1957. *Staat und Gesellschaft im alten Indien nach den Brāhmaṇa-Texten dargestellt*. Wiesbaden: Otto Harrassowitz.

Reinvang, Rasmus. 2000. A Critical Survey of the Dialogue between Yājñavalkya and Maitreyī in *Bṛhadāraṇyaka Upaniṣad* 2.4 and 4.5. *Acta Orientalia* 61, 145–202.

Renou, Louis. 1957. *Vedic India*. Calcutta: Sasil Gupta Private.

Renou, Louis and L. Silburn. 1949. Sur la notion de "Brahman." *Journal Asiatique* Vol. 237, 7–46.

Roy, Kumkum. 1991–92. Changing Kinship Relations in Later Vedic Society. *The Indian Historical Review* 18 (1–2): 1–17.

———. 1994. *The Emergence of Monarchy in North India*. Delhi: Oxford Univ. Press.

———, ed. 1999. *Women in Early Indian Societies*. Delhi: Manohar.

Said, Edward. 1985. *Orientalism*. Harmondsworth: Penguin.

Schober, Juliane, ed. 1997. *Sacred Biographies in the Buddhist Traditions of South and Southeast Asia*. Honolulu: Hawaii Univ. Press.

Schopenhauer, Arthur. [1818] 1969. *The World As Will and Representation* Vols. 1–2. Trans. E. F. J. Payne. New York: Dover Publications.

———. [1851] 1974. *Parerga and Paralipomena: Short Philosophical Essays Vol. 2*, trans. E. F. J. Payne. Oxford: Clarendon Press.

Sengupta, Padmini. 1974. *The Story of Women in India*. New Delhi: Indian Book Company.

Shah, Shalini. 1995. *The Making of Womanhood: Gender Relations in the Mahābhārata*. Delhi: Manohar.

Sharma, R. S. 1983. *Material Culture and Social Formations in Ancient India*. Delhi: Macmillan India.

———. 1999a. *The Advent of the Aryans in India*. Delhi: Manohar.

———. 1999b. *Aspects of Political Ideas and Institutions in Ancient India*. Delhi: Motilal Banarsidass.

Sharma, Shubhra. 1985. *Life in the Upanishads*. Delhi: Abhinav Publications.

Smith, Brian. 1989. *Reflections on Resemblance, Ritual and Religion*. Oxford: Oxford Univ. Press.

———. 1990. Eaters, Food and Social Hierarchy in Ancient India: A Dietary Guide to a Revolution of Values. *Journal of the American Academy of Religion* 57 (2): 177–205.

———. 1994. *Classifying the Universe: The Ancient Indian* Varṇa *System and the Origins of Caste*. New York: Oxford Univ. Press.

Söhnen, Renate. 1981. Die Einleitungsgeschichte der Belehrung des Uddālaka Āruṇi: Ein Vergleich der drei Fassungen Kauṣītaki 1.1, Chāndogya 5.3 und Bṛhadāraṇyaka 6.21–8. *Studien zur Indologie und Iranistik* 7:177–213.

Staal, J. Fritz. 1983. *Agni: The Vedic Ritual of the Fire Altar*. In collaboration with C. V. Somayajipad and M. Itti Ravi Nambudiri. Berekely: Asian Humanities Press.

Tambiah, Stanley J. 1976. *World Conqueror and World Renouncer: A Study of Buddhism and Polity in Thailand Against a Historical Background*. Cambridge: Cambridge Univ. Press.

Thapar, Romila. 1966. *A History of India*. Delhi: Penguin Books.

———. 1982. *Interpreting Early India*. Delhi: Oxford Univ. Press.

———. 1984. *From Lineage to State*. Bombay: Oxford Univ. Press.

———. 1994. Sacrifice, Surplus, and the Soul. *History of Religions* 33 (4): 305–24.

———. 1994. Aśoka and Buddhism as Reflected in the Aśokan Edicts. In *King Aśoka and Buddhism: Historical and Literary Studies*, ed. Anuradha Seneviratna. Kandy, Sri Lanka: Buddhist Publication Society.

———. 1999. *Śakuntalā: Texts, Readings, Histories*. Delhi: Kali for Women.

———. 2002. *The Penguin History of Early India: From the Origins to 1300*. London: Penguin Books.

Thompson, George. 1997. The *Brahmodya* and the Vedic Discourse. *Journal of the American Oriental Society* 117 (1): 13–37.

———. 1998. On Truth-Acts in Vedic. *Indo-Iranian Journal* 41:125–53.

Tull, Herman. 1989. *The Vedic Origins of Karma*. Albany: State Univ. of New York Press.

Upreti, G. B. 1997. *The Early Buddhist World Outlook in Historical Perspective*. Delhi: Manohar.

Urban, Hugh B. 2001. *The Economics of Ecstasy: Tantra, Secrecy, and Power in Colonial Bengal*. Oxford: Oxford Univ. Press.

Vivekananda. [1922] 1973. *The Complete Works of Swami Vivekananda*. Vol. 3. Calcutta: Avaita Ashrama.

Vlastos, G. 1971. *The Philosophy of Socrates: A Collection of Critical Essays*. Garden City, NY: Doubleday.

Whitney, W. D. 1890. The Kaṭha-Upanishad. *Journal of the Royal Asiatic Society* 21:88–112.

Witzel, Michael. 1977. An Unknown Upaniṣad of the Kṛṣṇa Yajurveda: The Katha-Siksa-Upanisad. *Journal of the Nepal Research Center*, no. 1:139–55.

———. 1987a. The Case of the Shattered Head. *Studien zur Indologie und Iranistik* 13/14:363–415.

———. 1987b. On the Origin of the Literary Device of the "Frame Story" in Old Indian Literature. In *Hinduismus und Buddhismus: Festschrift für Ulrich Schneider*, ed. Harry Falk, 340–414. Freiburg: Hedwig Falk.

———. 1995. Early Sanskritization: Origins and Development of the Kurus State. *Electronic Journal of Vedic Studies* 1 (4).

———. 1996. Little Dowry, No Satī: The Lot of Women in the Vedic Period. *Journal of South Asia Women Studies* 2 (4)4: 159–70.

———. 1997. The Development of the Vedic Canon and Its Schools: The Social and Political Milieu. In *Inside the Texts, Beyond the Texts*, ed. Michael Witzel, 255–345. Columbia, MO: South Asian Books.

Zysk, Kenneth. 1991. *Asceticism and Healing in Ancient India.* New York: Oxford Univ. Press.

———. 1993. 'The Science of Respiration and the Doctrine of the Bodily Winds in Ancient India. *Journal of the American Oriental Society* 113:198–213.

Index

This groundbreaking book is an elegant exploration of the Upaniṣads, often considered the fountainhead of the rich, varied philosophical tradition in India. The Upaniṣads, in addition to their philosophical content, have a number of sections that contain narratives and dialogues – a literary dimension largely ignored by the Indian philosophical tradition, as well as by modern scholars. Brian Black draws attention to these literary elements and demonstrates that they are fundamental to understanding the philosophical claims of the text.

Focusing on the Upanishadic notion of the self (*ātman*), the book is organized into four main sections that feature a lesson taught by a brahmin teacher to a brahmin student, debates between brahmins, discussions between brahmins and kings, and conversations between brahmins and women. These dialogical situations feature dramatic elements that bring attention to both the participants and the social contexts of Upanishadic philosophy, characterizing philosophy as something achieved through discussion and debate. In addition to making a number of innovative arguments, the author also guides the reader through these profound and engaging texts, offering ways of reading the Upaniṣads that make them more understandable and accessible.

Brian Black is Research Assistant at the School of Oriental and African Studies at the University of London.